The Roots of Literacy

The Roots of Literacy

David Hawkins

University Press of Colorado

Published by the University Press of Colorado
5589 Arapahoe Avenue, Suite 206C
Boulder, Colorado 80303

The University Press of Colorado is a cooperative publishing enterprise supported, in part, by Adams State College, Colorado State University, Fort Lewis College, Mesa State College, Metropolitan State College of Denver, University of Colorado, University of Northern Colorado, University of Southern Colorado, and Western State College of Colorado.

The paper used in this publication meets the minimum requirements of the American National Standard for Information Sciences—Permanence of Paper for Printed Library Materials. ANSI Z39.48-1992

Library of Congress Cataloging-in-Publication Data

Hawkins, David, 1913–
    The roots of literacy / David Hawkins.
      p. cm.
    Includes bibliographical references.
    ISBN 0-87081-595-4 (alk. paper) — ISBN 0-87081-596-2 (alk. paper)
      1. Education—Philosophy. 2. Learning. 3. Effective teaching. I. Title.

LB885.H36 H39 2000
370'.1—dc21

                                                                    00-044720

Design by Laura Furney
Typesetting by Daniel Pratt

09 08 07 06 05 04 03 02 01 00   10 9 8 7 6 5 4 3 2 1

Contents

CONTENTS

Preface

The present volume of essays on learning and teaching is a sequel to my *The Informed Vision*, which was published in 1974. Most of these new essays, like those in the previous volume, are "occasional," a term of the trade meaning prepared for special occasions such as invited lectures or articles. A few have been published, some given as lectures, and others just waiting.

The range of topics discussed in this new volume, as in the previous one, is wide, as it should be, if only to call attention to the deeper needs of our too-often dilapidated institutions of elementary education.

Perhaps a word about the author is in order. I had long been an academic philosopher with an amateur's interests in mathematics and the sciences. Then—still many years ago—I accepted a position to direct and teach a freshman-sophomore course in physical sciences—astronomy, physics, chemistry, and geology—for students who had successfully avoided these matters in high school. I loved it dearly, and spent many long hours preparing to trap my students into some investigative curiosity.

Once, in my first or second year, I worked to bring together the arithmetic and geometry they had already, quite separately, studied. "From square tiles, bring them together to make bigger squares: 2 X 2 = 4,

3 x 3 = 9, 4 x 4 = 16, etc." "So that is why they are called square numbers!" my students enthused.

Then I tried it with cubes: "How many cubes, one inch on an edge,
do we need to make a cube two inches on an edge?" "Let's see . . . four?
no, six?" Finally, I brought out the wooden cubes, and we did it: 8, 27,
64 . . .

"Wow! Is that why those numbers are called cubes?"

I brought the matter home that night, asking my wife why the problem of cubes was so inaccessible to them. And the answer, from Frances
Hawkins, a teacher of the very young, was, "Because they didn't ever have
a decent kindergarten!"

Since those times we have been collaborators, in one way or another, and much of my writing owes a major debt to her insights about
learning and teaching. We have worked together for many years, through
our teachers' center in Boulder, in tropical Africa, in England and Italy.

My strongest impulse is always to theorize, hers to look at the scatter—sometimes the wide scattering—of ways in which children actually
do learn. There are fields in which the best practice is well ahead of
prevailing theory, and the field of early education is one of them. I nurture the saying of Goethe: "Gray is all theory, and green life's golden
tree." But they belong together, always.

The Roots of Literacy

– 1 –

The Roots of Literacy[1]

In the nineteenth- and twentieth-century history of childhood schooling, there is a persistent failure to understand the roots of literacy, and thus to leave them unnurtured and disparaged—a neglect that the changing character of our society has exacerbated. I wish, by contrast, to illustrate various kinds of in-school context for children's rich engagement with text, and for the growth of literacy. Direct observation best defines the nature of this context and the adult capacities required to create and extend it.

In much of our public discussion, it seems taken for granted that the written word is the essential vehicle of education—as though what is a necessary condition were also sufficient. In the dictionaries the word *literacy* itself does just such a glide. Minimally, it means the ability to read and write, to decode and encode. Maximally, it means being well read, learned—hence, well educated. We may not intend this exclusive emphasis on the written word, but it is predictably going to continue to be taken that way, whatever the intent. In practice, literacy leads a life of its own, especially when it gets tied up in slogans and programs. More especially, this is likely when we are confronting educational systems already committed to the belief that the learning of history, literature, mathematics, and science is just a sort of printout in the minds of students. Unless we are emphatic in what we advocate to the contrary, I believe we will have another round of failure.

So it is education we should be talking about first, and only then the place within it for kinds and levels of literacy. For my part I wish to set forth, first, a statement of the aims of a general liberal education. Traditional views of liberal education are so book-centered that they leave too little room for discussing just what part in education the printed word *should* play.

With the industrial and scientific revolutions, it has come about that to live and work well, to be at home in this new world of ours, we need to have an education that is not limited to either the know-how of our jobs or to our duties of citizenship. The condition of "being at home" has other dimensions than these; it has all the dimensions of experience, and it is a meager and miserly puritanism that fails to recognize their import. Only with a secure home base are children freed for wonder and for exploration and enjoyment of what is around them. As children are well supported in their explorations, those from secure backgrounds are strengthened and those who lack early support and stimulation can be given their first opportunity.

Even adult curiosity flourishes only when in some good measure it has grown from a childhood that has found support for being at home in the world. Neither technical competence nor political judgment can grow, optimally, except from such a base.

This brief statement puts a heavy burden on the phrase "being at home," but the meaning is not hard to find or to expand. The antonyms are *estrangement, alienation.* Usually these words are used for persons cut off from participation, estranged from vital human associations. To be a part of life today, yet to live unacquainted with its newfound powers and the limitations that threaten it, is also to live in alienation and to have, in the end, no voice.

Literacy, in the narrow sense, is of course necessary to a good education. But it is surely not sufficient. That denial does not get the analysis very far, however, and I wish to extend it. The sort of literacy that is a necessary condition of good education is not an independent condition, not a sort of platform on which all else can somehow be built. The roots of literacy are many, not all of them obvious or even understood. But the metaphor of the platform is wrong. Literacy is more like a many-branching tree we must climb for some, but surely not all, of the fruits of education. Some of the roots of literacy lie near the surface. The mere transduction from words written to words spoken, or the reverse, is trivially easy for human beings, though difficult for computers. We make it difficult for many children by trying to program them as we program computers, ignoring their great self-programming capacities.

At a slightly deeper level lie the roots reached by the present-day diagnostic tests. Prevailing low-average scores show that much of our population lacks acquaintance with many matters sampled across a wide universe, matters familiar to those presumably well educated. I use the word *acquaintance* rather than speak of knowledge or understanding; one can score pretty highly without much of the latter. To serve the cause of education, one must dig for still deeper roots.

For my part, therefore, I will look primarily at our traditions and practices of early schooling through the age of twelve or so. There is little to come after, whether of joys or miseries, that is not prefigured in these years. The ills of illiteracy may have their infective agents distributed far more widely, but in these early years of schooling they come to a focus. Therefore, we can fix the time scale of needed reform, and even a generation is not enough. To begin and then consolidate any major change, we must try to modify the whole loop, the whole cycle. First, we need to give help to the work of teachers and children today. The latter will grow up learning to become tomorrow's parents and teachers, those who may then reinitiate the cycle, at higher levels of quality and for larger numbers. Indeed, *reform* is the wrong word for the many needed changes, each in the wake of others, many still problematic. *Evolution* is the better word—for a long-term commitment of effort and inquiry. Even such an evolution, however promising at first, can all too easily be reversed. It becomes irreversible only as its consequences permeate the fabric of our institutions.

It is easy, and ungenerous, to forget that this world of schooling, as we now know it, is new. In a period of four or five generations, no more, universal publicly supported education has grown at a rate that is a good multiple of that of our population, hence always calling on the too-thin resources produced by previous efforts. The style and presuppositions of this institution, moreover, have evolved from a still older Euro-American tradition in which schooling itself was mainly limited to the children of relatively educated upper economic classes. From that tradition there has been no significant change—change measured either by those needs it was once intended to serve, or by the new needs imposed by the political commitment to universal education.

The older institution of schooling, designed for a restricted and economically favored class of children, was no peach of perfection. From the records we have, and from the traditions passed on to later times, those schools were predominantly narrow, rigid, and coercive. Here and there the light did shine through, from some masters and mistresses, for some children. There was tutorial education for many of the wealthy. Here and there were the benefits of persistence for those children who by temperament or parental support could seize even mediocre schooling as their only chance. Benign apprenticeships could sometimes lead well beyond the narrow boundaries of a trade.

Through the nineteenth century and into the twentieth, as schooling gained public support and grew to offer some education for all, its failures drew increasing attention from reformers, exacerbated as these failures were by the increasing diversity of preschool backgrounds among the widening circle of its pupils.[2] This diversity needs to be spelled out. It includes radically varied family education and commitment to education. It includes all the conditions of social exclusion, especially—for the United States—the background of slavery. So there have been many efforts to reshape these tradition-bound institutions to some kinds of form and function more appropriate to a growing need. Beginnings of major reforms have dotted our history and have left here and there some marks of their passage, but by the measure of insistent need they are minor.

I mention just one example of an early and still prevalent failure, one surely central to the discussion at hand. In elementary schools there has always been a great emphasis on the rudiments of literacy. But books—other than a few schoolbooks—have been in short supply. Originally, it was apparently assumed they would be available, there in the home, waiting. For children from literate backgrounds, the motivation to read was taken for granted. They were presumed to know, even in the dreariest of school hours, what needs and ambitions the routine might serve. And then, as some schooling became nearly universal, those from other sorts of backgrounds were accorded the same narrow agenda. Some were from unremitting poverty, others from backgrounds that for other reasons placed little value on schooling as parents or guardians—sometimes correctly—perceived it.

Because of developmental and experiential diversity, the readiness to engage in reading and writing is always uneven among five- and six-year-olds. Correspondingly, however, there are many pathways toward that engagement, differing in substance as well as tempo, that can lead equally to success. Some children already read when they first enter school. Some almost read, and for them the schools can claim success. But the curriculum traditionally has provided only one pathway and one expected tempo as "normal." In former times, the wide distribution of children's acquired skills was simply accepted as such. In more recent times, accepting instead the proposition that all should somehow stay "on track," we have evolved a subculture of specialists to whose guidance and instruction children not on track should be referred. That sort of reference, however, involves some formal procedure of diagnosis, apparently modeled after hospital staffing. This formal certification requires that some euphemistic label be attached to the child, such as "educationally disadvantaged." So far as I know, schools themselves are not subject to "staffing."

In the absence of any lasting engagement in reading and writing outside school or after leaving it, those mere reading "skills" we work so hard at can be as soon lost as acquired. As alleged reforms have come along, there are indeed more books in schools, mainly unloved textbooks. Here and there are adequate school libraries, most often in prosperous neighborhoods. Our good public libraries, and teachers who use them well, have been only a very partial substitute for books in school. Imperfectly developed under one set of historical conditions, the institutions of schooling have undergone only minor restructuring through a century of radical change in those conditions and in the demands upon them. The story of books is but one indicator.

Since books themselves represent only necessary conditions of literacy, further conditions are what deeply need attention. For every text that comes alive for a child, there must be a live context—both over and above and down underneath the paper and ink. Those sorts of contexts need to come in part, of course, from the child's experiences before school, and from beyond it. But optimally for all children, urgently for many, the school itself should provide that context. It should be a rich context of material provisions, of relation to the world beyond, but also of atmosphere, association, and self-initiated work that skilled teachers can support. The major deficiency of our schools lies here. The ambiance that confronts children in school as they grow up rarely provides enough of this rich context of challenge, opportunity, and success to match the great qualitative diversity of their strengths. Nor does it readily stir the commitment for learning that, unless already severely damaged, they bring with them from their earliest years. The sense and importance of this deep relation of text and context is evident when confronted, but discussion can slide too easily past it.

The metaphoric origins of the word pair *text* and *context*, along with many other riches of our vocabulary, come from the ancient history of the weaver's trade. The elements of discourse—the words and the phrases, the transparent or translucent vehicles of meaning—are woven together to create *text*. But the text itself is always part of a larger text, a weft already woven, hence *context*. In this sense, still almost literal, each text is embedded in prior texts, or at least in prior discourse. I say *discourse* to include the oral traditions that are inseparably interwoven with the written.[3] How well a text can be assimilated depends on the reader's contextual store. It is the abundance of this store that distinguishes the art of reading, and the commitment to it, from the easy skills of decoding.

But beyond that literal meaning of context is another without which the whole discussion gets lost, often because so taken for granted as to be unavailable for any fresh imaginative guidance. It is, of course, the context of experience, above and below and beyond *all* text. But this very word *experience* cries out for context: the context that lively teachers of the young can supply; and unless one goes to observe classrooms, one cannot understand it. I choose the elementary years in part because I know them better than the secondary, but also because one can observe there the roots of literacy in nascent, branching form. One can see, above all, that children can learn to read and write with commitment and quality *just* in proportion as they are engaged with matters of importance to them, and about which at some point they wish to write and read. When such conditions are well satisfied, almost all children can teach themselves to read and to write, big words included, and need little of the baneful "sounding out" of the traditional reading lesson. The atmosphere of lively classrooms is thus charged with all the vehicles of communication.

I select from memory a composite fourth-grade classroom. There are books in a corner, some written, published, and bound by the children. On the wall is a graph of the guinea pig's self-selected diet, posted just above her classroom territory. There is a map showing birthplaces—children's, their parents', and their grandparents'—marked on a large world map. Two children are working on a graph of the numbers and their divisors. Two, bent on painting a potted tomato with the right leaf color, are carefully measuring and mixing pigments. The walls are full of children's reports of work completed. There is a computer in the corner for mathematical games and puzzles and other forms of self-help instruction. A traffic survey of children's routes to school is in progress, with a map of the school and its neighborhood, a surveyor's trundle wheel for the children to borrow for mapping. In the hallway a school play is being rehearsed.

Such schools and classrooms do exist, and obviously in greater numbers than one observer can find. Yet their existence supports rather than negates my criticism of our schools. These good classrooms are powerful demonstrations of possibility. With commitment, they can be evolved. They are not magical—just rare!

It is in such contexts, I think, that we can discern the deepest roots of literacy; they are just those of early education itself—not a platform but a tree. But it is not my part to expand further upon the ways good early education can (among other achievements) reduce the dominance of textbooks and workbooks and the "time on task" they steal from occupations more conducive to literacy. I wish rather to define a broader adult perspective within which this kind of criticism of our traditions of schooling may itself find context and support. Hoping to incite support from the reflections of academic readers, I draw it from classic texts. We are, after all, a bookish lot, suspect in principle of exaggerating the importance of text. So the texts I quote were addressed to others like ourselves, yet they manage to invert the metaphor I have been using, of text and context, and in so doing to help define just the style of early education our world needs.

The first of these writings is well known. It is from the pen of Galileo, a letter of reply to the criticisms of one Sarsi, criticisms directed at an account Galileo had published about the nature of comets. Galileo published this letter in his *Il Saggiatore* (*The Assayer*). Here is the text:

> In Sarsi I seem to discern the firm belief that in philosophizing one must support oneself upon the opinions of some celebrated author, as if our minds ought to remain completely sterile unless wedded to the reasoning of the other person. Possibly he thinks that

philosophy is a book of fiction by some author, like *The Iliad* or *Orlando Furioso*, productions in which the least important thing is whether what is written there is true. Well, Sarsi, that is not how matters stand. *Philosophy is written in this grand book, the universe, which stands completely open to our gaze.*[4]

It was a dangerous act, that publication, since clearly it might lead to questions about the earlier astronomical texts that had been more or less incorporated into the received theology or, by some extension, to questions about the Scriptures themselves. Galileo is a hero for science, for the defense of those committed to the art of reading the book of nature. In the same spirit, we can emphasize the need to support children's own attention and curiosity about that grand book, to the beginnings of their mastery of its grammar and syntax; so also we can emphasize the need to support their critical attention to the schoolbook. Among the authors of elementary school science texts, there are still Sarsis to be found.

What Galileo stands for is generally accepted, however imperfectly translated in early educational practice. Usually, however, it is linked only to the sciences. The concerns of early schooling in the humanities—history, literature, and the arts—are therefore still to be examined. This aspect of the curriculum, and the vitality of its introduction in the early years, has somehow been far less closely monitored than that of science and math. We have heard a great deal about the inadequacy of science education—if only for present and future research needs, job markets, citizen understanding of technological issues. It seems often to be taken for granted, however, that other educational deficiencies, if they exist, are less urgently in need of critical discussion. It is as though the growth of children's aesthetic capacities—their early cultivation of the historical, ethical, and political dimensions, their discovery and enjoyment of their own productive capacities—were of secondary importance or else less in need of educational support. It may be that teachers do a better job here, less intimidated by science and math phobias implanted during their own earlier schooling. Yet classrooms that foster such engagements with the humanities at a high level are still rare—rare for the same reasons as those that foster good science are. Often it is the same classrooms that are able to do both.

I wish to make the same kind of argument for the humanities as for science, to find the same reversal of text and context in which the book, however prized for itself, for its beauty or its depth, is still just context for some more alive and essential text—that of experience, which it can nourish and help extend, but not replace. To carry this emphasis further, then, I quote from the writing of John Donne. He was a contemporary of Galileo's, and what I quote was written, remarkably enough, in the same decade, possibly even during the same year as *Il Saggiatore*. It seizes upon the same metaphor, the same reversal. Perhaps it was a fresh fashion of the day among the literate. One of Donne's sermons announces that "the world is a great volume, and man the index of that Booke; even in the body of man, you may turn to the whole world." Then again, in his most famous devotion, he elaborates: "All mankind is of one Author, and is one volume; when one man dies, one chapter is not torn out of the booke, but translated into a better language. . . . God's hand is in every translation; and his hand shall bind up all our scattered leaves again, for that Library where every booke shall lie open to one another."[5]

The library, of course, is the Christian Kingdom of Heaven, which like the Happy Land of Shin Buddhism—all theology apart—is an image of a good society, one based on the mutual interchange of influence among its members, "open to one another." What I wish to make of it, however, is local and small-scale, nothing grandly conceived but only a description of that richly furnished classroom that I alluded to above, "charged with all the vehicles of communication." In such a world the diversity of children's strengths and needs can become manifest to a teacher for discerning and supporting their varied trajectories of learning. To each other, that same diversity brings recognition and enjoyment, sometimes a shrewd diagnosis of trouble or recognition of achievement that a busy teacher might miss. In their early readings of the book of nature, in their social play, their commitment to expression, one can see the point of those rather grand and lordly texts I have quoted, brought down to earth on a scale that permits analysis and understanding.

If the metaphor of the "booke" seems forced or strange at first, that is all the better for discussion. When one watches a young child's first efforts to pound a nail, or those of an older one committed to an accurate geometrical drawing, one doesn't describe the behavior—one *reads* it, rather, against a background observation, of familiarity with this particular child's ways of encounter and involvement. The posture, the motions of the hand and eye and facial muscles, are of course observed, but they are observed in the way that words are in a text: they are transparent—or at least translucent—to a perception of the child's intent. What one observes is act or action, not merely "behavior." Of course, the first intent is not to communicate, but only to seat the nail well or draw the parallels accurately; later it may become part of a request for help or even a display of competence. Only when the behavior becomes ambiguous to us do we give it attention in its own right. By the time we speak of "interpreting" it, it is in some degree opaque. Likewise, the words of a text first get seen as opaque marks on paper only when the text's fluent control of our thought or imagination brings surprise or puzzlement. Teachers must be skilled in behavior reading, and children who work together must become acute at it. For the understanding of human affairs, and of themselves, this is their first language. Stories told, books read, all the expressive arts can be motivated, enjoyed, and translated from that understanding and can profoundly extend it; but they cannot of themselves create it.

Children first achieve competence. Next, they themselves recognize and enjoy its expression. Finally, they can achieve social recognition through sharing with others what they have achieved. This three-step process is just what is meant by *expression* in adult discussions of the arts. Expression among children may take the form of an art normally recognized by adults, but it is potentially present in all of their achievements. It has the quality of spontaneity, but spontaneity achieved through work and practice rather than thoughtless impulse.[6] This is why expression is a first language—often far subtler for children than anything they can say in words. Expression in this sense can convey a child's first readings of Donne's great "Booke."

When provided for in the good classrooms, children's science often has an appearance remote from the usual recitational stereotype. Taken seriously for children's learning, Galileo's injunction gives them the same privilege that he assigned to "philosophy." Printed books may add, may indeed become indispensable, yet cannot replace the original. That this is as true for science education as for original scientific discovery may seem a dubious assertion. The knowledge of nature, once achieved, can surely be transmitted to others without repeating or paralleling the history, so often devious and slow. But this truism is beside the point. True, the classroom laboratory for elementary schools, like those for high school and college, is needed in some measure to certify that what is taught is so. The Sarsis should have no final say! That has always been the proud boast of science teachers, though the lab, with its cookbooks and exercises, does not always live up to it.

But there is a far more essential reason for students' involvement in the grand book of nature. Its language is that of the *phenomena* themselves, and it is those phenomena, closely observed, that give life and meaning to all scientific text and talk.[7] Without some deep engagement of observation and experiment, there is no growth of understanding, no enjoyment of the many novelties that lie just beyond the everyday world, no growth of the means of thought that shape choices, debate, and further learning.

From the earliest years children's innate curiosity can, at least for many, feed happily on a wide array of nature's phenomena. These involve light and color, motion and equilibrium, batteries and things they do, plants' growth and form, small animals' behavior, structures, siphons, bubbles, the sky, etc. The list of topics and classroom material that imaginative teachers can help evolve is practically endless—when they themselves are given adequate professional support. With some understanding that all those elementary phenomena lie close in one way or another to scientifically sacred ground, they can later become open doors to what is often, otherwise, seen only as a dark and forbidding pedagogical territory misnamed "science."[8] Understanding can also open doors to an ample and growing popular science literature that can give us all some entry to the walled cities of advanced and specialized research, so we can scale their walls and bridge their moats.

As I suggested at the outset, it is not just coincidence that the growth of public schooling has taken place over the same time period as the latter phase of the industrial revolution, the period marked by the growing impact of the sciences on technology. This period of the industrial revolution also saw a vast growth of population and energy consumption. A few wealthy countries gained and then lost control of the rest. Extremes of poverty in the poorest countries coincided with large pockets of economic despair even in the richest. The early educational reformers could not anticipate all this, of course, but they sensed that the older parochialisms were threatened, that the life-circuit of any citizen would traverse an ever widening territory of concern, and that this must be matched by the spread of education. What had been a culture of an elite minority must somehow evolve to become that of the majority. If they did not always understand the roots of literacy and the needed cultivation that their growth required, the ambition of the reformers was valid, and their efforts have shaped us all.

Parochialisms are indeed threatened, beyond all early anticipations: those of locality and region, of social class and ethnic isolation, of national tradition—even of Western civilization itself. The preservation of tradition is still vital—long live the "Great Books"!—but so is the more ecumenical scrutiny of its failures and its resources for meeting world crises. These are crises that none of the great traditions of urban society ever anticipated—crises of industry, war, agriculture, massive human alienation, and the planetary ecosystem.

For any adequate comprehension of such matters within our culture—our popular culture or even much of that which considers itself high culture—there is as yet very little readiness. Since many of the human and terrestrial crises that face us develop gradually and are still ill-defined and remote by the measures of inattention within daily life, there is time for an educational refocusing. The readiness to make any serious commitment to educational change must grow, however, far less slowly than ever before, and that puts greater demands on the media of literacy—the written word, first of all, and then on all the newer modes of communication, visual and digital, that now demand our attention.

Given the premise that the educational quality of literacy is an expression, a continuation, of its experiential roots, then one must look at these newer media with that same premise in mind, now applied not just to the book, but also to the screen. Books *are* digital. We'd never mistake their illustrations for reality. But the computer or video screen can come alive, can impart to education much of the visual impact of direct experience. That is an immense extension and potential boon—to capture the life in a drop of pond water, or the destruction of a rainforest, or to fly just above the nearby surface of the moon. But it can also blur the boundaries between reality and fiction, as some of our screens already too routinely do. There are Sarsis out there as well, in that camera-ready world. So it must be a figure of merit that in representing reality the screen should also lead us with fresh curiosity *back* to the concrete world of nature and of human affairs. Otherwise the screen confronts us with a danger far greater than any that confronted those of Galileo's time. In one classroom the teacher told me children were challenged to become serious "television critics." Along the way, as a result, they changed their viewing habits and inane recitations quite radically. In the same way, older children can be helped to cure themselves of addiction to adventure stories written by the plot machine of video and computerized game authors, but the addiction to the screen comes earlier, is far stronger, and is far more effortlessly acquired.

So here again, for this extended meaning of literacy, one must ask for context, for the primacy, in the curriculum, of experience. Confronted with the pseudoreality of the screen, we run a greater risk than books ever presented—that the program and the script should lose the name of education, lose the deep commitment voiced in their different ways by Galileo and John Donne. To match their seventeenth-century commitment, then, here is another text, from E. B. White, one of the more lively and literate writers of our own recent past:

> Those last days! . . . Children early formed the habit of gaining all their images at second hand, by looking at a screen; they grew up believing that anything perceived directly was somehow fraudulent. . . . I think the decline in the importance of direct images dated from the year television managed to catch an eclipse of the moon. After that, nobody looked at the sky, and it was as though the moon had joined the shabby company of buskers. There was never a moment when a child, or even a man, felt free to look away from the television screen—for fear he might miss the one clue that would explain everything.[9]

Notes

1. This chapter was originally published in *Daedalus* 119(2), 1990: 1–14.

2. Indeed, the essential content of the present essay can be found in a literature of reform, much of it buried, that goes back to the mid–nineteenth century. There is, to be sure, much chaff mixed with the wheat, but the good grain is there to be winnowed. The best reference is Lawrence A. Cremin, *The Transformation of the Schools: Progressivism in American Education, 1876–1957* (New York: Knopf, 1947).

3. Do we forget the illiteracy of Homer? Storytelling is a medium and an art seemingly today out-distanced by all the others; yet it can flourish where print is absent or inconsequentially present. What Homer meant in his times is still a kind of wealth that prevails in many parts of the world. I owe to the late Sohl Thelejane of Lesotho the wry remark that the "European" schools would prosper, in tribal Africa, only when they learned to compete with tribal schools: children going, on moonlit nights, to hear stories told by grandmothers. From our own recent history one should read the transcription of Nate Shaw's autobiography, *All God's Dangers: The Life of Nate Shaw,*

compiled by Theodore Rosengarten (New York: Knopf, 1974). This story was told by a man who, as one reviewer put it, was "illiterate—illiterate like Homer."

4. The quotation is from *Discoveries and Opinions of Galileo,* translated and with an introduction and notes by Stillman Drake (New York: Doubleday Anchor, 1957); the emphasis is mine.

5. The quotations are from "Sermon LXXX" and "Devotion XVII." They are reproduced in *The Complete Poetry and Selected Prose of John Donne and the Complete Poetry of William Blake,* The Modern Library (New York: Random House, 1941).

6. This formulation is that of John Dewey in chapter 2 of his *Art as Experience* (New York: Minton, Balch, and Co., 1934). I believe that Dewey's best writings relevant to education were often in his later works, but they are seldom, if ever, referred to in educational circles. The word *education* is not in the titles or even in any central way in his texts: *Logic, Art as Experience,* and *Experience and Nature.* They express his most mature thought about human learning. He was a great pioneer of "cognitive psychology" but is still largely unrecognized in that trade.

7. See Chapter 2 of this book, a reprint of my "Nature Closely Observed," *Daedalus* 112(2), 1983: 65–89, wherein I have tried to spell out the meaning of the title phrase.

8. There is much research, from recent years, that probes the troubled world of science teaching. Why do so many students fail to learn or soon forget? For a review, see George L. C. Hills, "Students' Untutored Beliefs About Natural Phenomena: Primitive Science or Common Sense?" *Science Education* 3(2), 1989: 155–186. The article contains a useful bibliography.

9. E. B. White, *The Second Tree From the Corner* (New York: Harper and Brothers, 1954).

~ 2 ~

Nature Closely Observed[1]

There is a marvelous continuity between the worlds of children's experience and the adult worlds of the arts, of the sciences and mathematics, of conduct and social life. This continuity is one of cumulative learning. Learning, in this educationally important sense of the word, is always in principle *spontaneous*. Man, said old Korzybski, is a time-binding animal. We store experience, well or badly, as the squirrel stores nuts. Not for a coming winter, though in a wintertime the store may save us. But learning is also always, in some degree, *induced*. In this chapter I wish to use both these words, in a sense as technical terms. For *spontaneous*, I go back to the Latin *sponte*, "of one's own accord," and still earlier to an Indo-European root *spon*, which is one of that vast collection of words derived from the weaver's art, "to spin."[2] In the hand of the spinner, the spindle is given an initial twist, but it continues for a time *spontaneously*, of its own accord or, as we may prefer to say, its own spin energy. Children only learn well of their own accord. In this case, we need not wind them up to start the process; nature does that. But in another sense, the learning they engage in can be induced; they can be led into association with matter that matches their readiness to assimilate and to make much of that which counts and that they might otherwise never gain access to.

15

Induced learning is still, for children, spontaneous, if they are led, not dragged. When children are only dragged, they learn to cope with a curriculum of intimidation. To teach, then, is to have the authority of the guide, of one who shows the way. To teach is not to drag, though some element of the imperative mood is always latent in teaching; the guide who shows the way is never merely permissive. When children have been brought into some fresh territory for exploration, and find in it some joy and satisfaction, they forgive the hand that sometimes had to push their noses into such milk. But mostly, the hand is not needed; trust can take its place. And an attentive guide is open to questioning, to the suggestion of alternative routes.[3]

So what anthropologists call the transmission of culture is not at all the sort of telegraphic imprinting that the phrase itself suggests, but rather an enormously complex and problematic concept. At its best, the continuity between generations means that babies can grow up to be inventive women and men; children who have been excited by learning can later become adults who infect new children with that same excitement, supporting their entry into the great world, maintaining and advancing the qualities of life, of all that which over a hundred millennia has increasingly set us apart from our sheer animal existence.

But there is also a dreadful continuity between the limitations and failures of one generation and those it visits upon the next. Under deprivation or duress continued too long, children are not able to find those affirmative choices that would enhance their lives. As they enter the streams of adult life, they often must take with them their miseries, their accommodations to failure, even to brutality. They then may themselves sow dragon's teeth, a crop their own children will in turn harvest and replant, sometimes in even greater measure.

Such connections, educative and miseducative, are powerful; they are the counterpart for cultural evolution—including the rise and fall of cultures and civilizations—of all the genetic transmissions and changes that evolutionary biologists are concerned about in the history of terrestrial life. As a product of that biological evolution, we are predisposed to care for the young for some major fraction of their whole lives, to bring them up and to educate them over the long years of infancy and childhood. Disposed in their turn to assimilate what the adult world can offer them, children may assimilate and respin its strands and reweave its wefts of competence and creativity. They may also, in self-defense, emulate its self-destructive capacities. If our best and most insightful nursery schoolteachers could be transformed by some magic into anthropologists and historians, I think they would look for a different sort of evidence than historians have mainly offered to explain the rise and fall of cultures and civilizations: they would look to the transmission of cultures and of the zeal to learn, or to the failures of education thus broadly defined. The task would not be an easy one; the detailed processes of culture transmission have long been practiced but seldom much noticed or recorded; the exercise of sheer habit can go for long unquestioned.

I have spoken about the extremes of the process, the best and the worst. More frequent than either, of course, is a pattern of partial education to which we have become too well accustomed.

In the total ambiance of children's lives, then, there exists always some educative potential of which the school is only one component. The other components of this potential for education or miseducation—family life, peer association, and the big world they increasingly respond to—are in many ways more powerful than schooling. Schools are, after all, only an institutional invention and, in the long sweep of history, a recent and still very uneven one. But even today, children of the well educated often likewise emerge as well educated, along pathways that owe less to their formal education than might appear. Teachers are prone to claim more in this regard than is really justified. On the other hand, where the out-of-school potential is low, school can be a vital alternative. This is often true for those from generally meager backgrounds; and where the educative potential of some major part of society is in fact low, then what can be learned in school can become a saving grace, ameliorating the dreadful continuity. In saying this, I do not wish to minimize those informal extensions of formal education, intended for adults and children alike, represented in our day by film and television and by museums. As extensions of schooling, they can enrich the ambience, at least for some.

I have begun with these rather wide-ranging remarks because I wish to discuss an educational domain in which the spontaneous potential of even our otherwise well-educated classes is on balance quite low: mathematics and the sciences. We are all acquainted with the extraordinary history of rapid social change that, over three or four centuries, has been coupled with the evolution of the special subculture of science. This subculture of science has owed its vigor, as a necessary condition, to its ability to reproduce itself on a scale that has steadily increased. This increase is in numbers, in detailed knowledge reduced to order, and in specialization. Thus an important part of the history of science has been the recruitment of the young. To this end, science has long since invaded the universities, and now in some manner can dominate them. Its influence is far less in the secondary schools, and almost negligible in the first six or eight years of schooling. Along the way, however, and perhaps as a necessity of rapid growth, the scientific subculture has developed such cumulatively special ways of learning, reorganizing, and communicating as to constitute increasing barriers to entry. The required preparation of neophytes has become more and more extensive and elaborate, and there is finally a threat of their sheer depletion. The well is not dry, but the needed talent level has been steadily lowered. Some of us have come first to a new concern for earlier and wider science education because of this threatened depletion, a threat to the continued prosperity of our craft. The wells of available talent must now somehow be refilled and maintained by earlier and wider and more effective science education. Such is the narrow view. The institutional statecraft of science has for a long time taken too much for granted, beginning its educational efforts too little, too late, and with too little attention to quality.

There is a wider view, however, concerned less immediately with recruitment than with the welfare of a society that on the average has so low a diffuse out-of-school potential for science education, but that depends crucially upon the institutions of science and upon their increasing symbiosis with industry, with medicine and agriculture, with government, and with the military. Our aim in teaching basic science should be to prepare all youngsters for eventual participation in the democratic discussion and reordering of ends; the narrowing, even the failure to broaden basic science education creates scientific and technological oligarchies, while the rest of us tend to become incompetent for democratic rule, to become—in the language of Arnold Toynbee—a cultural proletariat.

Both these honorable views, which have become very familiar to us, are clearly not incompatible. If the range of scientific literacy is widened, the diffuse educative potential increases, and the level in the wells of talent will also rise. Twenty years ago we argued—or at least competed for educational funds—in terms of the ordering of priorities as between upper-level professional science education and lower-level science for the citizen. Now, I think, this sort of debate seems rather stale and innocuous. We need both equally, each for the other.

But there is a third, a still wider view, growing out of good works that have often been attempted but not widely credited or understood. There are beginnings of it in the traditions of enlightenment; surely not, however, much reduced to widespread practice, and perhaps least so among the official austerities of present-day formal education. I think it is a view necessary to the empowerment of the narrower views I have summarized, but it has more important justifications as well. I shall elucidate it, as best I can, from the educational lives of children and of those who teach them. It is most accessible there.

In this wider view of science education, the central aim is to contribute, quite generally, to the improvement of *all* education. As such education should prove successful, it would of course contribute to enlarging the pools of potential scientific talent and enhance the qualities of intelligent citizenship. But such aims are thin gruel; they lack the kind of informational richness we need to guide our efforts. They may indeed only lead us today—in a new round of concern—to intensify conventional efforts already marked for failure. I propose to start instead with some account of what I believe to be our most successful experience. I cannot document it on any but a small scale, out of the experience of good teachers I have had the luck to know. It also fits a certain good theoretical mold, however, that supports it and that I shall try to sketch.

In singling out our present-day inadequacies for teaching science and math, and then in proposing a direction for remedy, I may seem to risk a false assumption: that all else is well in our early education practice. It is a risk made all the more obvious by the widespread talk of the deterioration of schooling, usually in the areas of reading, writing, and computational skill. But there is the opposite risk, that we fail to recognize the ways in which children's early involvements with the substance of science and math can open gates for them into all the domains of knowledge and enjoyment. I shall try to compensate for the first risk by doing what I can to avoid the second.

As a first step, a basic assumption: to lead children into domains of science and math can presuppose less, by way of any prior richness in their educative backgrounds, than is needed for other essential parts of a school's curriculum. History, for example, or literature, even reading and writing, can come easily to children whose family and social backgrounds provide them, early and steadily, with surroundings where such matters are valued as part of daily life. For those who lack that sort of background, these interests can be relatively inaccessible. There are exceptions, of course; but when we look closely there, among the children of poverty, we seem to find only rare, special circumstances that have opened the doors for them into the worlds of the written word, the arts, and the humanities. The sheer fact of poverty does not always exclude those drops of nectar in the sieve that can heighten children's taste for poetry, for fantasy, for storytelling, and so for the written word. Nevertheless, such engrossing interests presuppose an early richness of experience and of experience reflected upon, which the life of poverty can seldom afford.

If we follow this line of thought, we are led to the conclusion that there is more of the basic background experience for mathematics and science in the life of every child than for most other subjects in the early curriculum. These are the daily phenomena of nature that surround us constantly, early and late, and about which we all accumulate a central store of experience—of light and dark and color, of heat and cold, of motion and rest, of forms of matter and of life. In a trial course of geometry, the Gruppo Scuola e Universita in Rome, for example, introduced planes, lines, and points by slicing a potato at right angles once, twice, thrice.

But this conclusion seems in violent contradiction with the everyday wisdom of curriculum designers and of most teachers. Math and science are reputedly the most difficult subjects to teach. As a result, science is taught hardly at all, while math is reserved for the early hours of the day when children are, it is supposed, least fatigued. If this belief is correct—and it is surely based on massive experience of a kind—then something is very wrong with my line of argument, which implies that of all the traditional subjects in the curriculum, math and science should in principle be the most accessible to children from a wide range of backgrounds. But I prefer to take refuge from evidence of this sort. There is an old joke: "Don't confuse me with the facts!" I think the facts are there, but they are wrongly taken. Early math and science are on balance so badly understood and taught that the failures we know so well lie with the style of teaching and hardly at all with the children. School failures are typically regarded as children's failures, rather than failures of the school itself. There is very little evidence readily available to decide between my own belief and that which usually prevails; we have many would-be child doctors, but too few school doctors. Against a mainstream of opinion that I reject, I reaffirm my argument: the kind of experiential background in children's lives before schooling begins, or along the way, is more uniformly adequate to math and science than to most other school subjects. The poverty or riches of social background matter less here in the early years than in other school subjects. Math and science should therefore be the great equalizers, whether they are now seen to be or not.

I have said that in our elementary schools, science is seldom taught at all, while math is reserved for the early hours of the day. But that is inaccurate. I should have said that neither subject is taught, for the most part, at all. What is called school mathematics is not mathematics, or is barely so. The lives of children in elementary school are dominated during "math" periods by assignments that are only called arithmetic. A tiny bit is called geometry, but most of that bit dwells on the mere names of things unloved, such as triangles, squares, pentagons, and the like. Most of what is taught is called arithmetic, and children learn, soberly, to add, subtract, multiply, divide. They also may learn some bewildering rote algorithms about fractions, how to add or subtract, even multiply or divide them. They learn, in a fashion, to handle negatives or decimals. And this modest goal takes six or eight years of dubious battle; a thousand or two hours, central hours, of children's days for 10 or 20 percent of their lives.

The ancient Greeks made a distinction in their language between what they called *arithmetic* and what they called *logistic*. Arithmetic was the investigation of the world of numbers; logistic was a set of rules, to be memorized, for doing rote sums, differences, products, quotients. Arithmetic was a kind of science, always fresh and open to endless investigation. Logistic was a dull art, needed for bookkeeping and other such practices, that you could learn by rote. If you understood something of arithmetic, you could easily master the rules of logistic; if you forgot those rules, you could reinvent them. What we mainly try to teach in all those early years of schooling is logistic, not arithmetic. We drag, not lead, and the efficiency of learning is scandalously low. Of course, it is not all one way. In order to pursue arithmetical investigations and the many practical uses to which some can be put, it is useful to deal easily with sums or quotients. In some purely formal order of development, the rules come first.

But, in the order of optimal understanding, the intuitive grasp can often run far ahead of the computations necessary for completely reliable answers to questions that a budding curiosity has raised. We put poker chips together on the table in the patterns of triangles or squares, and find that these patterns can grow larger and larger, yet preserve their shape. It can be an invitation for counting, for tabulating, for seeing relations of sum and product and quotient. We begin to see a pattern of number growth in the patterns of shape; we predict and perhaps confirm; we find nice relationships between the visual world of geometric form and the step-by-step logical world of numbers. These are small examples of the vast array of relationships that cross-connect two very important domains within all our experience—number and form—which early schooling, if it treats them at all, too often treats in isolation. It is a simple and shocking example of this separation that, to most elementary schoolteachers in the courses I teach, the adjective *square*, when applied to numbers, has no perceived relation to the same adjective applied to forms. Even triangular numbers, not to mention pentagons, cubes, or tetragons, are then a complete surprise, as are other classes of number shapes.

Many investigations into the connections between number and form are quite accessible to children and bring new understanding. Along with the many practical uses of math that can engage children (carpentry, sewing, weaving, classroom bookkeeping, mapping, and measuring), the genuinely mathematical investigations can motivate the acquisition of computational skill, of logistic. This skill is, or should be, subordinate to real math, and when subordinated, can be learned more easily. In all of this, one can live and work in the style—often the very content—of the ancient Greeks before Euclid. In the three centuries before his works appeared, there were many little and some big mathematical discoveries made. Those early mathematicians, and many still later, used the letters of the alphabet for numerals and the abacus for computations, and drew shapes in smooth sand. The language they used was just the ordinary Greek; there was no elaborate shorthand symbolic notation such as we associate with present-day mathematics and force too early upon our children. But from such everyday beginnings, the ancients began to develop some powerful ideas and important questions, the beginnings of our own tradition. Children guided can do that, too.

A classroom in which this sort of real mathematics is pursued becomes a math lab—I call it the "Laboratory of Archimedes"—and by an easy extension, it can also become a science lab, with much of the simple apparatus for investigating physical phenomena (heat and light, sound and motion), and with space for various growing plants and sometimes resident or transient animals. And since all important matters that transpire in such a classroom must be related to what one finds in books, there must be a good library corner. Good things must also be reported on, with texts and posters. (A "nonreader" will learn to use them if they contribute to learning, and will learn to write if there is fresh excitement to communicate.) In its contrast with most classrooms we have seen, it may sound forbidding, but it is in fact the opposite. It is most inviting.

I recall with amusement a class in North Wales in which a group of ten-year-olds put old Galileo to the test. A children's science book had told the too-simple story of the unequal weights dropped from the Leaning Tower of Pisa, and had rather primly missed the whole point of it by insisting that the heavier weight would fall a bit faster. Those children devised a beautiful experiment that would have warmed the heart of Galileo himself; it was, in fact, one used first by Galileo's elder contemporary, Stevin of Brussels. They managed a tall ladder from which the two weights could be dropped onto a bit of galvanized iron. The ear (better than the eye) could recognize small differences in the time at which two weights, dropped together, would hit the tin. These Welsh children were treading sacred ground. Most agreed with what they were told was Galileo's conclusion, and explained away the very small differences they heard; two held out against this conclusion. Their teacher and I agreed that there was no need for us to straighten the whole thing out, at least that day. In his training, he said, he had been told that one should never leave children with wrong conclusions. But he thought children would never hold too strongly to conclusions of their own devising. The danger was that they might uncritically accept the errors that adults so often uncritically impose.

A central argument against the style of science and math education I am suggesting here is that there is no time for it; no time, they say, to reinvent the wheel. I cannot resist a first reply, which is that not everything is known, as yet, about the wheel, either the mathematics of it or the physics. I am thinking of the long and beautiful history, in mathematics and physics, of the circular functions, of the Fourier transformations that use them so elegantly, of the complex domain and the infinite scheme of the roots of unity. I am thinking also of the world of modern physics, in which one may learn to think of rotations that go twice around before getting back to the starting point. Today's children will do well *not* to close their minds prematurely on the subject of wheels.

Past experience must indeed be somehow summarized, must in some way be put in soluble capsules; it cannot be relived in its totality. If we had to relive all past errors and discoveries, it would be a commitment to absurdity. A part—indeed a major part—of the structuring of our minds must come from instruction. But this obvious statement leads much too easily to notions that are, I believe, radically false. Instruction by a teacher fails without a matching *construction* by the learner, induction without spontaneity, words without things. The lecture or the textbook passage that succeeds is one that meets an apperception well prepared. When we merely surrender to the textbook, we surrender to defeat.

What is essential, then, is that children should *often* be instructed, but they should *seldom* be instructed before they are prepared to engage, to criticize, and test at least some small part of what they are being taught. But how does a teacher, knowing such essentials, manage it all? Here, I think, we are most likely to fail. Good teaching is above all a preparation for the unforeseen, for the lovely things that can happen when one has faith that they will happen. When children are optimally involved, they bring to their interpretations of fresh experience a marvelous diversity of understandings from their own past; from what they have recurrently observed and put together and from what they have assimilated from adult associations, all mixed together in ways that are individually diverse but that have a common style. The teacher's job is not to fill some empty places in their minds with new knowledge. The human mind is never empty, though parts of it are often filled without those kinds of large-scale interconnections and reductions-to-order that education should seek to further. The teacher's job is, or should be, to help children sort and rectify. The great teaching art is that of observing and listening, of searching for clues, and of then providing that which may steady and further a budding curiosity, or failing, may lead to further clues. It is as profoundly inductive, in its own way, as children's own learning should be. Teachers, in their own differently ordered minds,

can often convict children of error, when in fact, the children's statements are right answers to questions different from those the teachers
thought they had asked.

Just here lies the central answer to the critics who impatiently say we
have no time to reinvent the wheel, and the right critique of that kind of
didacticism to which their thinking tends then to regress. Spoken or
written language, isolated from all immediate connection with what it
seeks to convey, has little power to excite those resonances in children's
minds that can call forth their full powers to retrieve the understandings
they already possess and that they can potentially link together in fresh
connections and analogies. I quote here a passage from Henry James,
used by Frances Hawkins in the broader context of a classroom atmosphere in which children of diverse interests and talents can learn well. I
use it for the related, but narrower, purpose of suggesting the way in
which closely observed natural phenomena can excite early curiosity and
understanding. "Small children have many more perceptions than they
have terms to translate them; their vision is at any moment much richer,
their apprehension even constantly stronger, than their prompt, their at
all producible, vocabulary."[4]

To this elegant statement I would only add a converse. The early-
evolved filing systems of children's minds, their resources of memory
and analogy and generalization, are often far more readily summoned up
by fresh input from activity and observation than by any of those thin
verbal streams that well-meaning teachers so often direct at them. What
is not within the range of their "at all producible vocabulary" is also not
readily excited by a teacher, however produced. The linkage between the
closely observed and the thoughtfully stated can only develop well in an
informal dialectic in which what is said, is said in the context of what is
seen, and what is seen, is seen in the context of what is said—contexts
linked in daily intercourse. If the classroom is bare of the materials and
phenomena discussed, this linkage is destroyed. When they are present,
the communication between children and teachers can acquire a second
and third dimension, indeed an nth, that the linear sequence of spoken
or written signs can never wholly replace. The phenomena observed in
classroom laboratories or field trips become symbols of themselves, so
to speak, literal parts of discourse; the talk about them is enriched and
informed. Children's grasp of them can be expressed in many ways, in
talk, but also in dance sometimes, or painting; the words themselves, of

children or teachers, can then be relieved of a freight that alone they cannot bear.

Let me illustrate. The textbook says that heat flows from hot to cold, or that light travels in straight lines, or that the earth goes about the sun; the teacher tries to elucidate, with questions and answers, with drawings, and through other means. But failure is often imminent. In each case, the intended communication is blocked, more often than not, by a radical mismatch between the presuppositions of the book or the teacher and those of the child. What the book and the teacher obedient to it try to communicate often presupposes (but fails to induce) a radical reorganization, in each case, of some common-sense category of experience. If our early grasp of motion is itself all geographical, then the earth itself surely does not "go." If our early understanding of light is in contrast with darkness, light may shine but not "travel." Heat may melt the ice or warm the hands, but it is not a "flowing" kind of thing, a fluid. In all such cases, one must, I think, demand an efficient division of labor between the spontaneous investigations of children and the planning and participation of teachers. When we try to describe the kinds of teaching that contribute successfully to children's reorganization of such big ideas as the earth's motion and the nature of heat and light, we find that the sheer amounts of time involved—time for induction—are large compared to what is usually allotted to them, but also that the growth of scientific understanding is then overall more rapid. When children can bring their own resources and spontaneous motivation to such learnings, their ability to break fresh ground can be enhanced beyond the range of any of the usual measures.

As for the kinds of phenomena to be brought together with the children and the teacher, there is a rich array, lying on the edge of everyday experience, that children can closely observe. For the beginning study of optics, we can easily provide a wide variety that bring illuminations and shadows center stage. Children (as well as many adults) have a vast background acquaintance; but they have seldom put the lamp, the object, and its shadow in that simple projective relation that has been there all along. It is a bit of geometry that has seldom been closely observed. With lamps and mirrors and pinholes for those strange inverted images, the geometrical abstraction of the light ray is within the reach and grasp of children, though it often takes a great diversity of examples, and some real time, to become compelling. A single classroom demonstration will often miss the point. Taken out of doors, there are new dimensions opened up, among them the daytime astronomy of the sun's motion and the most elegant of all sundials, the classroom terrestrial globe, flooded with sunlight, with its axis pointing to the North Star, and "Our Town" just on top. We cannot bring the solar system into the classroom, and mechanical models are confusing, because their introduction presupposes the very analogy they are supposed to show. But two string pendulums, hanging near each other, provide a diversity of phenomena that are among the closest terrestrial counterparts of planetary motions. With heavy weights and ceiling or doorway suspensions, their motions are only slowly lost, and they share the style of the heavenly motions, of Newton's sacred laws. Closely observed, they bring to the fore in children's minds a frame of thought very different from the common sense that Galileo and Newton had to overcome in establishing the laws of motion. But again, the phenomenal diversity needed is large, and the times to be spent with such things, in classroom or out, must be generously allotted.

Let me now speak of the very different ambience in which the biological sciences have evolved. Added to the Laboratory of Archimedes, plants and animals import one essential element, which Ronald Colton has repeatedly emphasized: respect for life. The term at first suggests only a detached moral commitment, one alien to the usual amoral stereotypes of science. But looked at closely, the obligations of maintenance are both profoundly moral and, so, instructive. The style of biology, unlike that of the physical sciences, begins with the conditions of maintenance that, over some billions of years, nature herself has supplied. To the usual biological and aesthetic sterility of the classroom, teacher and children must manage to add the necessities of plant and animal maintenance, and must do so with a degree of commitment that is absolute; otherwise, they die. Seedlings will grow in the dark, but not for long. What else is needed? Small animals will flourish under conditions that we must try to investigate, and be provided, to that end, with rich environments and choices of food, not just the bland commercial pellets (which will do for a start). Even colonies of bacteria and molds require some conditions of maintenance and care. And finally, again, the field trips are a widening exposure to the diversities of life, to the ecological web (again, a metaphor from the weaver's art), the flows of matter and energy that sustain us all, the interweaving of context and content without which none of the sciences of life—even molecular biology—would have any proper subject matter; it would have ceased to exist.

In 1980, Frances Hawkins and Ronald Colton offered a course for teachers called "Animals in the Classroom." It was a fascinating enterprise, a trial run of a large subject, one that brought together a great deal of experience. The range of animals maintained, or at least investigated, in the course was large, from guinea pigs to hydras. The latter lived in shallow dishes, and managed a living from another species, brine shrimp. The guinea pigs were benignly vegetarian, consuming lettuce and carrots from supermarket sources but, more educatively, the grass that was grown on their premises: seeds of wheat and rye and barley grown in their own territory, a large open steamer trunk of vintage 1910, filled with potting soil and peat moss, with rocks and logs and growing plants. They could have left their Eden, but they never did. There had been other ventures of this sort, such as a large and beautiful cage, in a Head Start classroom, for small mice, odor-free when the soil under their feet had the right bacteria and the living area per mouse was large enough. Out of this collaboration between two teachers who shared a deep understanding of the worlds of children and of other living things, there grew an analogy of proportions: only a good classroom, a good world for children, could sustain and care for a good world within it for small animals. Otherwise there would be only a surface interest, then indifference and neglect.

It is just here, I believe, that one can see the ways in which a good early education at the roots of science and math can nurture the concern for human affairs generally, for the arts and humanities. What I began to describe as the Laboratory of Archimedes has now grown, as it must, into a small human world linked in many ways to the large world of nature, but also to that of human affairs. Out of doors, in the schoolyard and beyond, is an environment rich in subject matter, crafted and natural, open to investigation. The town has a history, accessible from many starting points. Once, that I know of, the search began with a map of children's routes to school, then broadened to its valley and river, an older route to the sea.[5] It could as well begin with a map of ancestry, where each was born, then the birthplaces of parents and even grandparents. And the library corner can hold, for a time, good children's literature of history, of fiction and fantasy, as well as sober science, all sources for the enlargement of acquaintance and imagination. Craft work with yarn and clay and other materials is often relegated to spare time, but can be brought center stage through its relations to history and technology, to the stuffs and arts of everyday life, as well as to science and mathematics.

In all such children's work, guided by thoughtful and responsive teachers, there is a spirit of play. The adult conception of play is usually a stereotypic one: enjoyable activity devoted to no single or sober or serious end, and often disparaged for that reason. I think this definition of play is in fact a good one, but the disparagement is unwarranted. Children's play, closely observed and then steadied and extended by adult provisioning, represents a powerful organizer of their growing experience and, at the same time, a synoptic expression of it; it is an expression that is the precursor of all the established arts, wider in its range and never lost among those who grow creatively into the traditions that those arts represent.[6] But it is also the matrix out of which is born the capacity for the very definition of sober and serious ends, and the capacity to reconstruct them in the course of a worthy life. It is the unifying sphere in which all the major capacities of the mind are brought together in some potentially fruitful relation. In his *Critique of Judgment*, Immanuel Kant defined the aesthetic domain by reference to what he called "the free play of understanding and imagination," unfettered by the strict disciplines of cognition or the commitments of conduct.[7] The bachelor sage of Königsberg never explicitly included childhood within the range of his critical philosophy (as Rousseau later tried to do), but his analysis of the role of the arts required a conception of play that could have led him there.

I trust that my sketch of a classroom-laboratory-library-atelier is not taken to be giving some temporal priority to math and science, as though it would be expanded stepwise to include the other components only later in the game. There have been many good teachers whose work included nothing of math and science, at least nothing so called or so recognized. There have always been, and must remain, many pathways into the wider worlds of education suited to the special talents of teachers and of children. Good teachers differ more among themselves, and from themselves year by year, than do those who offer a meager fare. The universals of good teaching are invariants across a wide range of surface diversity. Bad teaching is more uniform and more easily described and condemned, and in recent times, we have had a spate of that sort of protest literature.

My argument for the importance of early math and science involves, then, only two logical steps. The first is the recognition that the doorways into these disciplines from the predisciplinary world of childhood are more widely accessible than others. The second is that in creating a school environment in which some of these doors are opened, teachers can evolve a penumbra and a style of inquiry that opens many other doors as well. To create such an atmosphere it is necessary—though by no means sufficient—to stock that classroom with diverse materials that exemplify or generate a wide range of natural phenomena in order to legitimate and invite children's curiosity. Printed paper, mass produced, is cheap and thin, and in its proper subordinate place, essential. It can never transmit more than a small—if necessary—part for the equations of understandings, even for adults. Yet if you conduct a census of materials in most of our classrooms (empty, on a Saturday morning), you find little else.

The classroom paper I despair of is not that of children's literature, too rarely present. Nor is it the vehicle of their written stories and journals, their early engagement with the disciplines of poetry and prose. If a classroom has two doors to a hallway, it should have a third, at least, a "lion door"—so a young friend once called it. The well-husbanded library corner, linked to the writing tablet and to a teacher-critic prepared to applaud and to question, can become a lion door. If nature closely observed can first extend children's "at all producible vocabulary," then the written language itself, closely observed and well used, can in turn extend the range of their perceptions. These extensions can reach in all the directions of experience, not least the scientific. And among the scientific extensions, not least is that of size and scale and complexity, which we represent, in shorthand, by the formal written code of the powers of ten. The dough of puff pastry is buttered, folded over, and rolled out repeatedly. Seven foldings make a flaky pastry. How many powers of two (or ten) to reach the thickness of an atom?

There is, then, an added, third step to my argument, which I venture to make in closing it. This step is one that bears on the need for fresh blood in the sciences and for a more informed citizenry, but that also extends the definition of those needs. On the one hand, the evolution of science since the sixteenth and seventeenth centuries has transformed our working relations with nature and has brought us, as a single biological species, to dominate—but also to destablize—the whole of our planetary world. We can learn to love it as a potential Second Garden or, by the turn of the screw, destroy it, and with it, ourselves. The love cannot come as a belated afterthought; it must begin in our early years with the onset of knowledge and wonder, of nature closely observed, observed first in detail and later conceived in powerful generality. Such love has always been a motivating force in scientific investigation, but it can get short-circuited in the pursuit of clever technologies, or is tolerated, in the halls of industry, as a useful eccentricity.

Yet the whole development of science, however motivated, has transformed for us any acceptable understanding of man's place in nature, and thus the framework within which we can adequately form or conceive our own ends and means. In these three or four centuries, our knowledge of the natural world has been extended upward and downward, in the scale of sizes, from the atoms to the cosmos. Begun in speculation, it was vivified by the microscope and telescope, radical extensions of our senses. The first major poet of this extension, awed and frightened by its implications, was Blaise Pascal, contemporary of Newton and of Leeuwenhoek. Pascal was a mathematician and physicist, abreast of, and contributing to, all those early developments of science. He was also one of profound ethical and religious commitment, who saw that nature, in its vastness, could no longer be regarded as only a set of theater props for the medieval Christian domestic struggle of good and evil. Another contemporary, Baruch Spinoza, was equally involved in, and affected by, the new world of science. Christian and Jew, both faced with the vision of infinite nature, concluded that man's whole dignity lies in the power of thought: the thinking reed can achieve some comprehension of the power of nature and of man's place. Pascal dramatized the uniqueness of man, while Spinoza sought to understand it as a mode of nature's own self-comprehension. But both acknowledged the new vision of science as a turning point for ethics and religion.

Today we can add a new dimension to that vision that fills it out and makes its import still more compelling. To the vast scale of size we can add the scale of historical time, a scale unknown and hardly guessed in the seventeenth century. In size we are almost halfway between the greatest thing we know and the smallest, as Pascal announced. More precisely, we are twenty-five powers of ten above the smallest things we know, and sixteen powers of ten below the largest.[8] In time, the scale is almost as great, from the briefest possible subatomic events to the duration of the cosmos in its now-estimated history. The duration of our own human least awareness is some twenty powers of ten above the subatomic minimum, while that of a human generation goes up by about nine further powers of ten. The duration of our species is about a hundred thousand of these generations, five powers of ten. For the duration of terrestrial life as a whole, we must multiply again by a thousand, the third power. On this scale, the earth itself, and then the whole cosmos, is less than ten times older, a single power of ten. If our dignity lies in the power of thought, as Pascal said, it is matched by a dignity of age; we and all our cousins in the terrestrial living world, though middling on the scale of sizes, are almost as ancient as the cosmos itself.

To have a sense for all these numbers, and the rich scientific story from which they are distilled, will surely suffice us not at all in baking bread or in coping with the destruction of our farmlands or the pollution of city slums. It will not of itself avert the peril of nuclear war, that terrifying stepchild of scientific advance. Nevertheless, we need that story as a framework for understanding, a framework that allows us first to acknowledge the issues that face us today, and then to work to understand and meet them. What we desperately need are the powers to cultivate the imagination far beyond the limits of everyday parochial life, and these surely include a sense for the many powers of ten. Our parish, our pueblo, our shamba—the neighborhood of each of us—has grown by many such powers, in space and in history, whether we know it or not. We need six powers of ten to understand the difference between a chemical explosive and a nuclear bomb; that is something even our great leaders, and the constituencies that elect them, have not yet adequately grasped. We need several powers of ten to frame the difference, in our imaginations, between our own years—six or ten or sixty—and those of the rocks we scramble over on a field trip or holiday. Again, it is six powers of ten to go from the perimeter of our school grounds to the distance to the moon, and a few more to span the distance to the sun. And so it goes, for the distance to the nearest star, then to Andromeda, and finally to the edges of the early universe. So it goes also to the distant past, in which we can see that all living things under the sun are cousins and all humans part of the same family.

As a final step, I wish to acknowledge a second sort of argument against much that I have said and against the optimism implicit in it. It is an argument that will rise most cogently in the minds of those wise in the ways of our present-day schools, and I must acknowledge it fully. I began with an emphasis on the continuity of culture, whether marvelous or dreadful or only drearily predictable, a continuity that is unavoidable in all our educative associations—and the schools are no exception. This argument is very simple: the educative potential of our schools is not high enough, and will not foreseeably rise high enough, to warrant any implicit optimism. To have such good education, except here and there and almost by chance, implies the existence of teachers who are themselves the products *of* that very education; while in fact the teachers we mainly produce are poorly educated. They are poorly educated with respect to subject matter, first of all. They are poorly educated with respect to the patterns of human development and the arts that foster it. And they are enchained within a school bureaucracy that has not learned to treat them as professionals in need of professional support and capable of a fully professional independence and accountability. They are treated rather as civil servants of a low grade, and the treatment is all too often self-confirming. In short, there is no way visible in which the antecedents of what we need can be matched to the consequents of what we have. So goes the argument of the critics.

Two decades ago, indeed, many of those who sought to improve our education in science and math were given to a false optimism based on the belief that the curriculum reforms then fashionable would be so potent that their effects would somehow bypass the inadequate education of teachers. This was an unjustifiable arrogance, and time has shown it to be so. The good consequences of those efforts lay mainly in those cases where teachers themselves became deeply involved in the reforms and showed us how to reduce them to practice. Help from the outside is of no avail unless, and in the measure that, it contributes to the growth and stature of the teachers, and they in turn contribute. That should be held to, I believe, as a firm axiom. We should judge all new proposals by it, whether for texts or guides or computer modules.

The continuity, then, is unavoidable, as is a certain pessimism concerning the probability of significant reforms. The optimism that many of us feel, the sense of romance about the potentialities of early education, is an optimism of the possible, not one of somehow calculable probabilities. But, I respond, possibility can be robust. Those of us who have been fortunate enough to sniff out and find the good classrooms, variations on the sorts of themes I have been suggesting, have indeed

found them, though rarely enough—have found them reduced to practice and thriving, guided by quite bona fide mortals, overworked but
happy in their craft. And here, too, there is continuity. Almost always in
the background or foreground of teachers there is some strong educative
influence, some professional support that they have assimilated and
modified, perhaps extended. No one person invented the wheel or the
telescope or the internal combustion engine. They have been evolved,
step by step, without any violation of continuity. And so can good education, though it is far more complex. The law of continuity is no warrant for fatalism.

In the biological world, there is a kind of theorem about the emer-
gence of new types and new species: they do not arise by sudden or
massive modification of older and dominant species, but appear, rather,
because some genetic variety, initially rare, manages to grow at a rate
faster than others around it when a new ecological niche appears that
favors it. That is why evolution is not predictable; it works through the
amplification of initially rare varieties that early go unnoticed. Good
ideas have that kind of history, too, and so we often see it only in retrospect. I should hope that we begin to think of the improvement of education in just these terms. If good patterns of work with young children
can be recognized early, while they are—as indeed they are—still rare and
all too easily lost, we can hope to create for them some systems of protection, support, and growth. Since they are rare, the initial investment
is moderate, and it can grow with the success it increasingly demonstrates. In our own search for the good sorts of early educational patterns, we have found them very unevenly distributed. Where they have
been thickest on the ground, we have found such systems of professional
support and encouragement, working high above the average level of
what is called in-service education or staff development, usually a per-
functory service with marginal budgets that can be most easily lopped
off in hard times. To say this is not an expression of pessimism, but of
outrage.

The continuing education and professional growth of our teachers is
of course not the only way of modifying the loop of continuity from
teachers inadequately educated to children poorly taught. There are others, especially those affecting the preservice education of teachers. Here it
is customary to blame the schools of education, themselves inadequately
provided for serious professional training. They are, to be sure, respon-

sible for some part of the failure. But a large part of the blame should be laid at the feet of our undergraduate arts-and-sciences colleges, which fail conspicuously to provide rich fare for future teachers of the young. Such students especially need what all college students could profit from—a wide and liberal exposure to the riches of genuinely elementary subject matter. This kind of provisioning is typically sacrificed to a pattern that leads as quickly as possible to advanced subject matter of sorts that have little relevance to the teaching of the young. With honorable exceptions here and there, mathematics and science are especially subject to this criticism. Future teachers are typically required to complete one or two courses, of which the content is regarded as so elementary as to be beneath the dignity of college lecturers; still formal in style, they are thin in content. Often those who teach such courses are themselves unfamiliar with the elementary riches of their own subject matter, and a typical course in the number system, or in remedial algebra, has little relevance to the needs or to the intellectual capacities—often substantial—of students bound for careers as teachers of the young. Knowing nothing of its enticements, they have often been turned off by such subject matter, and we do very little indeed to meet the challenge. Again, the treatment we provide is self-confirming: if they were any good, it is said, they would go into some more prestigious vocation.

The same pattern is visible in the sciences, with the same honorable but all-too-rare exceptions: Physics is taught mainly for future physicists, chemistry for those who might, with one chance in forty, become chemists, biology for future biologists, and so on. The upward draft, what physicists should recognize as an academic chimney effect, is very powerful, and not easily counteracted by the efforts of those few who have insisted on a wider view of their own professional commitments.

In all early education, then, the part played by the teacher is central and critical. It can be ameliorated by the enrichment of several kinds of support now on the whole very poorly provided, but only in the measure of its contribution to teachers' own continuing professional education, their growth of skill and insight, their morale. I believe we should accept this proposition as central and critical to the theory of early education. It can be derived from wide ranges of evidence; in the formulation of theory, it should be treated as an incontrovertible starting point. I have called it an axiom. In the history of mathematics, the word *axiom* came to mean an unquestionable truth from which others could be derived. Later it was bled of that meaning and stood only for some arbitrary logical starting point, a hypothesis whose contradictions could also be a starting point for some alternative logical theory. The original meaning of the word is, I think, more useful than either of these. In that meanmg, an axiom is a proposition most highly valued (*axiwma*, "a thing valued") and thus the last to be questioned in any further investigation.

When the central importance of the teacher is accepted as axiomatic, it provides a strong criterion in judging any proposed educational reforms. Thus curriculum development that robs teachers of opportunities for developing their own curricula, imaginatively matched to their children and their circumstances, should be weighed as negligible or negative. The sort of curriculum development that contributes to teachers' own critical and inventive powers should be supported; that which purports to replace their powers of invention with a dismal array of daily guides geared to dull texts and readers, and those endless workbooks that destroy all zeal for reading or expression—those should be destroyed. No ban against book burning should protect them.

In the hands of children and under their inventive guidance, the classroom computer can add more than one dimension to a teacher's repertoire as a glorified scratch pad for extending children's powers, as an *n*-dimensional kind of book, and as a sheer (though for some, powerfully addictive) delight in fun and games, sometimes educationally worthy. In its cheapest and now best-advertised programs, it robs the teacher of vital initiatives, and if our axiom is seriously meant, should be condemned. This does not exclude all routine uses, such as foreign-language practice, review of some imaginative arithmetic and geometry of the Pythagorean genre, or as a challenge to skill in estimation of numbers very large and very small. But because the computer is literally infinite in its potentialities, it can create the illusion that it is the real world, safely confined by the keyboard or even, in expensive versions, the light pencil. Einstein said that God is subtle but not malicious. We should add that commercial programmers are seldom malicious but never, in principle, divinely subtle. They are never even as subtle as teachers who know their particular children and guide them well. I quoted earlier the theorem that well-cared-for animals are possible only in a well-cared-for classroom. In the same spirit it should be added that a computer in the classroom can be well used only if there are other enticements there that will fully compete with its attractions. Much of its perceived addictiveness is only an escape from boredom. We should be thankful that there are such escapes, but there should be many more. The stuff for which computers can be well used, seldom discussed, is an abstract from the close observation of natural and human affairs; otherwise, they give us only another turn of the screw.

But there are other and more powerful conclusions from our axiom, and the chief of these is that teachers should by all means endlessly educate themselves in the substance of their craft and be well trained in its practice. The substance is to be found in the wide range of elementary subject matter accessible to children, from which teachers can, over the years, evolve increasing and impressive repertoires. The practice contributes as it is reflected upon and collegially examined, alone and with others, in the context of professional curiosity about human learning and development. And all of this—I repeat—implies levels of professional support, preservice and in-service, that we are as yet very far from providing.

The cadres who can support such growth are, then, the key. They may not now be numerous, but they are more numerous than our present readiness to enlist and honor them will admit. It is an encouraging fact that in recent years their ranks have been filled by increasing numbers who have come from such disciplines as mathematics or physics, willing to learn about children and about teaching them, and who believe that their own professions should be expanded to include such commitments. There are also many successful teachers who can be persuaded to spend some time, at least, in others' classrooms. Coming from varied backgrounds and able to learn from each other, such cadres can over time become a powerful agency of improvement in early schooling. Working through the colleges of education, they can guide beginners to good classrooms for serious apprenticeship. Working in the schools themselves, they can give personal support to teachers who seek it. Through workshops and seminars, they can bring to the schools something of the atmosphere of a learned society, the nourishment and morale of professional work and talk.

The secret of this whole process is a working association that is essentially personal, mainly one to one or to a few. As in the classroom for children, books and pamphlets and research reports can help, but only as supplements. Teaching as an art can be reduced to practice primarily with the help of others already skilled in it. Unfortunately, our schools of education have retreated more and more to a world remote from classrooms of the young, and those who spend much time there in violation of this tendency are typically less honored than those who publish many little papers. Even fewer and less honored departmentally are those who regularly visit from departments of math or physics, history or literature, though it might teach them more about college students. We have evolved an academic pecking order in which such ventures are vaguely demeaning. We might all learn more if we reversed it or at least gave serious support to interesting deviations from it. Even our public school systems are guilty, in the main, of a similar retreat. Principals used to be selected as principal teachers, the most skilled and successful, able to help those who worked under them. If the selection was not always wise, the criterion was. Supervisors and consultants and specialists have always been available in principle, though in times of tightened budgets, their ranks have mostly been depleted—unless their work has shifted to a more bureaucratic role invisible to the teachers they should be available to. Yet all of the professional support I have been speaking of is little more than a percent or so of the budgets from which they are now so frequently excised. Such budgets, of course, are not decisive, only necessary. What counts is the quality of professional support we offer to our now-neglected teachers, and that is where all of our discussion, of early math and science, and of all else in the curriculum, should come to a final and practical focus.

To start with the best we already know, toward a new species of early education, is to start small, putting the most effort where we find the greatest readiness for growth. This is unfortunately not a precept that fits our current fashionable notions of cost-effectiveness. To trim quantity to quality is often regarded as elitist, but it is not—not if it aims at growth. Some of our colleagues in these efforts, here and abroad, have deliberately sought out promising beginnings where the going is hardest, in the schools of city slums or regions of rural poverty. The work is harder there, but success is more conspicuous. That is surely not elitist. On the other hand, cost-effectiveness will usually be measured by some average changes (in test scores and the like), and in the early stages these will be buried in the numbers, the tyranny of the arithmetic mean. From this point of view, a long-term commitment of the sort we all might otherwise support is hard to justify. From small beginnings, the growth, in early stages, will always be buried in the sea of statistical noise. What can accrue over some years of growth is another matter, and that seems to require an act of faith, as indeed it does. Growth can follow the exponential curve for a good time at least, and before long will overtake all that begin large and, of necessity, are mediocre. And if faith cannot be justified by short-term statistics, it is all the more important that it be supported by knowledge. I have urged that we possess this support, that it lies in the axiom of the centrality of our teachers' own professional and human needs, now poorly met.

NOTES

1. This chapter was originally published in *Daedalus* 112(2), 1983: 65–89.

2. See Edwin Herbert Lewis, "What a Linguistic Contextualist Thinks of Philosophy," *Outlook* 20, summer 1976 (Boulder, CO).

3. David Hawkins, "What It Means to Teach," *Teachers' College Record*. Teachers' College, Columbia University, New York, spring 1973; and Chapter 3, herein.

4. Henry James, *What Maisie Knew* (New York: Penguin Books, 1974), p. 7. Frances Hawkins's discussion is in "The Eye of the Beholder," in S. Meisels, ed., *Special Education and Development: Perspectives on Young Children With Special Needs* (Baltimore: University Park Press, 1980).

5. A classic account of such work in physical and human geography is Lucy Sprague Mitchell, *Young Geographers* (New York: John Day, 1934).

6. See Michael Armstrong, *Closely Observed Children* (Richmond, Surrey, England: Chamelion Press, 1980). See also a fine new translation of *Tolstoy on Education*, selected and edited by Alan Pinch and Michael Armstrong (East Brunswick, NJ: Associated University Presses, 1982).

7. Immanuel Kant, *Critique of Judgment* (London: MacMillan & Co., Ltd, 1914). See also John Dewey's *Art as Experience* (New York: Minton, Balch and Co., 1934). Dewey is more Kantian here than he was willing to acknowledge.

8. These powers of ten are from *Powers of Ten*, by Philip and Phylis Morrison and the Office of Charles and Ray Eames (New York: Scientific American Library, 1982). The book is based on a film of Charles Eames of the same title.

— 3 —

What It Means to Teach[1]

A teacher I know commented recently that what held her to the profession, after thirty-five years, was that there was still so much to be
learned. A young student reacted in amazement, having supposed that it
could all be learned in two or three years.

It may be possible to learn in two or three years the kind of practice
that then leads to another continued forty years of learning. Whether
many of our colleges get many of their students on to that fascinating
track, or whether the schools are geared to a thoughtful support of such
endless learning by their teachers, is another matter.

To understand the dimensions of the teaching art, complex and inexhaustible though it be, is an equally endless commitment and one
that needs constant insight and renewal. In this chapter I shall try to
uncover part of the topic, a part that has fascinated me and needs much
further investigation. What we mostly know already comes from two
sources, one rather diffuse and one rather focused.

The diffuse source is our common sense, where all knowledge begins. By this I do not mean what at any given moment we happen to
believe. Honorifically understood, common sense is what we can be led
to see and acknowledge when our thoughtful attention is directed to it;

knowledge is already there, implicitly, and only needs elucidation and coherent form. It is the kind of knowledge that Plato illustrated in the story of the slave boy, who, it turned out, knew a lot of geometry though he had never studied the subject and didn't know what he knew. Needless to add, the philosophers are the traditional custodians of this art of teasing out and codifying the things we already somehow know. Though, I hasten to add, they often go off on other tacks, and surely they have no exclusive rights in this domain.

The more focused source is what teachers have learned when they have had cumulatively successful experiences and are able to bring sharp critical attention to the nature of the art they practice. It might be thought, I should add, that there exists a third source to our knowledge about teaching, that of professional scientific research. But when we ask what notable developments there are in our understanding or control of educationally significant learning, I think the verdict must be that we have very little from formal research. A parallel in the history of science might be nineteenth-century medicine, when most advances came from thoughtful practitioners, and when such novelties as the germ theory had not yet reached beyond the laboratory.

I should like to begin by observing that the teacher-learner relationship is at least as old as our human species, and that its formal institutional framework, though much more recent in origin, is only a stylized and often stilted version of something that goes on all the time among us, especially between the older and the younger. I want to underline the antiquity of this honorable relationship if only to remind you of the obvious—that it is a key link in the chain of human history and culture, and that without it we would perish immediately. Also, to remind you that it is not something on which anyone has a patent.

We in the United States are sometimes inclined to the view that nothing is known that is not known to a group of people campaigning to have it decided that they are the official knowers. In the past, this kind of claim was often buttressed with special credentials, and it was sometimes justified. In our own milieu it is likely to require certificates of proficiency in something called the scientific method. But the scientific method is also at least as old as our species, and we should remember that the uncertificated may possess a good deal of it. We have indeed seen a number of recent attempts to patent the idea of teaching. The way this is done is typical patent office procedure. You design something called a model, get a grant from a suitable public authority, "train" a group of people to operate it, invent a scale of evaluation, and then show that your model ranks higher on this scale than something else does. In this way, we have discovered the carrot, the stick, the blinder, the shoe, the collar, the bit, the curb, and many other refinements. Most characteristically, we have shown that a programmed computer works a little less badly than a programmed adult, and at least could be cheaper. We need to remind ourselves that all these kinds of things, including the program, if not the machine, have been in the public domain for a long time, and that we should replace the patent office with an institute for the study of educational antiquities.

Having suggested the antiquity of the teacher-learner relationship, and its necessary centrality in all the transmission and evolution of culture, I want also to characterize it in another way. It is a moral relationship; teaching lies inescapably in the moral domain and is subject to moral scrutiny and judgment. If teaching is good or bad, it is morally good or bad. This claim, as I intend it, is not a recommendation or a hoped-for view of the case, but is a claim of fact. The relationship, by its very nature, involves an offer of control by one individual over the functioning of another, who in accepting this offer is tacitly assured that control will not be exploitative but will be used to enhance the competence and extend the independence of the one controlled, and in due course will be seen to do so.

Of course, all distinctively human relations are moral in this sense, and perhaps also in the sense related to teaching and learning. John Dewey suggested, very profoundly, that the worth of any association and any institution could be measured by its educative value.

MASTER AND SLAVE

The simplest parody of the teacher-learner relationship is that of the master and the slave, into which the former relation sometimes degenerates. This is particularly easy in the relation of adults to children, and almost inevitable in performance-oriented schools and curricula that try to prespecify the control of children's behavior in a detailed timetable. The classic exposition of the dialectic of the master-slave relation is that of Hegel. What develops hinges on the fact that the slave, deprived of the opportunity to exercise his own powers of self-direction, and accepting his lot, finds himself idle in spirit, however busy in the flesh. In school we used to call this busywork, and its contemporary symbol is the work-book, designed to relieve the master of the tedium of detailed incessant instruction.

But idleness of spirit is a call to rumination and reflection. So the slave becomes reflective; the master, however, is too busy for reflection. The master thinks he is the master because the slave is a slave, while the slave, starting from the opposite premise, realizes that the master's role is itself an enslaving one and learns to manipulate it to his own ends, very much the way in which the cat is sometimes rumored to outwit the inventor of the Skinner box.

If we ask how the teacher-learner roles differ from those of master and slave, the answer is that the proper aim of teaching is precisely to affect those inner processes that, as Hegel (and the Stoic philosophers before him) made clear, cannot in principle be made subject to external control, for they are just, in essence, the processes germane to independence, to autonomy, to self-control.

A reasonable general account of the relationship is, therefore, that the teacher is one who acquires authority through a compact of trust, in which the teacher seeks to extend the powers of the learner and promises to abridge them only transiently and to the end of extending them. The teacher offers the learner a kind of loan of her self, some kind of auxiliary equipment that will enable the learner to make transitions and consolidations not otherwise possible. And if this equipment is of a kind to be itself internalized, the learner not only learns but begins, in the process, to become a self-teacher—and that is how the loan is repaid.

If you like the imagery of feedback loops and information pathways, you can describe the loan in those terms, though I think the human situation is inherently richer than such an analogy can easily suggest, and infinitely richer than the world of our present-day automata. For the enhancement of powers that a teacher offers has to be across the full range of experience—that of goal setting and goal seeking; that of thought and action; that of recapitulation and enjoyment. One of the extraordinary jargons of our time is that which separates education into "cognitive" and "affective," as though feeling were not the monitor of thought, or thought the vehicle of feeling. Pretty soon we will discover the faculty still untouched, and come back around the circuit of antiquities to conative education, the training of the will. God help us. In the old faculty psychology, the cognitive, the affective, and the conative were at least seen as inseparable dimensions of any human activity, and not reduced to separate and mutually irrelevant bundles of process.

So it is clear that a teacher does many kinds of things, and of course, the next thing is to say that these all involve communication, two-way interchange. However one studies typical school situations, one finds very little of that. What is found mostly is unidirectional flow, a truncated communication of "instruction" punctuated by fixed alternative responses. Hans Furth has directed all of Jean Piaget's big guns against this dominance of verbally codified unidirectional flow in our schools, but in the process he has managed not to reemphasize the importance of a different kind of communication, more properly so called, that is two-way and not predictable in its outcome from a perusal of the teacher's notebook.

I think the trouble here, as with much present-day talk about communication and so-called communication skills, is the truncation of an essentially three-term relation so that it is thought of as a two-term relation and, finally, I am tempted to use the absurd expression, a one-term relation. The three-term relation is that of teacher, learner, and subject matter.

Human beings are always engaged in something that William James called "flights and perchings." Sometimes, though less often, they are not only momentarily engaged, but are engrossed, concentratedly. John Dewey celebrated the continuity and culmination of this sort of engagement with his famous distinction between experience and *an* experience—that which orders and unifies, which is consummatory, which brings enhancement in its wake. Dewey elsewhere saw this kind of phase as a precondition both of artistic expression and scientific achievement, coming only, as he said, after long absorption in a subject matter that is fresh. Subject matter, then, does not mean, primarily or essentially, what is in books or lectures—and surely not what is in workbooks. Books and lectures have their place—even workbooks on some rare occasions have a place—but subject matter is not what is in them; it is that which they are or try to be about. Subject matter belongs to the universe, and books and lectures are only a small part of the discipline of being engrossed in subject matter. Have you ever thought about alternative demonstrations to the one in Euclid, that the area of a triangle is the product of any base times half the corresponding altitude? Two scissor cuts will do it, and I would not dare to guess how many other demonstrations might be found. They all belong to the subject matter, though only one to Euclid.

So communication is a relation between persons whose time tracks of involvement in subject matter are sufficiently parallel to have that subject matter before them jointly, or between them, or sustaining them; then they can both teach and learn. The truncation occurs when codified knowledge takes the place of subject matter in this basic sense. Such truncation is sometimes a component of good teaching, but only when the learner's involvement in primary subject matter has preceded and is temporarily suspended. You can understand a textbook only when you are at the point where you almost don't need to read it, where it helps you comprehend (if it is any good) some higher-order connections among things that you separately have already worked your way through or around. A young child can delight in a story about an elephant family because she can bring to this narrative a wealth of unorganized perceptions and insights that it enables her to recollect, as the poet said, in tranquility. The subject matter is not supplied by the novelist; he must rely all along the way on his many readers' unequal mastery of the implicit order within human affairs; he must design his tale so as to enlist their trust, their surrender of control over their own imaginations, and their ability to bring alive, at his subtly organized command, the inwardness of lives they have never lived.

The presence of subject matter, real or vicariously animated, is the sine qua non, the It without which I can know Thee not. People know each other through their common involvements and commitments. To be uninvolved and uncommitted is to have nothing to give and nothing to receive. Billing and cooing have their place, of course, but when you look at that place you see it to be full of complexities that you can only sort out when they take you back to the real world of humans and nature. We are so constituted that we amount to nothing without it.

ASYMMETRY

So I come back to the teacher and learner and the nature of their communication, which has a certain asymmetry required of it. This asymmetry is not the obvious kind, as though the roles could never be reversed. Indeed, the desired outcome is that full symmetry be established, and learners turn into teachers. Part of what a teacher learns along that thirty-five-year pathway is quite literally taught by the students. Nevertheless, the asymmetry, if transient, is still there, and we must try to analyze it in more detail.

Let me focus now on what might be called the differential aspect of teaching. This is a sort of short-term cycle that a teacher constantly reenacts. How does a teacher manage to "lend" resources that a learner will appropriate?

The most obvious metaphor is that of mind reading. In our philosophical traditions, the idea was dominant for a long time that mind was something private, inner, unobservable, and therefore mind reading implied some occult faculty, some telepathic invasion. What was available for observation of the ordinary kind was body, behavior. We might try to interpret from behavior what was going on in another's mind.

Now we must not object to this way of talking in everyday life, for the problem of discerning others' thoughts and intentions is often real enough. But the philosophers took it farther. Their analysis seemed to make a total and permanent mystery of what came to be called "the problem of our knowledge of other minds." What we observe is behavior, not mind or conscious existence. For all you know I may be an unthinking automaton, and for all I know you may be. But we can't all be, because I know I am a thinking reed; I also know you say you are as well, but of course you may only be programmed to say this. I hear your retort, and the symmetry of our dilemmas, each saying he knows, is a bit nerve-wracking.

Out of this marvelous philosophical stalemate—the idea that minds are unobservable and unknowable except by a question-begging analogy—came a number of other oddities, such as the subjective idealism usually attributed to Bishop George Berkeley, and its alter ego, "behaviorism." Psychology wants to be a science, and if we decide that psyche is intrinsically unobservable except by something called introspection, then although we can be polite and admit each other's psyches, we cannot observe them and, therefore, cannot be scientific about it. Behaviorism said, let's do away with mind altogether and just study behavior, calling the rest metaphysics. What the behaviorists failed to realize was that it was their own metaphysics they were attacking, and they have persisted in this unenlightened state ever since, in the remarkable belief that their own structure of categories is not metaphysics because it is something they call science. In fact, the word *metaphysics* tends to suffer from a trouble opposite to that of the word *mind*—it is something that only other people suffer from.

Once you reject the conception that minds are things concealed by and within bodies, the whole basis of behaviorism evaporates. It is not even a debatable assertion that human beings have been learning about each other's minds for as long as history, and they have been learning these things in the full context of their own and each other's behavior. Otherwise, we would never have the public concept of mind in the first place to get into philosophical troubles over, when reflection brought us to the point of serious philosophical gambitry.

The trouble with behaviorism is not that it threw out a useless metaphysical notion, but that it did not throw out the gambit that led to that useless notion. Thought words, mind words, words like *concept, idea, hope, intend, wish, feel, fear, see,* etc.—a very big part of the total vocabulary in all languages—do not refer to things that we know in subjective experience and can only (unscientifically) impute to others. They are complex dispositional nouns and verbs that have evolved over a long history of human communication as being precisely a way of making sense out of human behavior, our own included. Anger is at least as observable as magnetism. The inner subjective feeling, which I feel when I am angry, and you need not, is not the state we call "being angry." My anger is a complex, charged-up state of me that you and I both apprehend—so far as we apprehend it—in the same way. I recognize my state as angry because I am behaving in a way that is properly called angry, and this is true even when I am concealing part of the usual symptoms. If I could conceal them all from you, granted that you are a subtle observer, I would be concealing them from myself as well, and I might then not even know I was angry. And often, as we know, we can understand each other better than we understand ourselves.

So the behaviorists are not wrong in thinking that their subject matter is behavior. The error lies in thinking that the only way, or the only scientifically useful way, of describing behavior is in a version of part of the language of nineteenth-century physics.

Let me illustrate by coming back to mind reading. Let the learner be a young child not much given to long discourses, but present and operative in a material environment that the school and the teacher have provided, and let the child be singled out for attention because of any one of a variety of circumstances—manner of association with others in a specific activity, manner of involvement or noninvolvement with materials, content and style of communication, etc. The teacher begins to assemble such information over a variety of children, although for thirty the task is enormous, and even the best teachers will confess many omissions. Then there is a trial-and-error of communication, further observation, a gradual and still tentative sort of portraiture involving the child's style—strengths, weaknesses, skills, fears, and the like. I single out one aspect of this complex, the way a child comes to grips with some subject matter, matter originally provided because it matches the general level of interest and ability of a still individually unknown group—building blocks, clay, paint, batteries, and bulbs. If this subject matter represents something that the teacher has valued and learned from, and seen others learn from, then the teacher has a background for reading the behavior of that child. In a film from Cornell University, a series of kindergarteners come spontaneously to a table to play with an equal-arm balance and a large number of washers and other weights. In watching the film, one begins to recognize in oneself—if one is personally familiar with the large variety of balance situations that are possible here, and with some of the underlying ideas—the ability to read the levels and the specializations of interest represented in these children, no two alike. What one finds oneself doing (but only if one is acquainted with this kind of balance phenomenon and others related to it) is beginning to build what I would call a map of each child's mind and of the trajectory of the child's life. It is fragmentary, fallible, and subject always to correction. And next the observer thinks, what could I do to steady, extend, deepen this engagement I have glimpsed?

The important thing is that, as in all self-instruction, the participant does something. The diagnostic hunch leads to some special provision for this child or that twosome, some intervention, some special protection for a delicate and perhaps fearful beginning, some withdrawal of old materials and insertion of new ones. With large groups, the teacher must be a manager of great skill, evolving a context in which most are involved and self-directing most of the time, in order to really focus for a period on one or a few—discussing, joining, enjoying, directing, or deferring to a child's direction.

In every case, the aim is to repeat this cycle of diagnosing, designing, responding, and then rediagnosing from failure or from a child's confirmation of success. That's the cycle, and with variations it recurs over and over again, never twice the same in detail but with an assurance that will grow by what it feeds on—the finding of match and mismatch between children as the teacher reads them and those kinds of order and organization this reading has helped them extract from their world. I think that is the way it is, every day.

INTEGRAL TEACHING

But there is another level in teaching, which can be called integral rather than differential. A teacher knows and works with children over a period of time, which, from their perspective, is long. One swallow, or one fine day, as Aristotle observed, does not make a summer. If every day is the same, if there is no movement, no change of pace, and no cumulative history, the process has in some way failed. Many of us know teachers, know classrooms, where the cycle of a teacher's work comes to no apparent fruition in spite of good beginnings. What further conditions must be discussed? It is at this point that I would hesitate and turn the question over to those experienced and reflective teachers from whom, if we persist, we can learn much. But I venture two suggestions, two directions of further inquiry. The first concerns the relation between a curriculum and the teacher's repertoire, as I would call it. The second concerns the art of planning, an art that depends quite essentially on the nature of that repertoire.

The first suggestion is that the way in which a teacher needs to understand subject matter is much richer than that of the linear sequential order which we associate with outlines and syllabi and textbooks. These represent, at their ideal best, a stepwise organization of what has been learned. For a mathematician, it proceeds by steps of logic. For a historian, its steps are chronological, each narrative episode providing a context within which the next can be understood and interpreted. But no such formalized order should be supposed to represent the pathway along which learning does or can probably take place. The latter kind of order is determined by the antecedent learning and other resources of the learner. Very often this inductive order is the reverse of the logical or historical. In an overall sense, history starts in the here and now, a here and now sufficiently discordant with itself to awaken curiosity about how it came to be. Mathematical insight often develops first through involvement with a complexity of pattern and relationship intuitively grasped through practical experience. Aristotle remarked that what is first in the order of intelligibility is often last in the order of learning. In the mind of a good teacher that dictum has the status of a truism. Through practical experience, such a teacher knows the diversity of such pathways of learning and is alert to discover new ones. In the mind of such a teacher the organization of subject matter is a network of multiple interconnections, not a single sequence of topical steps laid out in advance. In the first place, that formalized ordering is never unique, as I have already suggested. The history or the Euclidean geometry could be rewritten with equal (or greater) cogency in many different ways. The Pythagorean theorem could be an early simple consequence of the flatness of the plane, and the story of slavery could surely be a part, more problematic and central than it now is, of the bicentennial record.

But in the second place, the network of possible learning paths is more complex and looser in its connections than any text. A teacher's growing knowledge of it (not to be more than started in a college course) can only be coextensive with the constant search for and recognition of learning opportunities for individual children with their unique abilities, backgrounds, and budding interests. Such a growing repertoire not only increases the target area for initially involving children in fresh subject matter, but facilitates that sort of transition and continuity out of which learning is deepened and extended, out of which education becomes more than a summation of unintegrated episodes.

In an early essay, "The Child and the Curriculum," John Dewey gave recognition to this need for constant reexamination and restructuring of subject matter, and called it, I think unfortunately, the "psychologizing" of knowledge. One aspect (but only one) of this task has been pursued in the traditions of child development, namely in relation to the concept of readiness as a developmental complex. Thus the educative value of young children's aptitude for play has gained recognition, at least in a good though small minority tradition. There, water and sand, clay and blocks, dolls and dollhouses do not need to be argued for. But one has the uncomfortable impression that such things are often valued lopsidedly, for only one part of their true worth. Play with such materials is seen as therapeutic and as contributing to children's social maturation among their peers. But the intellectual values of such play, as an exploration of intrinsically worthy subject matter, appears to me to have been typically overlooked. One unfortunate result, I believe, is that in the majority of our schools (in this case, nursery school and kindergarten) such materials have been cast out as unrelated to "pre-reading, pre-writing, and pre-arithmetic." In our own work, we have quite consciously and truthfully emphasized the value of play with such materials as encouraging the roots of early science and mathematics. But teachers will not know how to support such aspects of learning unless they themselves have been encouraged to explore and appreciate the manifold ways these simple materials of childhood play are related, as subject matter, to the style and character and history of the great world around us. Balance and flow, size and scale, number and form are all there to be enjoyed, wondered about, and put in place. Unfortunately, such subject matter, though enjoyed and appreciated by some of our best minds in research and scholarship, are not much valued in our college curricula; they are too "elementary."

It may be thought that this imbalance has been redressed through our increasing attention to the "cognitive" investigations of Piaget, and indeed that work is a valuable contribution to the need that Dewey defined. But just as Freudian glasses filter out much from one perspective, so those of the Piagetian schemes give us only a one-dimensional view of a potential repertoire that almost no one, as yet, has begun to build in its true proportions. And surely this repertoire, as skillful teachers will help evolve it, will provide in its network for all the human faculties, which it is the aim of education to cultivate. Such teachers need our respect, as they need our help.

NOTE

1. This chapter was originally an invited lecture at Columbia Teachers' College in early 1973. It was published in *Teachers' College Record* 75(1), 1973: 7-16.

— 4 —

Getting Into the Subject Matter:
A Missing Ingredient in Teaching

You can open a box from outside. You can imagine a box that can only be opened from the inside, and this is a paradox: How, unless born there, do you get into a box *before* it has been opened? Perhaps there are types of openings and keys that can resolve the paradox.

For a long time in our center for teachers we have wrestled with the problems of helping teachers gain fresh insight and knowledge about such openings and keys—in science, mathematics, social studies, and many other areas of study. Children and adults have to get *into* subject matter before they can learn to make their way around in it, and to have gotten into it is already to have fashioned some keys—of knowledge, of motivation, and of ways of looking and thinking.

Rather than talk about all this too generally, I will use the example of a recent workshop course given at the Mountain View Center for ten teachers from Boulder and nearby communities. Most of our workshop courses at the Center emphasize helping teachers get themselves into art or math or social studies or science at levels at which many children can also move freely. This implies that we ourselves have at least partly mapped such levels. We can sometimes find confirmation of our maps in the ways teachers respond, not just with pleasure and excitement but with expression—with freshness of thought and invention. We have sometimes been criticized for this emphasis on teachers' involvement in subject matter, by people who say that the primary job is to help teachers focus on pressing classroom problems and who seem to think that all this probing into subject matter is a luxury. We reply that children can't be educated until *they* are engrossed in subject matter and teachers can't well create conditions for engrossment without sharing in it, knowing where it can lead, and being able to extend its range.

If teachers can join us in mapping paths into subject matter, they are on their way to being able to do so for children. If they can't yet do so to some degree, they face a barrier to successful teaching. When we can help create an investigative atmosphere in a group of teachers, the way is open for discussion about children's own learning. Clearly, method and subject matter can't be separated.

The topic of one workshop course, which met for four weekly two-hour sessions, was "Heat and Temperature," a small part of early science that potentially is a key to many other questions, topics, and levels of entry into the modern world of knowledge and choice—a world from which their own education has excluded most adults, including elementary schoolteachers. Barry Kluger of our staff, an enlightened physicist, joined me in designing and teaching the course.

I should say first that this course was highly structured, in my own mind, around one question: How can we go back and forth between the rich, everyday, practical lore about thermal experience—in the world where adults and children live—and the formulations of elementary physics? I think all of our teachers were inexperienced in making this two-way passage, though one or two of them had some grasp of the physics. We began with a discussion of aims: to collaborate in investigating the relation between common sense and science in the chosen, small area, the relation between what "everybody" knows and the way "everybody" thinks about heat and temperature on the one hand, and "scientific understanding" of the topic on the other.

There was strong unanimous agreement that the relationship of common sense to science is supposed to be an instance of the way error is related to truth, ignorance to knowledge, confusion to clarity. One teacher's formulation was that "the more scientific you are the closer you get to reality." Barry and I put forth a different view: that "unscientific" common sense and science deal with the same range or overlapping ranges of phenomena but with different purposes and perspectives, and that each way of thinking seems strange and confusing when viewed from the vantage point of the other.

Our emphatic assertion that common sense is not wrong or "primitive" aroused unexpectedly strong enthusiasm among our teachers, as did the prospect that we outlined of reflecting on and analyzing common-sense ways of thinking. Barry and I were not just going to "teach physics" to the unenlightened, but rather were going to help them explore a new area, the *relation* between science and common-sense belief. This would generate knowledge that we all needed as teachers and would help us build bridges that could be crossed both ways.

We began work in our first session with large styrofoam cups and sizeable amounts of water—one large kettle quite hot and one very cold, near freezing. We issued a challenge: line up in order a series of cups containing mixtures of the hot and cold. There was a boycott on thermometers—fingers were to be the probes. One group lined up about fifteen cups from hottest to coldest. Another group, thanks to the absence of thermometers, began to name their mixtures—for example, "about like dishwater after the dishes are done." A third group was fascinated that there were small differences that some could detect and others could not, that the hot felt hotter when a finger had first been for a time in the cold, that the sensation changed over a few seconds, and that equal parts of hot and cold gave a mixture that was still noticeably on the hot side. There was much else. As usual, a branching flow diagram would show that our beginning could have gone in many directions. In a longer course we should have done so, but Barry and I were hunting some big game we thought was there and that's not always a mistake.

One thing we got into, and returned to in discussion as the course developed, was that what our temperature sense discriminates is *not* exactly the same thing the thermometer measures. Again, common-sense ideas are not *wrong;* they classify things in a more biologically useful way than can simple physics. From a common-sense point of view, physics is difficult; from a physicist's point of view, common sense is difficult. We *must* build those bridges.

In the second session, working within the context of a talk about the history of ideas, we introduced ice and thermometers. We now did some quantitative work with mixtures of hot and cold and found a reasonably satisfying relation between the amounts of water at two initially different temperatures and the final temperature of the mix. We did a number of other things, too. We melted holes in the ice with small containers of hot water. On the stove we heated a pot of ice floating in water and graphed the temperature change of the water against time. There was no appreciable rise in temperature until all the ice had melted. Then there was a steady rise to the boiling point and again no change in temperature as the water boiled away. Our graph showed clearly that constant heating caused no change in temperature while ice was melting or water boiling. We were on the track of "latent heat," but were not yet ready to deal with it as a concept.

In the first session we had talked about hot and cold as opposite qualities, about *the* hot and *the* cold as kinds of things—what the old philosophers called "principles" or substantive qualities. The teachers' contribution, helped by some questioning of their experience, was pure Aristotle—not a bad beginning and, we all now agreed, not far from the ingrained and reasonable patterns of common sense, including the common sense of most young ones.

The history we presented was some Aristotle, with jumps to the thermometer, to Galileo, and to the origin of "temperature," which was a sixteenth-century medical term signifying something also called the "temperament" of people, departures from a healthy state toward too much of "the hot" or "the cold."

Along the way we had occasion to notice in ourselves another common-sense habit of thinking about the phenomena of heating and cooling—that heat is not just a quality but is something that *flows* from hotter to colder, some kind of fluid. This was inconclusive because one could also think of cold the same way—cold *penetrates*. To underline this way of thinking, we went back to our earlier mixing of hot and cold, but now changing the equipment. We poured the hot and cold water into separate compartments in two plastic shoe boxes, one of which, *a*, was divided by a thin flat strip of aluminum and the other, *b*, by a much longer strip of pleated aluminum (see figure).

In both cases we got roughly the same result as when mixing hot and cold water directly—after a while the temperatures in both compartments were nearly the same intermediate value we had found before, though the two batches of water could not now mix. In box *a* the process took a lot longer than when the hot and cold were mixed together, while in box *b* the intermediate value was reached almost as fast as with direct mixing.

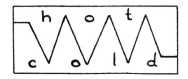

a   b

In this context we found ourselves thinking about heat as a fluid—it was no longer just the *water* that was hot—but a *second* fluid, invisible and imponderable, that could permeate the tangible fluid water but could also flow through metal, which water itself cannot do.

With the idea of heat as a fluid in mind, we were near to a clear sorting out of the relation between heat and temperature as the physicists define it. A lot of heat in a little water would give a high temperature; a little heat in a lot of water would give a low temperature, even cold. Of course, there is still the possibility of two such fluids, a fluid of heat and a fluid of cold, just as there can be two sorts of electricity, positive and negative. We laughed about that; we weren't trying to prove anything but were just learning to think in new ways and to think about our thinking.

As we were all trying to think about this mysterious fluid—it used to be called "caloric" in the heyday of its popularity—three questions emerged, two of which Barry and I were prepared for but one of which astonished and delighted us. This question was: Does the idea of heat as a fluid mean that the amount of heat is *finite?* If heat is a fluid that can be present in things in different concentrations, and if cold is only a relative absence of it—not a positive something in its own right—then you could imagine bleeding all the heat out of something so it couldn't get any colder. Suddenly our new way of thinking had shown logical power; it had suggested something genuinely beyond the range of common-sense experience, an absolute of coldness, an "absolute zero" of temperature. Is there also an absolute of hotness? Not in this way of thinking, at any rate. Everyone had heard that mysterious phrase "absolute zero." Suddenly it came alive, and we could meet over it as equals.

Other teachers immediately thought of another beautiful, related topic, the fact that the earth is a reservoir of solar energy flowing in from the sun and out again into the darkness of space. We had only touched on radiation as a flow of heat, but again the key was conservation. We weren't ready yet for the grand formulation, the conservation of energy, but the idea was there.

The second question was this: If heat is a fluid, what happens to it when it is being added to water but the temperature is not rising—as in the melting of ice or the boiling of water? I told the historical story of "latent heat," and we shared a puzzle with the nineteenth-century investigators.

The third question touched on modern-day physics. Another line of detective work in the long history of the subject of heat relates heat to motion—not a substantial fluid at all but a "form of motion," the internal agitation of the minutest parts of matter, as invisible as the fluid, heat. This theory, which can be traced to the Middle Ages, came into its own only in the last part of the nineteenth century.

Some of our teachers knew something of this now-established kinetic theory, and were concerned that the "subtle fluid" theory we had formulated must be wrong. We had had enough discussion of this difficulty to suggest what must be right about our fluid theory and to point again toward the idea of the conservation of energy, which might also explain the mystery of latent heat. But further insights were only a promised land; we did not get there.

A final discussion, prefigured along the way, focused on the interpretation of the animal and human temperature senses as being not directly a scale of temperatures but a monitoring of the inward or outward flow of heat. Thus we came back to the legitimacy of common-sense ideas about the hot and the cold. From common sense we had gone over to the physicist's way of thought; now we were coming back, beginning to travel the new bridge both ways. Since so much of our raw material came from everyday life, and consisted of experience children have in and out of school, we were also beginning to organize this material into a scheme of potential elementary-school curriculum. But since we don't yet know how children's thinking about heat and temperature will prosper, "curriculum" must, along with content, be a context for further investigation.

I have told this story in some detail because I want to illustrate from personal experience the existence of a need. Most college courses of the sort elementary schoolteachers have taken have failed to enlist their insight and intelligence. They have gone away feeling put down and battered, feeling "If that is science, it's not for me." So it is also with mathematics, music—and what else? It is fashionable to blame colleges of education for the poor preparation of teachers, but if delight and enthusiasm about the richness of elementary subject matter is still foreign to many of our teachers, the colleges of arts and sciences, with their pressures toward what they still regard as the "higher" professions, are equally to blame.

They pass by the genuinely elementary aspects of subject matter; they presuppose them without apparent appreciation of the fact that genuinely elementary understanding is also the deepest kind, that it must gestate, that it needs help in delivery, and that it is worth honoring. Until such dignity is accorded the genuinely elementary, generations of teachers, conscientious and devoted though they may be, cannot avoid transmitting to their children what has been done to them.

The only way we can interrupt this vicious cycle is by a cooperative kind of research into ways of penetrating the barriers that our history has constructed and that alienate so much of our population from the advancement of knowledge. Enlisting teachers to join us in pursuing such research is one of the aims of the Mountain View Center. The experience I have discussed is one example of how this can work. We have learned to think better, Barry and I, about something we already "knew." Our teachers, mostly feeling ignorant at the start, have explored a world of phenomena and ideas that are close to the domain of children's experience and thinking. Our next step will be to pursue this sort of investigation in classrooms, widening its range to encompass experiences of daily life such as weather and cookery, to take but two examples. This classroom research will involve much more than heat and temperature, but in such a context we can pursue our specific investigations further, adding to our own science repertoire and that of some teachers in the process.

Our center has many concerns, some superficially more pressing than those discussed here. But we wish not to lose sight of such investigations that are in the long run vital to the improvement of education. Science and mathematics, in their modern advance, have been structured for applications and research, not for access by growing young minds. The needed reconstruction that will make this access possible cannot be done by scientists alone; they usually lack the intimate knowledge of the furniture of most minds and the ways children can go about the furnishing process. Teachers alone cannot do the job, nor can historians or philosophers of science. But all have something to bring to such investigations, and the laboratory will be the living classroom.

— 5 —

Childhood Regained

In P. L. Travers's fantasy of Mary Poppins, nanny and magician, there is a story of the baby Annabel, a few days old, who still can talk with birds and still remembers where she came from. "I am earth and air and fire and water," she explains to a wobbly fledgling, whose starling father has brought it in the window and to the edge of the crib. And then the baby adds, "I come from the Dark where all things have their beginnings."[1] Only a week later, alas, that memory has faded away, and soon after that she can no longer converse at all in that marvelous prehuman language she had shared, at first, with the sunlight and the breezes and the birds.

An ancient and more famous writer, Plato, tells another version of the same story. In his dialogue the *Phaedo*, Socrates has demonstrated that a wholly untutored slave boy in a sense knows, and can be led by questioning to prove, a part of the famous Pythagorean theorem. Socrates then explains this seemingly innate knowledge by a myth of incarnation. Before birth the human soul has lived in a heavenly state of perfect knowledge. But to be born into the physical world, it is first bathed in the waters of Lethe, the mythical River of Forgetfulness. The newborn then enters the world in a state of forgetfulness that cannot be distinguished from total innocence and ignorance. With time and growth, however, things experienced in this life begin to remind us of those long-forgotten truths, and with help from those farther advanced, such as Socrates, they can be more and more fully recovered.

In *Mary Poppins* there is no possibility that Annabel should ever recover the lost language, that any child or adult ever does or can, except of course Mary Poppins herself, and she is no ordinary mortal. The newborn must become engrossed, with all her innate talents, in moving out to meet the world and learning its ways. The knowledge she was born with is thus buried and replaced by all the new impressions and the patterns they make. To learn, to grow, to achieve, means also to forget, to lose.

As Annabel, preoccupied with more urgent matters, lost the language of the birds, so we adults can lose the ability to communicate with children. It is not merely that we have put away childish things, concerned with matters of greater importance; we often seem to have put them away so carefully that we can't recover them again even when the need arises. Children grow rapidly and marvelously into the use of the adult language, but they see and understand much more than they can tell in it, to adults who hear but cannot read them.

I think there is something inevitable about our inability to maintain that sense of our own childhood or to draw on it as a source for understanding the ways of children. Yet there is a kind of recovery available to us, and that is where the myth of Plato is pertinent. What we once knew as children we cannot recover, but we can in some ways reproduce it—something acquired through imaginative association with children, long continued, and through study.

I don't wish to speak here about the scientific study of child development. That has its place, from Arnold Gesell to Jean Piaget and beyond.[2] But there is another literature of childhood that directly challenges imagination and can stir us to recover some of our own early lives, of the autobiographies that few of us will ever actually write. I think particularly of two autobographies, Maksim Gorky's *My Childhood*[3] and Sean O'Casey's *I Knock at the Door*.[4] The children in some novels or short stories can be important here too—those of Charles Dickens or Rudyard Kipling or Henry James or Thomas Mann. They too are drawn in part from recovered memory.

If we see the world as the storyteller truly sees it—I speak now of the world of adults as well as children—it is a world of inexhaustible diversity and novelty. Every human career is at some level unique in the pattern of its challenges, its responses, its gains and losses, its joys and sorrows. That is the secret of our endless curiosity about each other as human beings, and of the storyteller's endless popularity. The teller of tales extends our range to other times and climes, to situations of luxury or danger, poverty or tranquility we have never known. We somehow identify ourselves with the characters in well-told tales, vicariously leading other lives and seeking as much to understand them as we do our own.

And that is the perspective from which I wish to examine one of the besetting sins, as I see it, in our popular and would-be scientific view of childhood and child development. Children's lives are so different in so many important respects—obvious or subtle—that at any age their progress along any of the well-known developmental tracks is quite essentially uneven. A child who fitted close to *all* the statistical norms for his or her age would be a rare one, abnormal indeed. A child described as "average" is probably just one whose special talents and difficulties have been overlooked. In any classroom, as we well know, there is a wide range in any specific and measurable level of learning, and this calls for a kind and degree of individual work by children that our schools far too seldom afford. For the most important kinds of learning, those that go unmeasured, will work to meet the need for diversity in children's work, and for the orchestration that will create, from that sort of diversity, a community of learners.

Because we too seldom provide for this wide and legitimate diversity, we tend instead to provide children with a single fare and rank them on a single scale that the single fare requires. But then often the range is so wide that we are driven to create special categories of children, calling them educationally disadvantaged at one end of the scale and gifted at the other, and then to seek special programs for both groups.

THE CHILD'S PERSPECTIVE ON LEARNING AND SCALE[5]

Years ago I learned from one of my philosophy teachers an idea of great importance in the magic and folklore of some primitive societies. I think it is a deep idea, and not at all the sort to be labeled "primitive." Among the Melanesians, the word for it was *mana*. Mana is a kind of power possessed sometimes by things of an otherwise familiar kind: a stone or a mountain, a yam or a tree or a bird; sometimes a person. In all cases, the possession of mana turns the thing into something novel, something extraordinary, perhaps unsettling. That apparently ordinary thing suddenly does not fit our normal and routine expectations, but challenges them. The stone that resembles a mountain, the tree that weeps, the magpie that speaks with an almost human voice: all these must possess mana, say the Melanesians.

As we of another world may interpret this idea, mana is indeed a kind of power residing in things. It is the power to challenge our routine ways of seeing and thinking, to stir in us the feeling that still undefined potentialities exist within. The awareness of mana is a special kind of feeling, the kind of emotion with which we face something that challenges our established habits of belief. It is not the mere intellectual noting of exceptional shape or size or behavior. It is in its own way an experience of crisis and potential fulfillment. It is the source of all fresh desire to take things in new ways, ways that might enhance our understanding and our lives.

In our world, the stirring of that kind of emotion has been mainly the work of artists, but all teaching should share such work. One of the great arts in all teaching is to present familiar things in such a way as to stir this sense of mana in them. It is only when we are challenged in this way, I think, that our learning can become genuinely self-propelled, pursued with passion.

From my own childhood, the most vivid experience of mana I can recall was that of seeing the three-quarter moon through a friend's telescope. Suddenly that bit of familiar nighttime illumination was transformed, and so was I. Instead of looking *up* at the silver disc, I was looking *down* at a vast strange desert world of mountains and plains.

Changing the moon from a silvery disk to a vast planet was a major change of scale. Though I had already read about the moon in *The Book of Knowledge*, the words had not moved me as did the visual experience of the change of scale.

In Galileo's time, as in my own youth, this great power of surprise came only with the visual experience, not the book. In that time, the first telescopes were developed, and the Copernican revolution was under way. The bishops of the Church of Rome had read Copernicus. The idea that the Earth was a satellite of the sun had been around for a good many years, an interesting mathematical hypothesis that the learned could discuss. But when one bishop looked through Galileo's telescope and saw those lunar mountains and plains or the satellites of Jupiter, the mana hit him: he realized that the Earth-centered scheme might be only a mathematical representation of the heavens, while the scheme of Copernicus and Kepler might just be right. But that would be heresy! The mana gave way to fear and the condemnation of Galileo. Sharp mathematics and flat scientific prose have little power to stir the sense of reality until the mana of fresh vision has prepared the way.

All of our earliest experience and much of our adult common sense is focused on things in a medium range of sizes and durations. This guides us in daily affairs, for the most part not too badly. But there are things on the edge of common experience, greater or smaller than the ordinary, much faster or slower. Often, our common sense does not accommodate such things. In fact, looking closely at things that are very large or very small, very fast or very slow, may encourage us to remodel some cherished preconceptions. The Roman poet-scientist Lucretius looked closely at the dancing dust motes in a beam of sunlight that penetrated the gloom of a darkened room. Many have noticed that particular phenomenon, before him and since, but only in passing. Lucretius looked hard and conjectured that the dance was driven by still smaller invisible atoms of air. Imagine the mana centuries ago when seashells were found in high mountain rocks. That was one of the many bits of information that required stretching the time scale of history enormously, until even the lifting of those fossils appears as a fairly recent expression of the work of the giant plates of the Earth's crust, slowly climbing over one another, lifting and burying, squeezing and stretching, usually at a rate of centimeters per year.

Children are fascinated by changes of scale. For them, mana is possessed by elegant furniture for a dollhouse or by a miniature bonsai maple, ten inches high with leaves (almost) to scale. Recognizing the importance of the experience of mana for children's minds might help us understand their unremitting fascination with the great dinosaurs. As a teacher, one can share and extend that kind of emotion. But one can work well with children only if one can experience another kind of mana, that of fascination with the mind-styles of different children—so like and yet so unlike our own. Much of the world is still new for them, as it still should be for us.

In modern times, there has grown up a powerful yet simple discipline connected with the exploration of changes of scale: its arithmetic and geometry. Measures of distance and area and volume are needed for any serious discussion of changes in scale. These measures provide a frame on which we can hang those surprising changes of kind that large changes in scale so often reveal.

The basic mathematics of scale is simple, and its beginnings are accessible even to young children. But though children learn about multiplication and division, exponentiation, length, area, and volume, teachers rarely apply these skills to problems of scale. Neglecting such applications means missing a tremendous opportunity.

Some children have thought of a little dollhouse that could belong among the furniture of the classroom dollhouse. Many of us still remember our first close look at the Morton's salt carton with its picture of a girl carrying a Morton's salt carton. Such memories, like most vivid memories, are the afterglow of heightened emotion; not love or fear, in such a case, but mana. Repeated multiplication and division exponentiation can take you in short order from the world of atoms to that of the galaxies, or the reverse.

Do you know the art of making puff pastry? Roll out the dough, butter it well, and fold it over—then roll it out again. The cookbook tells you to repeat this operation (it could say, "exponentiate") seven times: making 2 layers of dough, then 4, then 8, 16, 32, 64, 128 layers! How many more times would we need to fold the dough to make a layer the average thickness of a single atom? In a workshop for elementary teachers, we once made the pastry and did the calculations: only fifteen or sixteen more foldings would have made a one-atom layer. One teacher said, "This is scary!"

Exponentiation can take us beyond the range of common sense into regions of frightening possibilities. Two calculations have convinced me that an understanding of exponentiation and scale is essential for everyone, not least our leaders. The first is a calculation that makes me aware of the scarcity of life. Living cells of plants and animals, by weight, are mostly water. If we compare the total mass of all life on Earth to the total mass of Earth's oceans, the ratio is one to one million. The second calculation makes me aware of the power of a nuclear explosion. For each pound of explosive, a nuclear explosion releases roughly one million times the energy of an ordinary chemical explosion.

The power of a nuclear blast, the fragility of the relatively insignificant quantity of life on Earth—these facts, when brought together, create the emotion of mana; they demand our attention and our respect. With the development of the telescope, the microscope, and other tools that let us venture outside the medium range of sizes and durations, we have stepped beyond the edge of common experience into a world that forces us to reconsider our rules and our traditions. When I consider my two calculations, some of our ancient and familiar military traditions seem also, suddenly, very strange. I believe we had better proceed with their most careful and radical revision.

NOTES

1. P. L. Travers, *Mary Poppins and Mary Poppins Comes Back* (New York: Reynal and Hitchcock, 1943), pp. 228-243, "The New One."

2. A profound study of child development is Sibylle Escalona, *The Roots of Individuality* (Chicago: Aldine Publishing Co., 1968).

3. Maksim Gorky, *My Childhood* (Baltimore: Penguin Books, 1966, orig. published 1915).

4. Sean O'Casey, *I Knock at the Door: Swift Glances Back at Things That Made Me* (New York: Macmillan, 1939).

5. This section was originally published on its own as "Learning and Scale" in *Exploration* 8(2), 1984: 13-15.

— 6 —

I Used to Wonder

I used to wonder about the Ice Age cave paintings of Altamira and Lascaux. Were they magic to attract fresh game? To propitiate the animal spirits? Adrenalin recollected in tranquility? Admiration for other predators stronger and swifter, yet somehow to be equaled? Lit by flickering lamps, was the scene reflective or orgiastic? I have finally given up, come to believe that those ancient participants might be just as confused as we are when confronted by the same attempt to understand our own concern about the arts. This chapter is not about the arts as such but about what we call the humanities, centrally about human history, back to the neolithic.

Knowledge has a kind of structure. Fluency of understanding implies a network interconnecting three domains. In the case of mathematics these are the domains of theorems, of concrete examples, and of ideas, mathematical concepts. In the case of history, one can see a parallel structure, but between mathematics and history there are radical contrasts. Mathematical knowledge is often conceived of as lying primarily in only one of its domains, that of the trunk-to-tail logical structure of propositions, theorems. That flattened structure by itself, however, is not adequate to account for either the creation of mathematical knowledge or what we mean by mathematical understanding. By the nature of logical order, theorums are strung out in linear array, a treelike structure in which each step presupposes those preceeding it. Mathematical *understanding*, however, implies a richer structure, connecting the theorems with concrete exemplars and with concepts, and can get where it is going in many fewer steps than the sequential structure of theorems would usually allow.

In conventional discussions of history there is often a similar flattening of three related epistemological domains into one, the sequential domain of the past. As in mathematics, one can be taught a great deal of history without understanding; without understanding, it takes a year to get from the founding fathers to anything close to the present. Historical understanding, like that of mathematics, implies a richer structure, a network connecting chronological ordering with two other domains. One of these is the domain of the present concrete world, including ourselves, when this world is seen as a source of information about the past, as contributing to the shaping of a story about what happened and how. The other is a domain of ideas, those that guide and discipline the reconstruction and the interpretation.

I remember a great sense of surprise, toward the end of a course in field geology, when I realized that we were really not studying the physical stratification or physical and chemical structure of the rocks except as an exercise in cracking nature's historical code, using some of the text that others had already decoded to refine further the search for evidence. I remember also how obvious were some of the guiding ideas, yet how powerful in the end—big crystals mean slow cooling; later strata are on top unless there is special evidence of overturning; missing strata imply periods of erosion. I remember especially the sense that one could now begin to see all those familiar landforms and outcroppings as a book to be read, and that even the literal textbooks we used were only a result of such modest work as ours, that of a few thousand geologists working worldwide over the century since Thomas Lyell and James Hutton. Above all, I remember gaining some sense for elapsed time, the years, in powers of ten, marked by characteristic changes. I remember learning to call the era of Altamira and Lascaux "very recent" and seeing evidence for stream deposits in billion-year-old metamorphics or the even older granites.

After such an exposure, all human history seems recent, but it involves a shift from essentially simple subject matter to the most complex, yet most familiar, that we know. As a discipline, human history involves the same problem of entry, of learning to sense the historicity of the present and the contemporaneity of the past, of learning what links the cave painters with Monet or Picasso.

What are the first steps toward historical understanding? The text-book, the summarized chronological story, is surely not the essential avenue of entry; it presupposes too much else. The dramatic examples of the growth of understanding are easiest to find. For one person I know, entry came through a biography of an admired artist, Leonardo da Vinci. Suddenly the past—much studied and much forgotten in high school and college courses—came alive. For another it was the grand sweep of rather speculative historians, Spengler and Toynbee, coming after two years of then-dull required history courses. But the best example I know is that of a child of five. The context includes much that I can no longer recall, but there was story reading and then a theatrical performance of *Under the Lilacs*, somewhat advanced for that age. There were also happy Sunday afternoons at the National Gallery in the late forties. The pre-cipitating event came after a visit to an extensive historical exhibit of costumes and to a gallery of portraits. For that child the costumes of those portrayed excited attention, climaxed by the strange and elegant ruff around the Elizabethan neck, marked, remarked, and much discussed thereafter. Something about that array of well-dressed mannequins and portrait costumes seemed to stir a new level of childlike imagination and thought, the awareness of a whole past world spread out in time, time before memory, even before the time Nannie was a child. For the moment, at least, a young child could meet the historian on his own ground. From this, or some earlier starting point unsuspected by parents, the fascination with the past would reappear from time to time, each time more developed, early sources of a later adult commitment that led even to a fascination with historical geology.

In these rather dramatic cases a key word is obviously *romance*, the sense of a freshly discovered and as yet unexplored world, a great con-tinuum of human experience in which one's own experience is somehow to be embedded.

This expanded space-time frame of human history is clearly shared with the sciences, all of which—even physics—are becoming historical in their mature development. But the content of our own history that requires that frame is of a special kind that contrasts with that of the sciences; it is the content of the arts and humanities. The historical interest is not primarily a scientific interest in the abstract regularities of human affairs but an interest in concrete and complex particulars, a vicarious expansion of acquaintance with life and its qualities beyond what a child or adult can ever directly experience. The historian, like the artist or humanist in general, is involved with the inexhaustible particularity of the past for its own sake, slow to generalize and quick to return to the specific case. In physics and in mathematics it is the other way around; we think of the particular, the concrete case, as illustrating the law or the theorem, or at best as a source of suggestion for new generalities.

The historical method is correspondingly different. It is to construct a model of past situations from which the state of the present will be most probable. A good historical model will not only account for some aspects of the present, including its records and artifacts, but will send us in search of new artifacts or records by which it can further be tested, filled out, or modified. As is true of the geological model, the human historical model is a way of seeing the present, of organizing our knowledge of it, in relation to the past. But such models of the past must meet another condition: they must be intrinsically believable; we must be able to live our way into them as into any good story, even when at first sight they seem inaccessibly strange. The principle is expressed by the Hindu law of sympathy, *Tat tvam asi*—That art thou. To the extent we can succeed in belonging vicariously to other worlds than our own, we become less narrow members of our own, which should then in its own turn come to seem strange.

I think it is clear that the third of my epistemological domains for history, that of ideas, is complex and hard to delimit. I mean it to include all of the terms we use in telling the story and all of the ways we link the story to the evidence it is founded on, including our common sense and more refined knowledge of the ground plan of human affairs, knowledge to which historiography may in turn contribute. Clearly there is much science relevant to refining this knowledge, and some stimulated by it. Astronomy, physics, chemistry, climatology, botany, medicine, archaeology and epigraphy, economics and sociology, linguistics, psychology—all can add to our resources for historical reconstruction. Information about the past decays with time, but there is more of it around than we have yet made use of, and scientific knowledge can help uncover it. Our whole world is an encoding of the past, as are we ourselves. Yet in the end the humanistic interest is dominant, not the scientific. We would not all be so interested in the reconstruction of a past that was not our own, inhabited by beings whose thoughts and motivations we could in principle not understand by the law of sympathy.

It is that personal interest, I believe, that justifies and explains the basic contrast between the sciences, including mathematics, and the arts and humanities. The historical interest is not a search for lawlike regularities in human behavior, though any believable story of the past must satisfy obvious causal conditions. Any human society at any time must meet the requirements of food, clothing, and shelter, of reproduction, communication, and education. But the central part of the story is one that finally relates it to our human subjectivity, to the ways in which we carry on what Howard Gruber aptly calls a network of enterprises, making room for or suppressing new ones, suffering or enjoying the consequences of our goal setting and goal seeking, intended or unanticipated. Even if it were possible to describe human behavior in terms of ideally adequate deterministic or statistically deterministic laws, that description would not match the needs of the historical interest or the conditions of historical understanding. Our capacity to deviate from habitual behavior in setting new goals and modifying the old ones is characteristic of our species and involves self-consciousness, which should always bring with it the recognition of a need for guidance initially lacking. Curiosity about other lives, other places and times, is a natural extension of that need, though like all such extensions of need it flourishes best when not under the pressure of immediate practical concerns. Like all fruitful interests in learning, curiosity must become an end in itself before it can minister well to the practical need that gave rise to it.

To emphasize the nature of the epistemic network involved in the development of historical understanding, the ability to move freely among its three domains, I have used a formula: history presupposes a recognition of the contemporaneity of the past and the historicity of the present. It is a knitting together of a story of the past from the life and evidence of the present, and a perception of the present as not only continuous with that past but as imaginatively projected into it.

If I were being a historian, I would not labor to produce such sententious formulations but would resort instead to the telling of stories. The first that comes to my mind is the story of John Dewey's Experimental School in Chicago, where the curriculum was derived from the known history of mankind, from hunting and gathering to agriculture to urban society. But it was not a curriculum in which children were taught *about* history; it was one, as Dewey explained, in which children relived that history in abbreviated fashion, facing its problems and participating as they could, and as able teachers could help them, in understanding the conditions and consequences of its innovations. I know also of a rural school in England, more recent, that did that sort of thing with the history of its own village, never before compiled, using primary sources, digging into the town records, the personal memories of its elders, and sometimes into the ground. The children and their teacher went from records to the story and from the evolving story to look for further artifacts and records. That work maintained continuity over several years, managing to find room in the process, as did Dewey's school, for all the standard components of a school curriculum.

I tell one final story that I think compresses the essence of what I have been trying to say in a very small compass indeed. It is a story from Frances Hawkins, my wife. She was working in a second-grade class in an industrial suburb. She had introduced the art of weaving on a circular cardboard frame, to be warped radially from center hole to edge, the weft to be a spiral pattern of changing colors. Like the other children, Maria struggled with the problems that weavers know, those of over and under, the odd and the even, of ending one color and beginning another, of sheer dexterity. But Maria caught on very ably and the outer part of her cherished product was elegantly improvised and finished. She came to Frances with it, expressing her dissatisfaction with the ugly early-woven central part with its skipped warp threads and random look, wanting somehow to redo it. Frances first replied, holding up the weaving, "Look at it from a little farther away; it's not a bit ugly." And then, from some adult resources of the kind I have been discussing, she added, "You could think of your weaving as a *history* of your learning to do it." This remark suddenly erased the frown from Maria's face. She sat silently for a long time, inspecting her work, and then got up and walked happily away.

— 7 —

Enlargement of the Aesthetic[1]

I once insulted a few professional educators by elaborating on a metaphor
I thought would please them. My metaphor was the tree of knowledge and, behind that, the ancient image of the tree of life. I had just had
my first serious involvement with elementary-school education. My audience was a general university audience, and I thought that I could have
a bit of fun by drawing a verbal cartoon locating various university schools
and departments within the tree. Naturally I put philosophy at the top,
next to the sky, where the footing is precarious and the earth almost
invisible except toward the horizon. Being firmly committed to the down-
to-earth movement in philosophy, I thought to praise educationists by
locating them in the middle branches, where they could be in readier
and more vital communication with the lower branches of education
and closer to the sustaining trunk, root system, and central circulation.
They took it, however, as a denial of some higher aspiration, as an all too
familiar expression of academic snobbery toward schools of education. I
concluded that some conciliatory insights are unavailing.

I hardly dare to mention my main subject, which has to do with the
place of the arts in our educational system. Fortunately the arts are sustained by sources outside the academic tree, but their representatives

within it are subject to some of those same gradients of prestige as are the educationists, and where the two overlap—in art education—the pressure can be considerable. University corridors and classrooms in general are not aesthetically pleasing. Some of nature's art may be seen through a window, although in many structures of more recent vintage the designers have managed to eliminate even that. The outstanding exceptions are the work areas, the ateliers of instruction in the arts and architecture. They are characteristically lively and inviting places full of diverse materials and of works in progress. Two stand out in my memory. One was at Makerere University in Uganda. In the sculpture department, full of students' unfinished work, I sensed the liberation into new modes of the ancient African tradition of stylized wood carving now expressing the new life of Africa in clay and bronze, wood and stone. Its vigor reminded me of the art of Mexico in the days of Rivera, Orozco, and Siquieros. The other, vivid in another way, was in a small English college of education. The English seem to believe that all primary schoolteachers should be competent practitioners and critics of the arts, and in that laboratory one could come to understand how this belief was carried into practice. Its stores were full of gorgeous simple materials: colored cards and paper, excellent tempera paints and expensive brushes, balsa wood and pine, clay, fabrics and yarns, and much else I cannot even remember. One wanted to settle in and get to work.

That impression was supported in some English and Welsh primary-school classrooms, well stocked with materials of all kinds, full of work in progress, and decorated with work recently finished: children's murals and calligraphy, illustrated reports of scientific inquiries, plans drawn by young surveyors of a nearby medieval castle. Where wall space was not sufficient, work hung at adult eye level from lines strung across the room. There was preschool and infant-school painting to rival our best from much older children; there was children's writing, fresh and uncoerced. In most such classrooms a small library was in constant use; dull primers had been replaced by excellent children's literature and reference books. Collections of found materials from home and field—snail shells and fossils, minerals and plants displayed with scientific nomenclature, drawings of microscopic wildlife—were arrayed with a certain dramatic flair, frequently with a sense for color and form. The teacher's hand was seldom seen, although often a teacher's personal investment was implied in fresh subject matter across the whole curriculum. Those excellent classrooms are by no means confined to England and Wales; they are just far more abundant there than in the United States.

Such classrooms, wherever found, are an aesthetic genre all their own. There is a strong adult presence, but no adult fakery to be found in them; the work belongs to children in style and content, and it draws you in, invites you to enter as a teacher. But you are likely to remain unnoticed unless you know how to join in some worthy science or math in progress or bring tempting materials of your own.

Two sorts of classrooms are unaesthetic. Although apparently at opposite poles, they merit a common diagnosis: boredom. One is quiet but dominated by mindless routine; the other is frenetic, lacking in governance, laissez-faire. Both create the problems they seek to cure: inattention, "discipline," the failure of engagement in learning. The classrooms I speak of, even the least impressive of them, were of a different sort. Children were not bored. They were engaged in diverse enterprises, moving about and talking freely, involved in honest subject matter. "I'll huff and I'll puff and I'll blow your house down" was being put to the architectural test by children in one infant class, with houses built of straw, wood, and brick. A class of older children was engaged in careful study of the ecology of a hedgerow, north side and south, classifying, counting, and preparing a final exhibit. I think any definition of aesthetic education that does not honor such involvements and such expressions must be discounted.

At one point a niggling American conscience (I have learned to call it "puritan") made me ask about such things as math and reading scores. No one seemed very concerned about the statistics. Devotion to such matters was not absent, but it was low-key and not at all test-oriented. Reading, writing, and computation were part of the life, but seldom isolated. Skill was valued but not mechanized. Primers were squeezed out by good storybooks and books of reference, abundantly used and always available. Routine computation was subordinated to the mathematical investigations in practical activity or with concrete math materials in which English curriculum developers have pioneered. Workbooks were as scarce as readers, but the three Rs were abundantly in evidence; nothing laissez-faire about that. So when one headmaster, in reply to my question, said, "We think that if a child has a good day every day, that's the best we can do for his future," I knew she spoke of the enjoyment of learning, not of just what we dismiss as fun and games. That is when I first became sharply conscious of our American puritanism, badly mis-named "scientific assessment." I still have not recovered from the reverse cultural shock I experienced on return. Our puritanism has mainly lost its religious sanction, but it flourishes with another ideology, settled in like arthritis in the joints of our public school systems, where we are all afraid of being criticized for letting children out of that narrow path we call the curriculum, herded along through those educational packages that someone outside the classroom ambience has persuaded us to be-lieve in and try to follow. The ideology is no longer the rooting out of innate wickedness as a preparation for life after death; the label of origi-nal sin has been replaced by a variety of quasi-medical labels such as dyslexia, hyperactivity, and the rest. Human judgment is replaced by paper things called instruments, and the package gives both the diagno-sis and the prescription.

In contrast with the best classrooms of England and their rare coun-terparts in our own country, the typical American classroom is domi-nated by one material: paper. Now paper is a marvelous material, not only for tempera and calligraphy but also for chromatography, many kinds of model airplanes, miniature houses, and much else. It can be made with a blender and screen from most plant materials and given your own watermark, bound in books of your own binding, or rolled into struts for a geodesic dome. Good books are printed on it, as are good illustrations. But most of these uses are unimagined or forbidden.

I had a student a few years ago, an artist and printer in her own right, who undertook a longitudinal study of elementary-school readers, de-cade by decade over a period of about a century. She looked at the quality of the stories, the illustrations, and the printing and binding. It was her surprised but considered judgment that in all these respects the quality deteriorated steadily. The stories were increasingly vapid, the il-lustrations increasingly stereotyped and hackneyed, the printing and bind-ing increasingly shoddy. From the examples she showed me, I could only agree. All hail McGuffey! This was in strong contrast with the pro-duction of really good children's literature—trade books—from Europe and America, which amid much dross continues to flourish, although few seem able to imagine that such literature might replace school readers.

Let me mention two telltale phenomena of our time. One is that the word *materials* used in school contexts now almost always refers to the two-dimensional kind, printed paper. An enterprising group of teachers in Texas recently lobbied successfully for special funds for materials in a more old-fashioned sense. At the last minute they realized that their appropriation would miscarry unless they qualified the noun with some very specific adjective. They finally came up with "three-dimensional." Paper is really three-dimensional, but it gets squeezed pretty thin. The other phenomenon, which I have confirmed many times in appropriate groups, has to do with the implicit metaphysics of the term "subject matter." It turns out that subject matter is conceived to be literally inside the book or package. For this reason we talk about students "going through" junior high school algebra or American history, and for this reason teachers can talk about "covering" a subject rather than uncovering it. The notion that the subject matter exists outside of the book or computer-storehouse and can even be investigated independently of it seems alien to our settled belief. And so we come to the final paradox: millions of children surrounded daily by little more than piles of printed paper, a large proportion thereby doomed to a meager literacy. Something is wrong.

The challenge to all of us is to take with theoretical and practical seriousness the fact that the thing called curriculum has no efficacy except as shaped by teachers, and those who help them, in the daily lives of groups of individual children. That is the central art without which all others, indeed all educationally significant learning, will fail. It is an art that requires the provisioning and reprovisioning of a rich material environment, one that gives access to subject matter and supports a cumulative engrossment in subject matter. But it also requires a many-sided adult involvement, with subject matter and with children jointly, and the evolution of channels of communication around joint engrossments. One is tempted to borrow from the vocabulary of performing arts and speak of choreography or orchestration, but such analogies are limited. Musical terminology might describe the rhythms and changes of pace, the occasional joint improvisation. For all of this Frances Hawkins has used the term *ambience*, for the shaping of which the teacher is centrally responsible. But she underlines something seldom seen as essential to the performing arts: the liberation, steadying, and eventual dominance of curiosity—children's curiosity about the world around them, in which the teacher joins, adding to it a fully adult curiosity about each child. It is here that the aspect of improvisation becomes dominant. Planning is required, planning with time constants from the year to the day and minute. Some elements of the yearly planning are prescribed. That is what the school system and the community understand by curriculum. But these elements lack power to determine the monthly or daily planning; they imply only a skimming off of certain end results, however achieved. At a more concrete level the daily sequence typically is offered, and sometimes seemingly also prescribed, in the form of what we sometimes refer to as instructional packages, which purport to relieve teachers of all but peripheral planning responsibilities. These can be, and frequently are, deadly. They represent, however, what some in the educational world generally understand as curriculum development.

The good classrooms, and the art that enables them, require sustenance of an entirely different kind. They need good books (not workbooks); they need three-dimensional materials and collections of ideas about the uses of materials; they need visitors with skill and knowledge who come to observe, discuss, or suggest. What it comes down to can be expressed by another term from the performing arts: the art of the teacher requires a large and growing repertoire. The wise use of this repertoire implies a wide understanding of elementary subject matter to match the diversity of paths along which children learn. Nothing less can shape the good curriculum, and any notion that it can be done from the outside is an arrogant illusion. Many of us who in the last decade or two have been involved in what has been called curriculum development have learned this, to our sorrow or, if we enjoy learning, to our joy.

To be explicit, we are seeking to support one of the finest of the high arts in a world that views it quite otherwise, as a job in which its knowledgeable discipline is reduced to prescribed routine and administered by lower-grade civil servants, meagerly educated, inadequately apprenticed, poorly supported along the way, and accorded little prestige.

If we accept this thesis, or even if we regard it as an exaggerated statement (which I do not) of a correct thesis, then I think there are enterprises of theory and practice to which we should commit ourselves. On the side of theory, the thesis suggests two major directions. One is to examine this assertion that teaching is properly to be classified among the high arts, classified there with no taint of hyperbole or mere metaphor. If this statement is to be taken seriously, it will involve some reconsideration of aesthetic theory, which tends to sequester the acknowledged fine arts as exhausting the range of aesthetic concerns. A reason for the neglect of teaching as an art is that its best practitioners are rare and mostly invisible to all but the recipients of their practice. Their work is not displayed in galleries or reviewed in newspapers. Many of us are probably fairly good teachers at a more adult level, but few of us have served an adequate apprenticeship in childhood education. One result is that when we offer help to teachers—and they do need help—we do it ineptly and sometimes arrogantly.

In my own work in curriculum development, we followed one firm rule: never publish, or even write, any materials to help teachers unless you have personally taught the same materials to a number of different groups of children. Following that rule was both exhilarating and humiliating. We didn't have—didn't initially know we needed—good teachers to guide us. Nevertheless, sometimes it sang; sometimes it was dreadful. When it sang it never did so twice in the same way. We began at least to learn to relax, to improvise, to seize the unanticipated development, to plan for changing our plans: we called it enlightened opportunism. By the end of that period in our lives, some of us at least were on our way to becoming good teachers of children. We still had something important to offer, much more to learn, and a profound uncertainty as to how best to help advance an art we were just beginning to acknowledge and understand.

There is unfortunately very little good literature on the teaching art. I think all of it is written by those rare skilled practitioners who are also skilled writers. One is Plato, the great dramatist of ideas, the philosopher's philosopher, the classicist's classic, but all too seldom the teacher's teacher. His pupils were mostly adults, but sometimes children.[2] Another is Tolstoy,[3] whose peasant children were all writers and artists. Not to compete with the great ones of the past, three contemporaries also belong in my list: Elwyn Richardson,[4] Frances Hawkins,[5] and Michael Armstrong.[6]

That is the first move: the teaching of children is in principle to be ranked among the high arts, and no consideration of the aesthetic dimension that excludes it will be acceptable! The second move is harder for many contemporaries. Put baldly, all the high arts are forms of teaching. To reject this statement out of hand, as some will, is to accept some un-Platonic conception of teaching that puts it at odds with the aims and services of the arts. The more we discuss the human importance of the arts, however, the more we erode these barriers of definition. If the arts are said to enrich our existence, to extend our acquaintance with the qualities of life or nature, to express and celebrate what is worthy of

enjoyment, are they not then educative in the finest sense and so justified? At times and places the arts have indeed been subjected to narrow
constraints, moralizing or otherwise narrowly didactic. Puritanism,
whether the individualistic puritanism of forebears or the socialist puritanism of contemporaries, does try to impose such constraints, as does
the marketplace. Artists should be autonomous though accountable to
their public and its critics. Indeed, that status is necessary to any genuinely educative function. So I would say that, as we understand better
what it means to teach, we also recognize the artist as teacher, whether
she likes it or not.

If you think this identification of teachers as artists and artists as
teachers has gone too far, let me admit that it has, or should have, some
awkward consequences. One is that it should be possible to speak seriously of the aesthetic dimensions of mathematics or physics or biology,
at least as these human concerns manage, if learned well, to retune our
perceptions and to achieve significant expression.[7] Although awkward,
this sort of talk has been going on for a long time. I think it is least
awkward in the milieu of children's involvement in learning more about
the great world; they have not yet settled into our specializations. And
that is the only real point of my argument. I have no wish to erase conventional distinctions; they have their place so long as we are somewhat
nervous about them.

In the same sense, aesthetic interests are relevant to all practical life—
to the craftsmanship out of which the graphic and plastic arts have
emerged without sharp separation; to the modes of association and communication in which all performing arts (storytelling, poetry, drama,
dance and theater, music) are rooted. Because all human life is pivoted
on the processes of selection or choice, the elaboration and celebrations
of morals and politics must be included in this survey of the aesthetic
realm. When the Lord had finished with his work, he drew back in
contemplation and found it good—aesthetically good!

In laying out the ground plan, the root and the trunk of the tree of
life, God was a mathematician, a physicist; but when it came to the
iterated branchings, out to the diverse leaves and flowers, he was clearly
an artist, and the whole creation was to become the stage setting for the
great moral drama. In any retelling of that old story, including the version now being so actively pieced together by cosmologists and radio
astronomers, by geologists and molecular biologists, by archaeologists

and the rest, there simply can be separatism neither between the arts and sciences nor between them and the activist concern for rerouting the presently dangerous paths of our history. It is a point of view that challenges our best critical faculties and moral concerns.

I emphasize so the inseparability and interpretation of distinguishable phases in experience and learning because of a conviction that no program for the improvement of any one component of the school curriculum can by itself be more than a means of entry, can prosper, without serious attention to the rest. If teachers are to be both the sponsors and critics of artistic expression as a more significant part of the life of schools and classrooms and to educate their students as artists and critics, this interest must affect all the curriculum in a substantive way. People in education talk a great deal about integration, but the only integration possible is to avoid disintegration in the first place. If separate curricula are laid down for reading and writing, math and science, social studies and art, they cannot thereafter by any magic be brought fruitfully back together. In the tree of knowledge you do not get from one branch to another by going back down to the branching point; the journey is too long. The tree of knowledge is not that kind of tree; it is full of cross-connections, anastomoses, like the veining of the leaf or the neural network of the brain. You can get to any part from any other part by a variety of pathways.

And here is a kind of contradiction. Young children most of the time—and all of us some of the time—learn optimally by these cross-connections, moving fluently from one focus of interest to others. They build structures of their own that can never be fully anticipated. A sensitive teacher may find that an intended lesson in geometry, with pencil-compass and straight-edge, turns easily and more fruitfully to one of decorative design, the geometry only implicit. Do you follow this indication or insist on the straight path? If you do the latter, you are likely to lose the last glimmer of children's understanding just as you get to your goal. If you do not, you may find that your lesson is realized more fruitfully in some later context, when what had been only implicitly learned emerges more fully formed. Slow can be fast, and good teaching an art of indirection.

But there is a place for discipline, and never too early. You cannot impose it blindly; it must be accepted as a means to some persistent goal you have helped to steady and deepen. Then you must transiently block the side branches and insist on the straight course. This phase of teaching and learning can powerfully facilitate the more anastomotic kinds of learning later, but when made absolute it degenerates (e.g., coloring between lines, painting by numbers, doing algebra by rote). At its best, however, it has an aesthetic of its own, that of order, elegance, and organizing power. When Van Gogh struggled successfully to get the white of those grubby peasant caps in the dim interior, he was on the same plane as Poincaré, to find just that equation that would summarize his findings. To concentrate is to isolate, but to isolate fruitfully is only to define better what will then be one node in a larger and freer network. What we too often call discipline, that is, rule and routine, does not merely block the side branches but cuts them off, and what is said to have been learned is filed irretrievably in the wastebasket.

I have argued for two initial moves in aesthetic education, both of them implying that this odd label be used to indicate a style in all education. One is to recognize teaching, and I mean the act of teaching, as inherently one of the high arts, although institutionally unrecognized and unsponsored as such. The other is to place all the recognized arts, whether practiced out of schools or in them, as modes of teaching, as in a fresh and proper sense didactic. If both these moves can be accepted, we will find ourselves unable to regard aesthetic education as other than good education that not only values the acknowledged arts but sponsors them and that recognizes the aesthetic dimension as vital to all educationally significant learning.

Why this should be so I have not philosophically tried to say, and a fuller argument I can only suggest. In any adequate phenomenology of experience the term *aesthetic* has a reference far wider than the recognized arts. That which is routine, self-automated on the one hand or mechanically constrained on the other, may be taken as unaesthetic. Such experience is inevitably a large part of our waking lives. By contrast the experience that is cumulative, that leads to some reduction of the tensions of disorder, some unifying grasp of perceptions or plan of procedure, has aesthetic quality, is suffused by a distinctive emotion. Aesthetic experience is in this sense synoptic, integral. Its quality is in one sense indifferent to subject matter; the outcome may be practical or theoretical, and may in such matters be communicated to others in prosaic style, as instruction or argument. These may serve their purposes well while entirely failing to communicate the emotion that has sustained their creation. It is lost by the wayside, not an object of attention in its own right. When on the other hand such emotion is steady and powerful, it seeks to communicate itself through some form of expression that can evoke a direct or vicarious reliving of the experience or experiences that have sustained it. At some such point we enter the domain and disciplines of the arts, the genres of which are in principle as various as the characteristic phases of collective experience, and which can serve to extend our acquaintance with the qualities of life and of nature far beyond the constraints of direct individual experience.

If this outline is valid, then any concern about the educative experience of children (or adults) must be centrally concerned with matters of aesthetic quality and aesthetic expression. In the ambience of the good classrooms I spoke of earlier, you can directly experience the ways in which they generate significant expression and in which that expression, central in attention sometimes and always peripherally influential, supports and extends the involvement in subject matter. What would you say of a display of decorative small weavings in which the yarn was dyed by plant dyes collected on a local botanical field trip, the patterns related to the life of the Anasazi and their present-day descendants and also to some investigation of the combinatorics and geometry of braiding and weaving? Where are the disciplines? Three or four of them are there, and without them it would fail. Yet if they place themselves apart, the failure will be equal. Mathematics was not in the syllabus; it was considered too advanced. Native Americans belong in social studies, for paper-and-crayon headdresses and pictures of teepees. Weaving belongs in art if the teacher chooses it as a skill to be taught sometimes. Botany and extraction of dyes are science, but this year we are studying the weather.

So I return to the starting point, the practical tasks confronting us in education. I have tried to make the circle big enough to contain some ideas. I would like to end with a quotation from John Dewey. In his last major works he did not address the subject of education; but one of them, Art as Experience, is immensely relevant.[8] I intend this quotation to support my pleas for the centrality of the arts and for the nondisintegration of the curriculum:

> Works of art often present to us an air of spontaneity, a lyric quality, as if they were the unpremeditated song of a bird. But man, whether fortunately or unfortunately, is not a bird. His most spontaneous outbursts, if expressive, are not overflows of momentary internal pressures. The spontaneous in art is complete absorption in subject

matter that is fresh, the freshness of which holds and sustains emotion. Staleness of matter and obtrusion of calculation are the two enemies of spontaneity of expression. Reflection, even long and arduous reflection, may have been concerned in the generation of material. But an expression will, nevertheless, manifest spontaneity if that matter has been vitally taken up into a present experience. The inevitable self-movement of a poem or drama is compatible with any amount of prior labor provided the results of that labor emerge in complete fusion with an emotion that is fresh.[9]

NOTES

1. This chapter was originally published in Martin Engel and Jerome Hausman, eds., *Curriculum and Instruction in Arts and Aesthetic Education* (St. Louis: CEMREL, Inc., 1981).

2. All of Plato is relevant, but see especially *Meno* and *Republic*. For a rewarding comment, see D. Wheeler, "Teaching for Discovery," *Outlook* (14), winter 1974.

3. See Tolstoy's works included in volumes such as Alan Pinch and Michael Armstrong, eds., *Tolstoy on Education* (East Brunswick, NJ: Associated University Presses, 1982); and *The Life and Teaching of Leo Tolstoy* (London: G. Richards, 1904).

4. Elwyn Richardson, *In the Early World: Discovering Art Through Crafts* (New York: Pantheon Books, 1964).

5. Frances Hawkins, *The Logic of Action: Young Children at Work* (Niwot, CO: University Press of Colorado, 1985), and *Journey With Children: The Autobiography of a Teacher* (Niwot, CO: University Press of Colorado, 1997).

6. Michael Armstrong, *Closely Observed Children* (Richmond, Surrey, England: Chameleon Press, 1980).

7. I have tried to suggest the place of science in a genuine contemporary culture in the following: David Hawkins, "The Creativity of Science," in H. Brown, ed., *Science and the Creative Spirit* (Toronto: University of Toronto Press, 1957); "Science as a True Mythology," in S. F. Seymour, ed., *Washington Colloquium on Science and Society*, first series (Baltimore: Mono Book Corp., 1967); *The Informed Vision* (New York: Agathon Press, 1974).

8. John Dewey, *Art as Experience* (New York: Minton, Balch and Co., 1934). I believe that Dewey's unacknowledged inspiration for this work was a classic he (quite typically) criticized, Immanuel Kant's *Critique of Judgment*. Aestheticians who can read their way into an eighteenth-century German pietistic taste, and a great philosopher, will find in "the free play of the imagination and the understanding" a powerful argument for the unifying role of the aesthetic in human experience.

9. Dewey, *Art as Experience*, p. 70.

— 8 —

Reconstruction in Education:
A Perspective on Dewey's Development

In speaking about John Dewey, I always suffer a mixture of confidence and diffidence. The confidence comes from long but indirect association. I never met him, though he was the age of my father. But among my teachers and older colleagues in philosophy were several who had been his students or younger associates, knowing his thought through personal association. The two who influenced me most—H. W. Stuart and H. C. Brown—had grown up in the atmosphere of the University of Chicago and later of Columbia University, which Dewey helped create, and had contributed to *Studies in Logical Theory* in their early careers. Such is the source of my confidence; I could always read Dewey with the assumption that I knew what he was about.

My diffidence, on the other hand, comes from the actual reading of his work, even with the assumption of prior understanding. I find it usually an unsettling experience; I question and argue; but a written text, as Plato long ago wrote in the *Phaedrus*, is deaf, it only repeats itself. There is perhaps also a simpler reason for diffidence, which is Dewey's literary style. One of my professors at Stanford, Harold Chapman Brown, told a little story that may illuminate Dewey's style. Dewey was a firm believer in the equality of the sexes, and as a good experimentalist tried to contribute equally, with his wife, to the menial tasks of the household, including the dishwashing. Above the sink where he washed he had fastened a writing board and pencil, and there he could commit his thoughts to paper. This may explain some of the fluidity of Dewey's style, turgid and sometimes turbid, the stream of his thought, the hot and the cold, the continuum of experience. Dewey does not so much want to argue for conclusions as to involve us in the critical process itself, itself part of the flow. This process, and with it Dewey's philosophy, is not easily or properly reduced to summary form.

But I have another and stronger commitment to Dewey, which is his long preoccupation with the theory and practice of education. He is one of the very few important philosophers since Plato who brought the subject matter of education to center stage. As did Plato, he says more than once that in one way or another concern about education requires response to all the basic philosophical questions.

To put Dewey in historical context as a philosopher is no easy task, and it is not my main purpose to do so. But there are a few philosophical liaisons that I think help us to understand him. The first of these comes always as a surprise to persons who know only his persuasive writings. It is his strong liaison with the Greek classics, particularly Aristotle. As a teacher of the classics he was remembered by his students as an exacting taskmaster, disciplining their too-easy interpretations by endlessly sending them back to read the texts more carefully, never content with facile interpretations. This liaison is in fact the original source of Dewey's naturalism, his opposition to all dualisms in metaphysics, epistemology, or ethics; Aristotle is the source, I believe, of his ideal of a unified vision of experience and nature.

The second major influence, much better known, is his deep youthful commitment to Hegel. Though Dewey early grew away from the then-prevailing American version of Hegelianism, he also kept and developed something important from it, from the Hegel of *Phenomenology*, perhaps also of *Logics* and *Philosophy of Right*. Many critics have sensed in Dewey an unresolved conflict between his naturalism and his characteristic resort to a dialectical development of the phenomenology of experience.

A third liaison, in some ways the most important, was with the content and methodological spirit of the scientific world of the late nineteenth century, the latter interpreted by Charles Peirce, one of Dewey's teachers at the newly created scientific university, Johns Hopkins. This is the origin of Dewey's instrumentalism, but even more importantly, I think, it is the origin of his deceptively broad conception of the scientific method and his belief in its universal applicability. Darwin's work, he said, opened to science the gates of the garden of life; it "freed the new logic for application to mind and morals and life." One should mention also, in this connection, the work of such anthropologists as Lewis Henry Morgan, those who formulated in grand outline the major phases of postbiological, cultural evolution from ancient small hunting-and-gathering societies, thus vastly extending the meaning and potential range of human history. In Dewey's experimental school for children at the University of Chicago, the curriculum was in essence a scheme in which children *relived* (and thus in part reinvented) that newly discovered story of human cultural evolution—a story so much grander in scale than the story of the Garden of Eden, though essentially similar in its intent.

The last of these liaisons I wish to mention takes us back to the eighteenth century, to Jean-Jacques Rousseau and the French and American Revolutions. For this liaison (not being a thorough scholar) I have little direct evidence, so I mention it as a conjecture that is useful to my present purposes. Dewey seems never to have been fully caught up in, or therefore to have recovered from, the nineteenth-century socialist critique of capitalism. He knew very well that the growth of industrialism created a need for profound social reforms, and in his long career he was party to reformist efforts, an intellectual leader for many who were sometimes even more actively involved than he. But I think he mistrusted any but piecemeal efforts at reform. He never addressed himself in major writing to a detailed and substantive critique of Karl Marx, who anticipated him in speaking in the name of science, and of the unity of theory and practice. Dewey's central political concern was the furtherance of democratic commitments and institutions, and he accepted no framework of political thought that reached beyond that which is available, or can become available, to democratic liberal reform. That is why I take him back through the nineteenth century to the figure of Rousseau. Rousseau's great achievement, though in paradoxical form, was the development of the theory of government through participation and consent. I think Dewey's *The Public and Its Problems*[1] is Rousseau's best twentieth-century analogue, though analytical and conciliatory in style rather than polemical. If there is to be a *planned* society, it must also be a *planning* society (a very brief formulation I have heard from the Italian philosopher Aldo Visalberghi), one in which decisions are responsive to the discussion of ends, a discussion in which everyone has some voice.

Rousseau also attacked two other eighteenth-century institutions, those of religion and of education. Rousseau's anitclerical battle had been won for us in the American Constitution, and again Dewey's parallel is conciliatory rather than polemical (in his *A Common Faith*[2]). The liaison with Rousseau in the philosophy of education is, of course, the one I wish to develop. Here, moreover, the counterpart of *Emile* and of *Lettre à M. de Beaumont* is a whole major part of Dewey's life and writing.

DEWEY AND THE PROGRESSIVE TRADITION

Rousseau was an eighteenth-century gentleman who seems callously to have discarded his own illegitimate children, and who I believe had no personal curiosity about any living children. His writings on the subject embarrass us, they reveal the very artificiality that he attacks in defense of the natural child. Yet in the curious web of his mind there was a golden thread. He did not observe children, he invented them; but that invention was a necessary link in his conception of the natural order, new to his age; it was a link in which children's education in the arts and sciences would be, at the same time, the expression of their natural bodily development, their growing talents and curiosities, their growing capacity for self-expression. In his own way he first invented, and then dramatized, the very idea of child development. Dewey in his own time was sharply critical of Rousseau's ideal—often sentimentally expressed—of the natural in opposition to the artificial. Rousseau's contemporary François Quesnay made use of this same opposition in his critique of the taxation policies of the French monarchy, and out of this critique laid the foundations of the *tableau economique*, of modern political economy and quite incidentally of the doctrine of "laissez faire, laissez passer." Rousseau's educational doctrine, in which the coercive shaping of children into an artificial mold was to be replaced by the nurture of their natural development, appeared equally to imply an attitude of educational laissez-faire. I believe that Rousseau's basic thinking was better than this, though it was and still is the easy interpretation of his writings.

Indeed Dewey himself, because of the popular vulgarization of his views, seems sometimes caught in the same trap; he is often seen as an advocate of educational laissez-faire, though in several places he repudiates it: I choose his 1899 *Lectures*, a Chicago talk to parents ("The Child and the Curriculum"), and his later, more mature work, *Experience and Education*.[3] In these writings, spanning two decades, the laissez-faire ideology and the view of human nature it implies are described as an *incorrect* way of recognizing the essential autonomy of the learning process, and of children's innate curiosity and capacity for the exploration and mastery of any worthy subject matter that matches their development powers.

In "The Child and the Curriculum," we see Dewey's characteristic dialectic at work; he starts with the polar opposition of the child-centered ideology, with its emphasis on spontaneous and undivided curiosity on one hand, and on the other the unchildlike nature of a logically organized and formalized curriculum, with its basic commitment to a compartmentalized, didactic, and ultimately coercive process of instruction. In *Experience and Education*, Dewey relates this same polarization of educational belief to two implicit metaphysical commitments. The first is expressed by the preformationist nativistic, horticultural metaphor of unfolding, "development from within." The second is behaviorist, environmentalist: the child is clay, to be shaped from without into the patterns of adult knowledge and virtue.

Dewey clearly rejects both of these metaphors and the views of human nature and learning they respectively imply. But between Rousseau and Dewey there is another kind of historical connection that I wish strongly to emphasize. Rousseau's views on education, whatever their merit when seen in retrospect, triggered in his time a series of small explosions, both of denunciation and of accord. Out of the latter there grew a minor but persistent tradition, associated early with the names of Johann Pestalozzi and Friederich Froebel, that attempted a reduction to practice of a style of childhood education that matched Rousseau's newly articulated perception: that the estate of childhood is not an inferior version of adulthood to be pushed or hastened through, but one with its own developmental style and character, its own tempo, which education must respect and understand, and by which it must be disciplined. This practical tradition I speak of includes many unsung heroines of childhood education, whose contribution was seldom in writing but most often in the pupils they educated and in the training of their apprentices. It gave rise also to a number of perceptive theorists and advocates.

All honor to these pioneers; they often showed great insight in matters of child development and learning. They also, unfortunately, tended to elaborate detailed systems for others to follow, and thus to create premature and rigid orthodoxies from which obedient followers were fearful of departing. Nevertheless, the practical tradition did continue to develop, though always limited in size. Over a hundred years ago, the Froebel Kindergarten came to the United States, and soon there were many of them, small private schools scattered thinly. Nearly that long ago my mother was a pupil in one such kindergarten. Her teacher, Susan Blow, was a Hegelian philosopher and student of Dante, debarred by her sex from academic life. She was a colleague of William T. Harris, founder and editor of the *Journal of Speculative Philosophy* and later United States Commissioner of Education. It was the high point of my mother's formal education, and as her children in the "cowboy" West, we were in turn subject to the gentling influence of the Froebel songs, games, and gifts, though always in competition with more vigorous wild-west pursuits.

There were other successful small-scale reforms in American education, for older children, and during the period when compulsory public education became a reality there was much stir and advocacy of these reforms, though little general understanding or practical support. Such was the context of Dewey's first involvement in childhood education. Dewey's contribution lies in the way he synthesized two streams of influence. One of these was a vigorous American tradition of theory, in psychology and philosophy; the other was that still minor and obscure, but authentic and already successful, tradition of childhood education that I believe came to Dewey through the experienced teachers he worked with.[4] It was not his creation, as is widely believed, though he became its major philosopher and practical advocate.

Very often in the history of knowledge important forward steps have occurred when the various barriers to communication between the academic traditions and the traditions of skilled artistry or craftsmanship have been breached. The knowledge of the skilled craftsman is organized for immediate use; it is not transmitted through learned journals and conferences but through his productions and his apprentices. Thus I suspect the Emperor Claudius knew from experience and reflection on gambling more implicit mathematical probability theory than any mathematician before the Renaissance, though we have lost his treatise. The metallurgists Agricola and Biringuccio knew a better chemistry than any alchemical theorists of their time. Aristotle somewhere observes that for the earthbound astronomer the cause of the eclipse is a matter of learned geometrical inferences, while an observer from the moon could directly perceive it. The craftsman, like Aristotle's lunar observer, can sometimes directly see what for others is only a late and learned inferential achievement. Our knowledge of the world is dependent on the nature of our practical relations to it. This is indeed a thesis central to the epistemologies of Aristotle and of Spinoza, of Marx and of Dewey.

On the other hand, the confluence of such often-separate traditions, of theory and of practice, can bring about developments and transitions that unaided practice or unaided theory would seldom accomplish. Such a confluence, I believe, is at the core of Dewey's importance for education. He assimilated the spirit and style of an already flourishing craft tradition called progressive education; he criticized its shortcomings; he gave it a far richer epistemological and psychological guidance than was available in its earlier trappings, borrowed from Hegel and Schelling, of Froebelian thought. His writing and personal influence gave intellectual stature to the new movement, and a vital sense of intellectual romance. Lucy Sprague Mitchell, an important American educational leader in the early twentieth century, has told how her whole sense of commitment to the teaching art was shaped by youthful association with Dewey. Her book *Young Geographers*[5] is one of the classics that illuminates the teacher's art, the art of a teacher who is master of the curriculum rather than its slave, one who leads children to a deep involvement in the exploration and understanding of the natural and human world around them.

Dewey's influence on the academic world of teacher preparations was even greater, at least on the surface. After his experience with the Experimental School at the University of Chicago, he went to Columbia University, where his commitments became a powerful influence in shaping the development of its long-influential Teachers College. His influence was in part responsible for the commitment to research within it and other pedagogical training colleges, thus legitimating their increasing affiliation with the universities. Most of this development took place in the first third of the century. When Frances Hawkins was a student and young teacher in the early thirties, prepared in an excellent pedagogical institution in San Francisco, the whole movement to which Dewey had given such powerful support appeared to be on the ascendency. As a young academic philosopher, I was thus also exposed through her work to the educational power of this tradition, as then reduced to some of its best practice, and to the conceptions of child development and learning that were implicit (and partly explicit) in it. In later years, when I became involved practically in matters of early education, I came to realize that I was myself excited about some possibly important transactions between the academic world of theory and that of a successful, though still very small, minority practical tradition.

DEWEY'S CENTRAL PROGRAM, THEN AND NOW

But by 1960 the directions of educational change in the United States had altered profoundly. The influence of the earlier progressive education tradition had waned rather than grown, indeed had almost disappeared. Though that movement had never penetrated far into the world of the publicly supported schools, it was now in full retreat. Fresh beginnings could be found here and there, but the elegant craft traditions themselves were virtually lost. These fresh beginnings were often ineffective, and what had been learned before had to be learned all over again. The guiding traditions of theory were lost or ignored, or were first vulgarized and then rejected. Research and training in the colleges of education marched to other drums. Educational research became increasingly dominated by a narrow scientism in which something called scientific methodology was more important than substance.[6]

There are, of course, some honorable exceptions to this doleful story, but they are not numerous. However, our very size and pluralism in the United States may sometimes save such exceptions from total extinction; there are always some cracks in the pavement where the green grass can still grow, and sometimes flourish again.

Dewey's influence moved, of course, to other countries. During a year spent in England, where the practical traditions I speak of continued to grow and flourish after World War II, we found that the guiding influence of Dewey was more widely acknowledged and more adequately understood than in his native country. During recent years we have even observed, with a sense of irony, a minor reverse influence in which Americans eagerly sought to learn more about, and indeed to import, "The English Infant School," in apparent unawareness of their own American traditions now lost. In characteristic American fashion it has been supposed that some of those good English schools could just be torn from their own developmental roots, placed in pots, and transported across the Atlantic.

In view of the obvious lack of widespread recognition for the movement that Dewey sponsored and extended, one must very seriously ask today whether there is not some deep inadequacy in his synthesis and in the practice that has tried to remain faithful to it, or whether, on the other hand, our puritan traditions, reinterpreted and amplified by a narrow educational utilitarianism of costs and benefits, would have defeated even the most enlightened and effective traditions of schooling. To insist upon the educational importance of playfulness in inquiry and upon the long-term consummatory joys of self-propelled learning is almost surely to be disparaged in, or even banished from, a world dominated by moral futurism, whether secular or sacred in its measures of utility. Dewey himself saw the threat and devoted much analytical attention to challenge this presupposition that education is only a preparation—whether for life after death or for life after schooling makes little difference.

In order to pursue properly the question of the adequacy of Dewey's schematism of education, I shall try to say something more about his style than my opening joke. First of all, it was a revelation to me when I realized that he was often what we nowadays would call a phenomenologist. One can, of course, catch many echoes in Dewey of Hegel's *Phenomenologie des Geistes*, and thus of the notion that understanding evolves by stages, and that the life of reason is a life of endless self-transcendence. This is, of course, not the phenomenology of recent Europe, though there may be more affinity than meets the eye. Dewey's phenomenology is literally a following of characteristically evolving patterns in experience, it is a reflective description and analysis of characteristic phases within self-conscious experience. If you have trouble reading Dewey, you should just relax and let him remind you of the patterns you have been, or can become, aware of in your own experience. I don't think, to be sure, that Dewey would readily admit to this description. In his day phenomenology was firmly bonded to the traditions of idealism that he had come to repudiate. In his metaphysical commitments, Dewey wanted to be, and in some ways was, an Aristotelian naturalist. In our day, however, this bonding has dissolved. Dewey was a naturalist indeed, if that means repudiation of the Cartesian split on the one side, and of post-Watsonian behaviorism on the other. *Experience and Nature,*[7] however successful or unsuccessful as metaphysics, is enough to convince us of this; of the mindfulness of nature and the naturalness of mind. Dewey's version of human behavior was as literally mindful, and in the phenomenology of behavior Dewey is concerned with the agency and growth of an inquiring intelligence; never with the limiting abstractions of stimulus and response. Indeed, his critique of the S-R schema, in "The Reflex Arc Concept,"[8] has hardly yet been improved on.

The affinity with Hegel, thus detached from Hegelian systematics, stands out, I think, very clearly in Dewey's philosophy of education. It is revealed repeatedly in his critical treatment of educational polarities and controversies, a treatment that in each case illustrates his dialectical method. I propose to discuss four examples from Dewey's writings about education. There are others, but these among them will also serve to convey a central part of his educational commitment. What he does, procedurally, is to seize upon every controversy he sees as important, upon every polarization of beliefs that gives any surface evidence of deep underlying conceptual disturbances. Dewey then digs deeper (to extend the metaphor) looking for those basement weaknesses, those inadequate presuppositions that the opponents in controversy can be shown to share. To undermine the standard rigid oppositions is thus not to reconcile or to palliate, but rather to extend understanding and the ranges of experience it can comprehend.

The first example concerns the understanding of child development and goes back, therefore, to the time of Rousseau and to his perennial detractors and defenders. Here Dewey elaborates the opposing conceptions. On one side we can think of human development in the sense of behaviorism, or (from the anthropologists) of cultural determinism. In this version, when biologically considered we are but clay, shaped entirely in our actual character by external forces. In *Experience and Education*[9] Dewey presents this metaphor of human nature as the metaphysical basis of an all-too-familiar conception of education: an activity of teachers directed at students, to inform their passive minds and shape their ductile characters. If students are in any way co-agents of this process, it is only by way of submission or recalcitrance, much as clay might resist or accept a craftsman's attempt to shape it. In some form, this metaphor reflected a mistaken notion of original sin, an anxiety over the mischief of idle hands, etc. Children must be taught to shape up and fly right, and the devil will inevitably take the hindmost. I am embellishing Dewey here a good deal, though I don't think he would mind. I think the most neutral and valid expression of this shaping metaphor is, simply, the recognition that human cultures have often been transmitted from generation to generation with a remarkable degree of invariance, even across apparent interruptions and discontinuities.

In total opposition to all of this way of thinking stands the basic biological—or better, horticultural—metaphor, that of development from within, of unfolding, of self-realization. The plant will not grow without sunlight and water and air, to be sure, and it can prosper under cultivation or suffer from neglect. But it cannot be shaped to other than its own specific natural form except in some superficial and unreproductive way. Aristotle had said it for the plant and animal forms; he was a better geneticist than anyone between his time and the twentieth century. But no purely biological endowment was for Aristotle a sufficient condition for the appearance of human virtues; those evolved only through experience, through instruction and practice. Modern romantic reactions—following Rousseau—against the shaping metaphor and the manipulative or coercive didacticism associated with it misrepresent the social character of learning, as it accrues through association in joint endeavor, experience and instruction interwoven. Dewey's own dominant image of education is one of apprenticeship—it captures the essential ternary relation involved in educationally significant learning that is suppressed in both views he has criticized. It is the relation between an active learner engaged with some primary subject matter that has been made accessible through the art and engagement of a teacher.

Subordinate to this central interactionist view of the learning process, Dewey's second attack upon the either-or in education is that of the individual versus the social. One wing of the self-styled progressive movement associated the horticultural image of unfolding with a sort of individualism, while its opponents could acknowledge and emphasize only the communality of knowledge and culture, to which individual differences could contribute nothing except some harassment of instruction and inequality of outcome. Here Dewey's interactionist position allows him to remind us that individuality among our human kind is primarily a social attribute; individuals are valued not for sheer differences, but for the differing ways in which they can optimally learn, contribute to, and benefit from the world created by their association.

The third polarization is again implicit in the first: it is the perennial conflict over freedom and disciplines. The conception of discipline shared in such debates is of a kind of performance that is unfree, while freedom is equally taken to be undisciplined. In many places, Dewey expresses his recognition of the fact that in education, freedom without discipline leads only to the unsteadiness of transient and superficial curiosity, or to a routine and repetitive performance that learns little and ends in boredom. The kind of discipline that directs and steadies and extends curiosity is inherent in subject matter, and thus no enemy of freedom but a condition of its achievement. Here again the dissolution of the either-or comes about not through a kind of purely formal dialectic, but through a thoroughly empirical investigation in which each of the initially conflicting conventional categories of behavior is exploited as a kind of search warrant, leading to a more discriminating account of the other. As he pursues it, this becomes a method of successive approximation, in which new questions are born out of the resolution of older ones and new investigations are suggested.

My fourth and final example is of yet another polarity implicit in the first. It is the contrast between learning conceived as a creative act of the learner, a fashioning of insight or intuition from the raw materials of primary experience, and learning conceived as sheer transmission, as that which is received and recorded in a form more or less unaltered from some already learned source. Here again, of course, the resolution is one that follows the logic of interaction. If children should not be required, in each generation, to reinvent the wheel, it should be observed also that the last word in wheels is hardly in as yet, in technology or physics or astrophysics or mathematics. The secret of resolution is to recognize that the transmission of old knowledge should come always with a fresh curiosity about the means of testing or extending it. And this leads Dewey to what I believe is his sharpest and most insightful line of analysis and criticism. In his 1899 *Lectures in the Philosophy of Education*[10] and in several other writings, notably in his elegant little popular essay "The Child and the Curriculum," he makes a very emphatic contrast between two modes of pedagogical organization in the curriculum, one of which he calls "logical," the other "psychological." In the former work, "Lecture XIII," I find the most detailed statement. The logical mode of organization is one that "surveys the subject matter in its highest stage of development," detached from the process and order in which it has been evolved and, more importantly, from the diverse sorts of process and order by which it might be evolved again in the minds of individual learners. Curricula and textbooks—what in the United States we now call "instructional packages"—may be more simplified for more immature learners, but the essential order is typically the same. Pedagogy based on the adult logical—transitive—order of the knowledge typically suppresses the many developmental pathways for achieving that order. "The logical statement of the subject matter simply *states* the (educational) problem, it does not solve anything at all."[11]

Here Dewey uses the example of geometry, though as usual with almost no attention to the kind of illustrative detail that would show the power of his argument. To solve the pedagogical problem, for geometry, Dewey says, we must indeed first fully understand the subject in its logical organization. Next, we must "study the child in his present environment, until we find the actual concrete things in *his* experience which we have in this highly elaborated and objective way worked out in *our* geometry;" and finally, "having found out these things we must see how to utilize them so that they will develop with the least waste and the greatest amount of positive movement toward this ideal which we wish to reach."[12] This is what Dewey meant by the "psychologizing" of subject matter. In view of the dominant later development of American psychology, the term is unfortunate, though clear in meaning.

In this same lecture Dewey refers to the partial successes of the progressive tradition, precisely through its efforts to reconstruct the substance of science, history, and literature, so as to provide new pathways of access for children of primary-school age. But, he says, now surely echoing Rousseau, "Throughout the educational system, for the most part, the assumption is that boys and girls are simply little men and women, they are simplified, less capable editions of the adults, and consequently should have simplified editions of the subject matter which the adult has succeeded in getting."[13] In this and the following lecture he makes it quite clear that the mere reorganization of textbooks according to a more psychological order, while it would help, is by no means the goal of his reforms. No textbook could ever be adequate to the needs of different children. These needs can only be met, Dewey says, "if the person teaching has a thoroughgoing broad knowledge of the whole field and so surveys it that he can see just what facts, at each particular period, the child can get hold of, the facts that he really needs in order to make his own interest valid and permanently valuable to him." And here, for emphasis, is a final warning to his own followers: "The so-called

new education, in realizing the value of children's interest, has not sufficiently realized the need of advanced and thorough and specialized scholarship, in order that the interest may be really effective in the educational
process."[14]

Dewey's emphasis on the needed reconstruction of subject matter,
reconstruction with the aim of giving the greatest and most fruitful access to it from the diverse starting points of children's individual talents
and experience, is stated again in other and later writings, but I for one
am not satisfied. I think he greatly underestimated the magnitude of the
problem of reconstruction and of the consequent education and support that teachers need; I refer especially to what he describes as the
"thoroughgoing broad knowledge of the whole field" that would also be
of such a kind that the teacher can indeed readily "see just what facts, at
each particular period, the child can get hold of, . . . to make his own
interest valid and permanently valuable."[15] For it is just this combination of fluent understanding of subject matter with the simultaneous
ability to grasp children's thought and experience, and thus to build
bridges between them, that our educational system for the early years (in
Dewey's time or our own) does not provide and hardly as yet ever seeks
to provide.

There was, indeed, some later American research effort in the direction in which Dewey had pointed. It was called "the psychology of subject matter," but it became unfashionable among American psycholo-
gists, who thought it more honorific to develop a completely general
theory of learning, one independent of all possible subject matter. And
Dewey himself, so far as I know, never developed this program much
farther. To do so would indeed have required the collaboration of the
best minds and most skillful practitioners in the arts, the sciences, and
in teaching.

In his later years, in his most mature writings as a philosopher, Dewey
did not, to our loss, return to his earlier detailed concern with formal
education. His basic idea of reconstruction, however, grew in its scope,
and dominated his most mature thinking. All human institutions, he
says, are finally to be judged by their educative influence, by the measure
of their capacity to extend human knowledge and competence. The
growth of industrial society and the transformations inevitable within it
will lead only to widespread misery and destruction unless the institutions of power and the institutions of intelligence[16] can be increasingly

brought together in the unity of interaction that Dewey first explored, in detail, in the small but central world of childhood education. We find this theme extensively developed in *Experience and Nature*, where it implies a reconstruction in metaphysics, a new sense of the unity of man and nature, and a new framework within which to understand man's evolving place and the problems it generates. We find it in *Art as Experience*,[17] where Dewey's earlier conception of consummatory experience is transformed into a theory of aesthetics and, indeed, a new version of his theory of knowledge. We find it in *Logic*,[18] which proposes a reconstruction of the very canons of rational inquiry. In the last two of these works, Dewey explicitly discusses the alienation of common thought and experience from the modern world of science, too new, he says, "to have penetrated into the subsoil of mind."[19] As a result, we now live within a society whose members are for the most part alienated from the very means by which they live, excluded from the intellectual and aesthetic potential that those means provide, and therefore from full and democratic participation.

Dewey is often accused of being a utopian philosopher, one whose reformist efforts presupposed the very means that only those reforms would bring into existence. But of course all of us are utopian in some such sense. Dewey was indeed one who could describe the goal without claiming omniscience about the detailed means for reaching it. He was in this sense an experimentalist who insisted on the test of practice for all proposals, including his own. He was a *skeptical* reformer.

In the lectures I have quoted from, on the philosophy of education, Dewey says that there are three phases of planning for the curriculum. The first was fully to understand the subject matter to be taught, in its logical organization. The second was to search for that which, in the legitimate experience of the naive learner, would give this learner access to that subject matter. The third was to discover how to utilize what had been thus found in effectively bridging the gap between "the child and the curriculum," and it is this central task of educational research and innovation that I think Dewey underestimated, and that his followers have too often ignored.

In redefining that neglected task we must first recognize that immediate concerns for the education of children and youths exist within a larger situation, in which those who teach are themselves the product of the very education they seek to ameliorate, and this fact is itself only one expression of the still larger alienation that Dewey later spoke about. In concluding his discussion of "Common Sense and Scientific Inquiry," in *Logic*, Dewey calls this the outstanding problem of our civilization,

set by the fact that common sense in its content, its world and methods, is a house divided against itself. It consists in part, and that part the most vital, of regulative meanings and procedures that antedate the rise of experimental science in its conclusions and methods. In another part it is what it is because of the application of science. This cleavage marks every phase and aspect of modern life: religious, economic, political, legal, and even artistic.[20]

If we take this latter-day conclusion seriously, then Dewey's early conception of reconstruction is indeed inadequate. We cannot simply contrast adult knowledge and childish ignorance, as though the former were already adequate. The cleavage affects us all. We must recognize the historical loop that ties together the past and present, the child poorly taught becoming, without reconstructive professional support offered all along the way, the teacher who teaches poorly. But who among us will know how to provide this help? One should be reminded of Marx's recognition of this loop, that the educators must be educated. If education were really a one-way process, this would imply an infinite regress of educational wisdom. Rather, ends and means must interact. We must see the graph of the process not as one directed downward from above, but as a web, as a network of transactions that is grounded in the radical unevenness and specialization of our present-day culture, and recognize that reconstruction is a process in which we all need both to teach and be taught.

Unable as we presently are to comprehend the powers that the sub-culture of science and technology has placed in our hands, the success of this commitment has surely become a condition of our survival.

NOTES

1. John Dewey, *The Public and Its Problems* (New York: H. Holt & Co., 1957).

2. John Dewey, *A Common Faith* (New Haven, CT: Yale University Press, 1934).

3. John Dewey, *Lectures in the Philosophy of Education*, 1899, Reginald Archimbault, ed. (reprint, New York: Random House, 1966); *The Child and the Curriculum, and the School and Society* (Chicago: University of Chicago Press, 1956); *Experience and Education* (New York: Collier Books, 1963).

4. Two books that throw partial light on this connection are Katherine Camp Mayhew and Ann Camp Edwards, *The Dewey School: The Laboratory School of the University of Chicago, 1896–1903* (New York: D. Appleton Century Co., 1936); and Joan K. Smith, *Ella Flagg Young: Portrait of a Leader* (Educational Studies Press, Chicago, Ill., and the Iowa State University Research Foundation, 1979).

5. Lucy Sprague Mitchell, *The Young Geographers* (New York: Bank Street College of Education, 1971).

6. This methodology was mainly from the traditions of Karl Pearson, R. A. Fisher, and company, elegantly applicable to the study of small-sample phenomena affected by not too many and not too long-term well-defined variables, and relatively independent of all the etceteras we call context. The classic examples are from agricultural research, the worst from the study of important human affairs, including what is vital in education.

7. John Dewey, *Experience and Nature* (LaSalle, IL: Open Court Publishing Co., 1958).

8. John Dewey, "The Reflex Arc Concept in Psychology," *Psychological Review* III, 1996, pp. 357–370.

9. John Dewey, *Experience and Education* (New York: Macmillan & Co., 1938.

10. Dewey, *Lectures in the Philosophy of Education*, Reginald Archambault, ed. (New York: Random House, 1966).

11. Ibid., see Lecture no. XIII, p. 128.

12. Ibid., p. 129.

13. Ibid., p. 128.

14. Ibid., p. 141.

15. Ibid., p. 141.

16. To use a distinction of Bert Morris, a colleague of many years.

17. John Dewey, *Art as Experience* (New York: Minton, Balch & Co., 1934).

18. John Dewey, *Logic: The Theory of Inquiry* (New York: H. Holt & Co., 1938), pp. 178–179.

19. John Dewey, *Art As Experience*, p. 97.

20. John Dewey, *Logic*, pp. 78–79.

– 9 –

Not to Eat, Not for Love

It was in these words—"Not to eat, not for love"—that a famous New England writer spoke of the aim of four snakes he saw wandering in the woods.[1] I want to talk instead about persons, mainly children. My aim likewise is not to eat, and not for love, but for theory. It is to isolate and define a kind of human motivation that I see as crucially important for education and that, unrecognized, is characteristically suppressed in our schools. It is a result of the failure to recognize, and of the suppression, that we produce a self-confirming system of schooling that operates at a far lower level than is possible and good. This system is not anyone's invention, and it is not a place for blame. On the other hand, if we are to destabilize and remodel this system, the "we" who can do that are ourselves products of the system, and the efforts to perturb it must come in that sense from within. One of the things we can do is to unlock the school door and look beyond it for resources, for freshness and novelty that will help us. And these resources must be of a kind that will arouse some answering potentialities from within: from children and teachers first, and then from those who are the connective tissue of the system and its links with the community.

One of the things we need is more adequate and better-grounded theory relevant to both learning and teaching. By theory I mean theory in the full scientific sense, a wide and adequate summary of what we know that will, in particular, help us define what we do not yet know and how we might yet learn about learning and teaching.

Central to such theory is an adequate account, or at least an adequate framework for an account, of motivation. Prevailing theories, especially those that are appealed to in the justification and planning of curricular materials and teaching strategies within the present system, are inadequate. When I say this I mean to include under the term *theory* not only some general propositions about how learning takes place, but also the application rules, explicit or implicit, by which those general propositions are related to the design or testing of concrete learning and teaching situations. Let me look first at the theory widely practiced in school long before its later formulation, the theory of operant conditioning. This theory, in anything like the form in which it has emerged from the matrix of laboratory psychology, presupposes an external reinforcement in the form of a reward that can be administered independently to a subject, at a point where goal attainment can be specified by an experimenter. The theory of operant conditioning is linked, by the very form of its statement and experimental evidence, to reinforcement of a particular pathway from goal seeking to goal attainment. It presupposes that the subject is in what scientifically can be called a "prepared state." Thus, for example, the cat in the puzzle box must be hungry, which means that some internal biochemistry has switched on a behavioral system that can be called food seeking. Then if you put goodies outside the box within sight or smell you can hope that the cat will try to get out of the box, and when he does the goodies will reward him.

Now you can try to embed such a very restricted theory in a wider context, one in which the reinforcement is described as *intrinsic* to the attainment of a goal. So for example, if someone sets you a puzzle to solve and you happen to accept solving that puzzle as your goal, then the finding of what you recognize as a solution is reinforcing, intrinsically reinforcing, and that may mean you will tend to try the same pathway again if the puzzle again interests you, or if another similar one does. There may, of course, be the other, extrinsic reinforcer still present. Perhaps your goal wasn't really to solve the puzzle but that was only a means to extract adult approval, in which case you might also learn some puzzle solving or equally some appearance of puzzle solving. On the other hand, you may be seeking an adult's disapproval, and that may make it unlikely you will learn about puzzles unless the relevant adult happens to disapprove of puzzle solving.

In either case, however, you find that there are questions relevant to learning that are not answered within the framework of the original theory, which thereby shows itself to be inadequate to the needs of the real situation. Let me discuss two of these. The first is the need to incorporate, within the framework of theory, just *how* the child comes to be in the prepared state of purposing to solve a particular puzzle. When the prepared state is that of being hungry, in the cat or the human, we can take it for granted because it is a standard, recurrent, biochemically induced state that we are all familiar with and one easily induced except when overridden by, for example, anxiety.

We don't think of food seeking as a function of education, though we might. But when the goal is directly that of puzzle solving we do have to inquire into the *setting* of such goals. It won't do to say the goal is set by the adult, the teacher, because that does not make it a goal for the child; that only makes it a possible means or obstacle to another goal. Of course it may be that if this goal is set by the teacher it may become a goal for a child. Thus a child may get into the puzzle because the pathway to compliance lies that way, but he then becomes involved with the puzzle and the original goal is displaced by the attractiveness of the more immediate one. Learning theory has not said anything about how the child may come to set such a goal for himself, and thus for a time to set aside the goal of manipulating or pleasing the adult. It has said nothing about this subject because it is a theory that can only *talk* when there is a goal, a pathway to be defined, and a reinforcement at the end. It can consider goal *setting* only as if it were goal *seeking*. Operant conditioning theory can be modified to include reinforcements intrinsic to goal attainment, but it always ties motivation to a preestablished goal being sought. Otherwise, it doesn't know how to be a theory.

This limitation leads to the second question, which has to do with the breakdown of the sharp distinction between goals and pathways to them. The truth of the matter is that learning theory has developed these sharp distinctions because, while they are more or less commonsense distinctions, they represent presuppositions of a certain type of laboratory method, not conclusions based on evidence. It is only when

you can identify the goal that an animal or a human is set upon achieving, that you can promptly observe and measure the amount of his learning. If your imputation of a goal is quite wrong and the subject is quite
otherwise occupied, it is very unlikely he will exhibit the learning you
expect and are prepared to clock. Of course if you just *watch* his behavior
you may begin to get some clues to his goals—if at the moment he has
any simply definable ones. But then that stops being laboratory psychology in the usual mode and becomes observational, nonexperimental,
and some would say less scientific; certainly, indeed, it is less neat, less
subject to the mass-production of data. Now if, as I think we all know,
there are very important aspects of learning that do not fit the goal-
dominated paradigm of learning theory, so much the worse for that
paradigm. And if, as I shall argue as well as I know how, the intimate
interrelation of goal seeking and goal setting is central to educationally
significant learning, then we must move beyond the confines of learning
theory. The general idea of reinforcement will remain, but it will lose
the explanatory power it has in the narrow special cases that have been
studied. For the question cannot be settled about the causal role of
reinforcement: roughly speaking, whether we learn because of reinforcement, or whether there is reinforcement because we learn. Another way
of putting this question comes from the examination of what is involved
in exploratory behavior. If we want to say that exploration is a goal, we
also have to say that exploration is the means to that goal, so you can't
make a time separation between means and ends. Or if you want to say
that the goal is future, is to *have* explored, then anything you explore
and map is automatically a means to the end, and there is no criterion as
to what will not be reinforced. Suppose a child is playing with food
coloring and soap film, the combination having come into his hands
because the two materials happen to be available at the same place and
time. He drops a drop of dye onto a soap film (hoping to make it turn
green) and it falls through the film without coloring or breaking the
film. Far from contributing to the solution of a problem, this phenomenon will probably attract attention from a ten-year-old simply because
it is a surprising one and it may even give rise to a problem. Indeed, I
hope it intrigues some of you enough to try it. My point is that this
phenomenon and many others like it are of some importance in the
economy of learning, whether they happen to be found in a context of
problem solving, in a context of problem setting, or in a context where

they are merely noted with wonder and stored away, available for some future recall. And this last is the most probable description among children and among adults, simply because explicit problem solving or problem solving are special transition phases occupying a relatively small part of any such biography as measured by the clock. We will do a disservice to them if we assume that such activities as the soap-solution dyes of my example may provoke are to be counted as significant only in the context of explicitly raised questions of why and how. Indeed, I would expect that some children would come back to this phenomenon, and that one or more of them might, perhaps with a teacher's judicious intervention, keep trying to make a green soap film, or on the other hand think of dropping other liquids though a film—water, oil, and alcohol for example—and along either track get onto some very interesting investigations. For others, the experience will be primarily an aesthetic one, and we might decide to value it as such, giving a substantial wealth of such experience due and proper place in the lives of children.

What we know, from the experience of practitioners, is that amid such wealth many sorts of engrossments develop in children who will not otherwise become so engrossed, whether intellectually, artistically, or practically. What we do not know is how, or when, or in just what way this will happen with any one child. My point at the moment, however, is that if such a component of education is valuable, it implies a different theoretical framework for our valuing it than that provided by operant-conditioning theory. I have now suggested three phases of experience, all properly I think, called learning, of which only one satisfies the conditions for application of current learning theory—and that one satisfies the conditions explicitly only when abstracted from the fluid integral context of educational experience.

Let me now discuss a framework of learning theory more adequate than the above. It is a framework formulated and familiarized by John Dewey, and adhered to over many years by him, from his early educational writings to his latter-day Logic.[2] It is not easy to criticize Dewey, because when you do you usually find that he has made the necessary qualifications somewhere else in his vast writings. So I shall distinguish the lesser Dewey from the greater Dewey, or Dewey the theorizer from Dewey the perceiver and qualifier. Here, I am discussing the former.

In Dewey's familiar account of thinking and learning, thought or inquiry is a phase of experience that deals with problem solving and begins when our normal, ongoing habitual activity is blocked in one way or another. Literally or figuratively, activity is blocked by a stone wall that we find across our path—and the drive of our ongoing activity now is diverted into new channels, the channels of investigation, of problem solving.

I will only briefly remind you of the familiar phases of the thought process thus initiated—of defining the problem as a problem, of the search for relevant hypotheses, their testing, and the final hoped-for resolution by which psychic energies drain back into the channels of overt action, with the stone wall surmounted, bypassed, or tunneled under.

This analysis of thought was employed by Dewey as a basis for the critique of much conventional teaching. In emphasizing the way thought flows out of antecedent overt activity and tends to reestablish such activity, Dewey was able to argue for a greater emphasis on the organic continuity of knowledge and acting, on thinking and learning as growing out of the child's overt active interests and leading to their enrichment and redirecting. In an important sense, Dewey is providing an alternative to the laboratory-oriented theorists' notion of the prepared motivational state of hunger, etc. Problem-solving behavior is "switched on" for Dewey in much the same sense that food-seeking behavior is, but not on arbitrary external command. The problem a child will see and formulate will grow out of the child's needs, at the child's level, clothed with the child's experience—the child will define it and own it and work significantly at solving it because it matches both needs and resources. This means that what the child may learn in such a phase is a dependent variable, not imposed or imposable by a school timetable, except as that timetable may in a very broad sense succeed in steering the child' s active interests toward specific curricular areas. It is the teacher's job primarily to assess the learning-readiness of a particular child at a particular time, and to see that educationally fruitful problems will arise along the track the child is in fact following.

Because goals are set by children out of their ongoing activity—with the help of teachers but not injected by teachers—the content and order and style of learning will differ in general for each child. This will make for diversity and autonomy within a group. When recognized and exploited, it will also thus create possibilities of significant cooperation and division of labor, significant communication and development of critical capacities. Important areas of learning will be traversed many times by children in the course of their unique problem-solving activities. Abstraction and systematization of knowledge so gained will come along as a late-stage process. The order in which things are learned, and the order into which they are finally systematized, should never be confused. Because fundamental learning takes place in a way connecting it with practical work and involvement, what is learned is richly cross-indexed to applications, and this fact becomes the basis of Dewey's theory of the transfer of learning: what has been learned in many connections is reapplicable in many ways, while what has been learned only in the isolation of formal instruction remains disconnected and largely unusable.

So far, I think, we can have no quarrel with Dewey's general scheme. But at the same time it advances no farther than operant-conditioning theory in one important respect. (In view of the historical order, I should rather say that operant-conditioning theory has retreated no farther, in this respect.) The motivation of problem solving is quite explicitly derived from and limited by the drive of interrupted overt activity, much as water flowing downhill will, if suitably interrupted and diverted, turn wheels that generate power, light lights, or operate computers before it resumes its downward flow. Not only is the problem to be solved defined by the end-in-view that comes to focus when habitual activity is interrupted, but inquiry ceases when ways are found to reinstate that activity. Dewey replied to criticism of this by saying that of course the resumed activity was characteristically different in quality from what had been interrupted earlier, more informed, more competent. But as far as I know he never conceded on the point that the *motivation* of thought could be more than the ongoing drive of the activity that obstacles had, willy-nilly, interrupted. To admit any independent motivation for thought would have seemed, I suspect, to threaten Dewey's vision of the seamless web of thought and action, and to threaten some dangerous reintroduction of forbidden dualism. And yet his position clearly invites that vulgar pragmatism he so often repudiated, that thought is and ought only to be the servant of immediate action.

The limitation I see in Dewey's specific analysis of thought as goal-dominated problem solving, a limitation it shares with the far more restricted viewpoint of operant-conditioning theory, is that it fails to do justice to the humanity of essential processes of goal setting, and thus also to that third phase of experience that I called exploratory and in which goals do not figure immediately in either direction, as being sought or being set.

Let me first try to develop a little farther the description of what is involved in the process I call goal setting. In Dewey's analysis of the means-end relation, the reconstruction of ends-in-view begins with the definition of some problematic relation between means and ends, some perception of uncertainty in the situation calling for action. Ends get destabilized and redefined in the attempt to work out detailed means of achieving them, and means get evaluated, in turn, in relation to ends as these come into sharper and more realistic definition. But as I read Dewey, at least, there is no place for the questioning of ends as such, or for the recognition that experience may directly suggest new goals, in situations where the suggestion itself is reacted to as vivid, surprising, even disconcerting. We can find abundant examples in our own lives, and in literature. But because my subject is education let me describe a pattern in the work of children in school that has been rather carefully recorded in a number of cases, namely in the work of the Nuffield Junior School Science Project in England. The pedagogical goal here is to help children on the path to educationally significant goals fabricated out of involvement in exploratory learning. It has been the purpose of this group to enlist teachers in a cooperative venture whose harvest is a system of materials and ideas for the junior, i.e., upper elementary, years. The members of this project had no intention of producing either a curriculum in the received sense or any lockstep, trunk-to-tail instructional guides for teachers. They had the old but nowadays surprising idea that the curriculum should only be defined by rather broad areas of subject-matter, concept development, skill, and appreciation and that the professional job of planning and daily organization belonged with teachers, and children in individual classes. What the Nuffield group has done is to harvest such work by teachers, which they helped stimulate and guide, in the form of case histories. The collection of these case histories, in turn, is what the group proposes to give other teachers to help them on their way, without intruding on the teachers' own prerogative of helping each child and group to evolve their own individual styles and patterns of work.

The result, in each of the case histories gathered by the Nuffield group, is a fair account of developments day by day and week by week, together with lists of equipment, or for example, a detailed description of a child-made pottery kiln, etc. And for each there is a brief summary in the form of a special type of flow diagram. This diagram charts the progression of topics of investigation that get started from some initial exposure of a class, such as a visit to a beach, a Roman fort, a piece of waste ground, an old railway station; or a beginning may be found in the classroom, with a study of shadows, mirrors, pin-hole images and prisms, or with the growth of seeds and cuttings.

Whatever the beginning, it will commonly and characteristically happen that interests and exploratory pathways will diverge and, as the teacher is able to make provision, within a short time new topics will have developed. From a field trip there will have come plants, insects, rocks, a long piece of rusted iron pipe. From the pipe there develops a project of making chimes, which leads to consulting a book on sound, and a design problem, to decide the lengths of pipe to produce desired tones. There also develops an investigation of rusting, with nails, wire, and steel wool. A rock collection is begun and added to, and this leads to a project of comparing rocks as to "heaviness" and a disentangling of concepts of linear size, volume, weight. This in turn gets connected to graphical representation of weights and volumes, and a grouping of rocks arises, with the concept of density just around the corner. Three children interest themselves in rocks, soil, and weathering, and a project for the manufacture of sand develops. Two become involved with man-made rocks, with bricks and clay, with cement powder, with sand going back into rock via some flour paste. Another group gets involved with the taxonomy of plants. Discovery of strong color in one plant root leads to a return trip to look for vegetable dyes, and this leads to problems of extraction, dilution, mixture, and the effects on colors of various household chemicals. I won't follow the flow diagram farther, but I hope the style and atmosphere are well-enough suggested.

You may well ask how this pattern I have sketched differs from that described and advocated by John Dewey, and built into the program of the Chicago Laboratory School. I do not know exactly, but certainly there is a family resemblance. Self-selection by children is an initial key that increases the probability that a particular child will select phenomena or subject-matter that has some match with his momentary readiness to pursue, to investigate, to assimilate. Thus the continuity of development that Dewey was concerned with is not guaranteed, but given a good chance. But first-round interests are not likely to be deep, and to deepen them a teacher must try to assess the character and level of these interests, and to give a particular child new choices in the range that assessment indicates is probably fruitful. It is in that interplay of choices, children's and teachers', that the whole process gets started and gets sustained and deepened. Reference to Dewey most commonly raises the image—for which he was not responsible but others associated with him—of "progressive" education as meaning "permissive" education. Since Dewey is only a myth to most contemporaries, substitute A. S. Neill and his book *Summerhill School*[3]—his basic philosophy for dealing with children is one of heroic permissiveness outside the classroom.

Now it is a fact about readers, typically, that they hear mainly what they are already prepared to classify, and turn off what does not fit easily. I know this is sometimes true of myself, and am eager to declare you not guilty. At any rate I want to try very hard to say that the pattern of teaching and learning that I have tried to suggest in the description of the Nuffield Junior Science classes is *not* permissive, and neither is it authoritarian, nor does it represent the whole of education, but only a phase. If you were to watch those classes and failed to notice the teacher preparation and planning that went into each day's work and the pattern of intervention and guidance, but saw instead only the work of children, you would indeed think it permissive—you would see an atmosphere that was hardly ever coercive, with children mostly decoupled from the teacher, who is usually somewhere else, working with another child or small group. There is noise, not the threatening tomblike silence that is prized in many schools. But it is workmanlike noise, not the runaway noise that develops when the quiet classroom has its lid unexpectedly removed. There is an abundance of material and equipment, mostly filed in the room where children can get at it and replace it. There is discipline in all of this, but it is the discipline of involvement in subject matter, not mainly an arbitrary discipline imposed by a powerful adult. Children are neither compliant nor rebellious, but busy. The point I want to make, and it is a point that Dewey never denies but never relishes or emphasizes, is that the teacher is *constantly fulfilling* the many-sided role of teacher; at one time assisting, providing; at another time advising and explaining; at still another time questioning and assessing, but always furthering the ongoing work; sensing here a lack of involvement, there the need for protecting a child from untoward pressures. This role is in the highest sense a role of authority, but not in the disparaging sense of the word "authoritarian." The teacher is looked to as an authority, as one who can and does assist, advise, provide, question, and sometimes answer. The role is not imposed but earned. An authority in this sense is one looked to for the furtherance of life, an adult figure who facilitates the good work and who invests it with adult value. There is affection in this relationship, sometimes immediate personal warmth; but the basic attitude is better called respect, both ways—respect for the adult facilitator who makes it all possible and respect for the resources and potentialities of the child, for his or her unique personal style, which will here and there blossom. The common classification of classrooms along the authoritarian-permissive axis is too crude and too irrelevant a classification to catch the essence, and we ought to be ashamed to use it.

I would add only one thing to this description. The teachers involved in this work, of which I have given a composite impression, are not giants with respect either to their own formal education or to their academic grasp of subject matter. Typically they lack the British A.B., and are academically often rather simple people. But their morale is extraordinary. Their morale is high because they are evolving some success, and old rudimentary failures are disappearing. A pattern that started with science or mathematics or art has spread; scheduling is gone or is on its way out; gross failures in reading, writing, and math have almost disappeared; and the more complex and challenging problems are coming to definition. What one sees repeatedly, in many an older and younger teacher, is this sense of professional competence and address to new problems, and it is engendered by success.

If I may now return to the central theme of motivation in learning, I would like to make use of the images I have suggested to fill in a pattern I outlined at the beginning of this chapter. I said first that prominent current American theories of learning fill only one little part of the field, and are cut off by their a priori framework from relevance outside of it. To appeal to them except in very special contexts is like using Babylonian astronomical theory to solve the problems of planetary motion. We do not have, and will not soon have, a formal dynamic theory of human learning adequate to the obvious demands of education; but we know some things about the necessary character, shape, and scope of such a theory. Dewey's work, still honored in discussion if not in practice, represents one delineation of a wider field in which thought and learning on the human level are linked significantly with other phases of human operation and experience. This theory makes it plain that goals in prob-lem solving cannot be imposed by external input, but must be evolved, fabricated, set out of the antecedent, ongoing activity of the learner. The "must" here is not a moral "must" but a plain necessity. Learning at significant human levels—including conceptualization, evolution of func-tional logical schemata, and the capacity for planning and organizing of conduct—is only effected through the autonomous activity, the self-orga-nization of the learner, including the capacity to assimilate significant resources from others, from the available cultures.

When we ask what motivates such learning, and through what path-ways of spontaneous or planned experience it prospers or languishes, the Deweyan motivational funnel is, as far as I can see, wholly inadequate. For it leaves out of the account altogether what I can only describe, once more, as the phase of exploratory activity, activity guided by no standard organic need and by no such definite goals as obstacles could interrupt. The stone wall across the pathway, an obstacle to one late for an ap-pointment, is in another frame an invitation into the forest, where one may find deer tracks, an orchid in bloom, or other marvels unguessed. What motivates exploratory behavior, in a deep psychological sense, one cannot well say. For myself, I would like to label that motivation, how-ever connected with others, as being provisionally of an independent category; not, as Emerson said, to eat and not for love. The word I would use is *aesthetic*. It is a mode of behavior in which the distinction between ends and means collapses; it is its own end and it is its own reinforcement. Or rather the reinforcement comes to it because of what is found along the pathways of exploration: for infants, in their expand-ing capacities to elicit from the environment those marvels of sight and sound out of which they fashion the stable patterns of early perception and control; for older children, the patterns of order and equivalence and symmetry out of which a grasp of the big world and their place in it can become consolidated; and for those still older, going on to adult-hood, the capacity to systematize their learning, to institute long-range curiosities and investigations, and to see themselves steadily as the steers-men and organizers of their own lives. By how much our education fails or succeeds in provisioning this extraordinary potentiality I will not try here to say; but one thing, I think, is clear: it is out of the unpressured but well-guided exploration of the environment and their own develop-ing capacities and interests, assimilating the means of further exploration as they go, that children develop best the human capacities we all admire; it is in this same way that they harvest the raw materials for significant purpose and for steady involvement. By that measure, I think, we must say that our educational institutions fall far short of their potential just when, in a world increasingly threatened by disorganization and alienation, we have most need of it.

NOTES

1. *The Journals of Ralph Waldo Emerson*, with annotations; Edward Waldo Emerson and Waldo Emerson Forbes, eds. Vol. 3, entry for April 11, 1834. Included in *The Complete Works of Ralph Waldo Emerson*, vol. VII (Hougton Mifflin, 1903-1904).

2. John Dewey, *Logic: The Theory of Inquiry* (New York: H. Holt & Co., 1938).

3. A. S. Neill, *Summerhill School: A New View of Childhood* (New York: St. Martin's Press, 1993, originally published ca. 1960).

– 10 –

Investigative Arts:
Science and Teaching[1]

From a variety of points of view we come seeking to investigate the ways in which our philosophical and historical interests in the sciences may contribute to the substance and art of science teaching—science teaching at all levels, beginning perhaps most fruitfully with childhood.

In the background of these interests we share there is, I believe, an increasing anxiety. We associate this anxiety with the recognition that science education, so far, has failed to achieve very much of what has come to be called scientific literacy. In the words of John Dewey, science is still too new, among human affairs, to have penetrated into the subsoil of the mind. Yet we are deeply committed to the institutions of science—they have become part of the fabric of society. With enhanced self-consciousness we must look at the sciences in new ways to help us understand the nature, the preconditions, and the altered technologies of a sustainable human future.

Until the special culture of science becomes more deeply embedded in our general culture, however, with at least the more elementary ranges of scientific understanding becoming widely and informally accessible, we will as a society remain in a state of alienation from the very substrate of our lives. In his famous fantasy *The Time Machine*, H. G. Wells most vividly defined just that state of alienation. His story projected the fate of a pitiable society, one that lacked the commitment that the real time machine, the ongoing life of our planet, requires of us.

This alienation, I suggest, is the source of our anxiety today. It should lead us to a self-conscious criticism of our traditions of science education. In this connection I shall put forward a very simple thesis. My thesis is that a still-dominant style of science teaching is radically inappropriate to the cure of our alienation. This style has been set for us by the intellectual habits of some professional scientists who often cannot retraverse the sometimes crooked pathways by which they themselves, as beginners, have come to their present understanding and competence. What many of them, and their textbooks, consider to be elementary is therefore often inaccessible to students who have not yet traversed some part of those same or equivalent pathways. They forget the double meaning of the word *elementary*. Sometimes it means just where one begins, where one enters a discipline. Sometimes it refers to the elements, the essential abstractions—and these may be the deepest of all, not where one begins, but hard won along the way. So my focus is on the art of helping students get *into* important subject matter.

There have always been some beginners who can enter a scientific discipline and swim with the didactic current, more or less easily meeting its challenges. Their numbers, though relatively small, have sufficed heretofore for professional recruitment, but not for widespread literacy. I have heard members of a prestigious science department remark that only one in forty beginners really catches on, but that is sufficient. That sort of snobbery is rare, but it comes from a history in which the advancement of certain kinds of knowledge has depended upon a special social status, isolated from the common language and culture, and yet prestigious. Over the long run this combination of isolation and prestige is not a healthy one.

Imagine now a world in which science, to use Dewey's phrase, had penetrated into the subsoil of the mind. Just what does that phrase suggest? Such a mind, surely, would not be ordered like a collection of lectures and textbooks, all in linear array. In the life of the sciences, texts and lectures are only some among the means of communication, a small part of the ambience. The actual, productive mind of the scientist is not like that. It is not linear; it would not be productive if it were. But that sort of narrow track is often what students and the public are led to expect.

The metaphor of soil and subsoil suggests, rather, a mind for which novel phenomena are accepted as seeds to be nurtured with attentive curiosity and with the marshalling of available resources of understanding. That sort of understanding can be organized more accessibly and informally than any textbooks allow. For that kind of organization there is another metaphor, which I borrow from the great novelist Henry James, who speaks of the *web* of experience. He had in mind a taut spider web catching new experiences and resonating with them. The structure of the web is that of a network, a graph—nonlinear connecting nodes of past experience and understanding, against which new experiences, new phenomena, may be examined and tested. Being brought into the net they sometimes fit neatly, sometimes contribute to changes in its structure.

When we go as teachers to the sciences with such a perspective on what I am going to call the investigative art, then we wish more of that same perspective for our students. If we scan the bibliographies of professional research in science education we find, generally, a lack of attention to the intercourse between subject matter and the way of teaching—as though the subject matter were somehow given. I believe that the ways in which we seek as teachers to invest our subject matter depends often on our own understanding of it, of turning points that can lead into it, of barriers that can block that entry. To this end both the philosophy and the history of science can acquire a new vitality for us.

I wish to emphasize this new interest by way of contrast with the style of the history of science as I first encountered it in the 1930s. At that time, the history was still primarily a narration of some sequence of discoveries, marching through time like a string of elephants on parade, trunk to tail; or sometimes as an account of past errors ending in the present, quite remarkably, with the truth. In those histories, there was little or no concern for understanding the sometimes devious pathways of discovery or invention or frustration, and little for the backgrounds, the intellectual and practical repertoires, of those whose discoveries were being celebrated.

The philosophy of science, similarly, was preoccupied with questions, quite legitimate perhaps, as to the logical organization and verification of scientific belief, and very little with what may be called the logic of investigation, the logic, sometimes the capricious logic, implicit in the investigative art.

In its formal aspects, this logic is entirely familiar. I propose to remind you of it with a quotation from a famous eighteenth-century philosopher celebrating discoveries made during the previous century or so. Immanuel Kant's first *Critique of Judgment* was clearly inspired, as he earlier stated in his second introduction to the *Critique of Pure Reason*, by the character and growth of the physical sciences in his time. I quote:

> When Galileo caused balls, the weights of which he had himself previously determined, to roll down an inclined plane, when Torricelli made the air carry a weight which he had calculated beforehand to be equal to that of a definite column of water; or in more recent times, when Stahl changed metal into lime, and lime back into metal, by withdrawing something and then restoring it, a light broke upon all the students of nature. They learned that reason has insight only into that which it produces after a plan of its own, and that it must not allow itself to be kept, as it were, in nature's leading strings, but must itself show the way . . . constraining nature to give answers to questions of reason's own choosing.[2]

For Kant, then, scientific knowledge is not the passive reception of sensory information but an active or constructive process involving the generation and testing of hypotheses. It is not hard to see that a great deal of the philosophy of science has followed in Kant's footsteps, developed sometimes by those who did not realize how Kantian they were. But what Kant left out, and others since, is the source of those good questions that the students of nature are able, sometimes and somehow, to persuade nature to answer. We all know research, do we not, in which nature has been constrained to answer questions that are perhaps not much worth asking. To focus attention on the ways in which test-worthy questions can come to be generated is, or should be, one of our major philosophical concerns.

But how can we hope to answer that sort of question? One answer, surely, is to be found in the study of history, in the imaginative reconstruction of just those sorts of episodes that Kant alluded to. It is the sort of study that may offend the narrow historian; since it has to be somewhat speculative, its aim is not so much to bring the past into the present as it is to take the present back into the past. What I mean by that is that we can, in our own time and place, be confronted by the same questions that confronted Galileo or Torricelli or Stahl. We can quite literally repeat their investigations as they described them.

We cannot so easily know the thought processes of past investigators, though detailed reconstructions may give us important clues. Even so, the fabric of their investigative art remains a matter for conjecture. But we can understand their curiosities and pursue them as if they were our own. This can lead to the same or to related investigations—some that might have taken place but seemingly did not, or some they might have welcomed had they possessed the means. Here are some examples at a level appropriate for older students generally, and especially those who might in turn become teachers.

The suction pump has been around since antiquity. In Galileo's seventeenth century, those who engineered the pumping of water from mines knew very well that such pumps would lift water vertically only some meters. The proposition that "nature abhors a vacuum" was available to the learned who discussed how such a pump worked, but this bit of Aristotelian thermodynamics from twenty centuries before had no explanatory value.

Galileo got the question right: why does nature's abhorrence of the vacuum always fail to lift the water more than that distance? His own first hypothesis was that the cohesion of a column of water, adhering in turn to the piston of the pump as it was raised, might be strong enough to lift water just to that height; like a suspended rope that would break under its own weight when it was long enough. It was the right kind of explanation, but off by two or three factors of ten, as Galileo soon found out. We know it will work for pipes minute enough in diameter, as in the circulatory system of trees. Galileo died with this problem unsolved. His successor Evaniste Torricelli found a wholly different answer. They demonstrated something new and striking about what had been for some time familiar.

A mercury column, with a density thirteen times that of water, could only rise, under the vacuum, one-thirteenth as far as the pump could lift water. Therefore, for a given column diameter, the weight lifted was the same. The proffered explanation was that the force lifting the liquid column, in either case, was a push, not a pull. It was the weight of the atmosphere sitting on the surface but unperceived by us who swim in it. This explanation was confirmed when Blaise Pascal asked his brother-in-law to carry a mercury tube—a barometer—up a mountain. Perrier saw the height of the mercury column decrease with altitude, and that was the final evidence.

It was a development rich with consequences, as I believe it can be in some of our own teaching. The news of the discovery and its proffered explanation, the weight of the air, attracted widespread attention among the learned in many fields, none more so than astronomy.

Although not unchallenged, Aristotle's proclamation of an earth-centered universe was still widely accepted. He described a cosmographic sequence of the four elements: earth at the center, then the surrounding sphere of water, then air—more properly, *atmos*, vapor—then finally the fires of the heavens. In Aristotle's scale of substantive properties, solid Earth was heavy, water only less so; air was light, and fire lightest. Thus the properties of the elements ranged from gravity to levity. The sphere of air, the atmosphere, supposedly extended, weightless, all the way out to the celestial world of fire.

Torricelli's mercury column made the new order of things not only visible but, quite literally, ponderable. Air had both inertial and gravitational mass. That was the excitement. Yet curiously enough others, including Descartes, had already announced that the solid Earth and the oceans were surrounded by a finite shell of gas held down, like the water, by its weight. Thus Torricelli's idea was not really new, but neither had it been vividly apprehended. New astronomical theories required it, but only the barometer gave it reality and measure. It had been a node in the web of not a few investigative minds, but so far without any reorganizing influence. What had still been missing was any instrument that would measure this weight. The weight of the air does not stretch a spring, nor tip a merchant's balance. These were the only previously known measures of weight, and like our bodily sensors, they seemed to confirm the common sense presumption that the air is weightless. This was common sense long before Aristotle, the very philosopher of common sense. Torricelli's tube of mercury provided the first operational definition to the contrary. The evidence of the barometer was a kind of unanticipated detail, but it led in the history of science to many extensions of experience and understanding. For teaching at certain levels it can, as curiosity directs, generate a whole tree of further investigations, as it did in history.

Among the ancient Greeks, the atomists distinguished sharply between matter and space, atoms and the void. Lucretius, the great Roman poet-scientist of the first century B.C., was utterly opposed to Aristotelian ways of thought. Yet he argued that the moon could not be as far away as the astronomers claimed. The clarity of our vision of mountains decreases, he observed, with their distance; a very distant moon could therefore not appear so sharply defined as in fact it does. Those Greek astronomers got the distance to the moon from eclipse data that show it is some sixty earth-radii away. They trusted the geometry; Lucretius didn't. He trusted, and they seemingly ignored, his common-sense objection: How can it be so far, yet look so near? He knew very well the material reality of air. Atoms, he said, dashing around randomly in the void. But he did not consistently ascribe weight to the air, and took for granted that it filled the space between Earth and moon.

So I come back to Torricelli and the seventeenth-century excitement about the ocean of air. It was not just the Aristotelian cosmology still lingering in the minds of the learned that this new vision of the atmosphere dispelled. That was part of it, but it was deeper than that. What lingered was a common-sense ambivalence about the very nature of air and its properties, its relation to other forms of matter.

In this case, what we have to take back to the time of Galileo and Torricelli is not just the expression of our own investigative art, but rather a recognition that their discovery and its implications are still deep for most adults and children. There is in our time also a widespread ambivalence about it. Indeed I think we all recognize it. When the water is all poured from the pitcher it seems empty, not full of air. Air is the medium of our lives normally omnipresent and unnoticed. After three and a half centuries the simple physics of it remains, for many, in the same state of obscurity that prevailed before.

My own teaching experience with college freshmen, with ten-year-olds and their teachers as well, has indeed seemed to confirm that we live mostly in that pre-Torricellian world. For this reason a wonderful beginning has evolved in our laboratory experience associated particularly with the phenomena of the siphon, equally known since antiquity. We both drink through straws and start siphons by suction. Nature indeed abhors a vacuum! But why does the siphon continue thereafter when the suction has stopped? And in how many other ways can you start a siphon? The very question is almost always received with surprise. So for young and old the siphon can initiate many investigations in the classroom ambience. Of course it can lead back to the story of Torricelli when the time is ripe, but it has other riches as well, all associated with the fluid states of matter.

On some occasions I have started with the barometer, pouring mercury into the barometer tube and inverting it. Why does it fall just so far, oscillating a bit, but no farther? One or two know the name *barometer*, but that's a word, not a clue. I try to fish for the analogy of the balance, for some idea of equilibrium, but half of that balance, the weight of the air, seems missing, invisible and impalpable. I could have just explained it all, and was tempted. That is the tradition. But I knew that a week or a month later, for most if not all, the traces of that explanation in my students' minds would be weightless.

The siphon was better. You could start it in different ways, play with it, mark the flow of water with drops of dye, change elevations, reverse the flow. Now, moreover, there was some searching for analogies, which the barometer did not easily evoke. A teacher-student offered this one. She said the water in the tube was like a rope over a pulley, the longer side would fall and pull the shorter side up! She was in excellent company—that was precisely Galileo's hypothesis. Could we have disrupted the siphon, and this fine and partly correct hypothesis, by reducing the pressure artifically? We did not try. But we did finally weigh a batch of air. The great Italians could have done that, but I don't think they thought of it; we could remind them. I finally told the story of Galileo and Torricelli and Pascal. It took a day or two to catch up with them. As a sort of grand finale we made a siphon with two buckets of water, one higher than the other, in a basement stairwell with a hundred-foot plastic tube connecting them, half of it coiled in each to start with. The siphon still flowed until raised well up in the second story when, with much bubbling of dissolved air, it stopped—and we had turned our siphon into a water barometer.

One could think of the mercury barometer as the visible arm of a balance, but this appears to be, for many, a quite inaccessible analogy. Oddly enough, this deep and simple concept of the balance has been badly treated in most science pedagogy. In elementary-school science it is usually represented by a simple equal-arm affair of limited virtue. For those ages, the more generalized balance of Archimedes is a topic rich in challenges to children's investigative imaginations, but even that is constrained. It can be fruitfully generalized toward even three-dimensional configurations—as in the one-point suspension of a broken tree branch, or a complex mobile design. I think that hours invested in all these diverse phenomena can dig pretty deep. In all later scientific inquiry the concept of equilibrium is a vital one, but it can hardly be generalized as a tool of thought unless we help students to invest in it. It is central to the great tradition of Archimedes, for mathematics and for physics, with Galileo and Newton following, and much else. As students of Archimedes know, there are many simple topics from modern experience we can take back to discuss with him.

All this work or play takes time. I could have explained the essentials of the barometer, quite carefully, in half an hour. We have often heard in discussion of science education that there is no time for such playful wanderings. They say that one will never get through the course that way. In response to that, Victor Weisskopf, a physicist, says the point in such matters is not to cover the subject but to help uncover part of it. For the time being I'll rest my case there.

My own teaching experience has seldom taken me into the biological world, so I lack honest biological illustrations for my thesis. But I cannot resist one more important example of communication with the elders. It concerns the physiology of green plants and a way into it accessible to beginners, and therefore the possibility of conversation with Stephen Hales and those who followed his work in the eighteenth and nineteenth centuries. He seems to have been the very first to probe the essentials of plant nutrition and growth. This subject has arisen in the teaching experience of some of us simply because of the prevalence of preconceptions about it, which are very durable. "Preconceptions," "alternative conceptions," and "critical barriers" can become an "open sesame" for student investigations.

Two young college students revealed their belief that plants generally, and trees in particular, grow "up" out of the ground (mushrooms do!), and generate their new growth in the center. These are very common beliefs—we have found them even among farmers. We challenged the students to see what evidence they could find by examining and dissecting the trunk of a small dead tree. For each observation they made they managed, for a time, to convince themselves that their belief was correct. When the new wood grew in the center it somehow expanded the outer, and older, layers. Only the outermost layers (bark) split under this pressure. It was only when they assembled all of their data that they began to visualize the skeletons of the previous years' trees, inside the more recent, and began to see how plant growth determines plant form. It was a beginning for them of curiosity. They had, I believed, relied on a common-sense analogy. Trees are living things, animals are living things; hence the growth and development of trees (less familiar) should be more or less the same.

Stephen Hales was the first person to show by simple experiments that plants draw through their leaves some part of their nourishment from the air,[3] and indeed showed that a great proportion of the weight of the plant was from the air. From his time down to the great work of D'Arcy Thompson, On Growth and Form,[4] there is a rich record of investigations, many of them accessible to simple investigation that can lay bare the profound differences between plant and animal physiology and the even profounder similarities.

The stories I have told thus far, rather randomly selected, are intended to suggest a style of science teaching at any level that is seldom adequately understood outside the circle of those who engage in it. Its principal concern is that important subject matter be introduced to students as a challenge to their own investigative curiosity and art, with enough diversity of ways into that subject matter to match that of the students' talents and potential interests, their different strengths and trajectories of curiosity.

To do this well requires a teacher whose own understanding of the subject matter is deep enough to recognize some variety of ways into it, and to have at hand a repertoire of possible means to support students' own investigations. It is a large order. But remember, please, I am speaking of the need to provide for diverse ways into scientific subject matter, to set traps to catch the talents and interests to be found within any group of students, at any age and level of previous attainment. This does not eliminate the need, at some point, for the more formal side that we call instruction, but it can radically alter its style, frequency, and quality. Of course there is an unavoidable tension between the process of getting into scientific subject matter and what is vulgarly called getting through it, as though you went in at one end and came out the other. More properly, there is a need to acquire mastery, acquire the organized knowledge that distinguishes science as science.

It has been my intention to urge renewed attention to the history of investigation and discovery as a resource we need for constantly mending our ways as science teachers. This attention may often involve a kind of imaginary but carefully informed discourse with those of the past who have been responsible for turning points in the early development of our subject matter. Very often, I believe, our appreciation of their investigative art can guide us to find ways of stimulating the curiosity, and the latent investigative talents of our students. When we can learn to do that, we may be on the way toward some cure of the prevalent alienation of our culture from the scientific vision—the always growing vision of time, and space, and history.

NOTES

1. This chapter is an edited version of an opening address given at the 2nd International Conference on the History and Philosophy of Science and Science Teaching, Queen's University, Kingston, Canada, May 1992. I was honorary chairman of the conference.

2. Immanuel Kant, *Critique of Pure Reason*, abridged edition, Norman Kemp Smith, tr. (London, Macmillan and Co., 1934). Preface to the second edition, p. 15.

3. Stephen Hales, *Vegetable Staticks* (London: Macdonald & Co.; New York: American Elsevier, A *Classic of Botany*).

4. D'Arcy Thompson, *On Growth and Form* (Cambridge, England: The University Press, 1942).

– 11 –

On the Improvement of Education in Our Schools: A Modest Proposal

At a time when the whole country is once more engaged in discussion about the failures of its public schools, it would seem important to focus attention primarily on improving our contributions to the professional welfare of our teachers, and thus on giving them the kinds of education and support that can at all meet their needs. All other reforms ought to be in support of this one. I would like now to address a particular kind of program that seeks to give teachers the continuing support they need, and far too seldom receive. It is, I believe, a kind of program that can help us define just what it means to say something too often given only lip-service: that teaching is a genuine profession.

The program I would like to describe can properly be called advisory. It involves a kind of work that Frances Hawkins and I have observed, and have been a part of, over many years. She is herself a kindergarten-primary teacher of many years' experience, whereas I come from the university world of philosophy, of the history of science and math, with a special interest in the fascinatingly different ways in which children can get involved and committed in understanding such matters. Our advising experience is limited to the elementary-school years.

The purpose of an advisory system comes from the recognition that successful teaching of diverse children can be a high art, one in which the more one learns, the more one can enjoy the prospect of more to be learned. Teachers can learn from academic courses, from research studies, but all that learning must be reduced to practice with children. In this process, great help can come from many sources and be tested in the classroom; and especially from fellow teachers, chosen colleagues: collegial help.

The title of adviser, in certain school systems, has been given to a few persons whose work is "advising" others. The way advisers relate to other teachers is quite different, first of all, from that of supervisors. It is not the adviser's job to report on the quality of teaching, but to contribute to it. Advisers are, above all, fellow teachers. Might an adviser then also be called a mentor? In Homer's *Odyssey* there was a wise man, named Mentor, who was the trusted friend and adviser of a young hero, Telemachus. That story gave us the word *mentor*. So the two words, *advisor* and *mentor*, surely have the same meaning.

But today *mentor* has come to be used differently. Mentors, in school systems I am aware of in the United States, are far more numerous: more senior teachers in a building appointed, part-time, to be of help to beginners. Advisory work, as I shall explain, is on a different plane. One obvious difference is that in any sizable system there will be many part-time mentors available to help beginners. The reason for so few advisers lies in the very nature of their work. Though chosen from among the most experienced and successful teachers, they also must be catalysts, their work in effect to add to their own ranks, spreading a new spirit of professionalism throughout a school system; thus not simply to add, but to multiply. Thus their abilities are more important than their numbers.

In the beginning of their work, advisers will pay visits to all the elementary schools in their district. They meet first with each school principal to explain that they are available to help, to work with teachers who ask for help with classroom matters: problems with individual children, of finding fresh ways into subject matter, or of enlivening what has become too routine; classroom organization and management; or any other professional matter. If in a given school the principal seems to think the proposal unneeded or invasive, work in that school is, for the time being, deferred. If the principal shows genuine interest in advisory help, a later meeting is arranged, to let teachers know that help of various kinds may be available.

An early result is that the first requests for help come mainly from the liveliest principals and teachers, those already regarded as the best—not yet from those who would be judged most in need. This principle of selection has been criticized, but the response has been that as the program succeeds, so will its attractiveness to those at first withdrawn from interest in it. Beginners of course need help, and in good schools this sort of help is traditionally provided from within the building, from other teachers, whether or not these are called "mentors." What I will discuss and illustrate herein is a different sort of help. A good principal will, of course, have some knowledge of teachers' strengths and weaknesses, but a basic advisory policy requires that the request for help must cone from the teacher; it must not be imposed. That is an old and established principle. We can encourage the desire to learn, but without it no help can avail. It is as true of teachers as it is of those they teach. It is a principle well established in all human affairs, as in therapy, but one often set aside or forgotten. It is the whole basis of any good advisory program. Help is effective only to those who seek it; and comes best when given only from teacher to teacher.

Our experience and observation of advisory work has been varied; some of it in England, in Canada, in Italy; mainly in England and the United States. But very briefly I must mention one high point. Twenty-five years ago we were invited to observe schools in Budapest, Hungary. That was during Soviet domination. We heard a May Day parade in the distance, but most parents were boycotting it and, with their children, enjoying the holiday in a park by the river. We visited a few schools. In one first-grade classroom the children were about to do a chemical experiment, to make a "volcano." They were at tables in groups of four, with materials in the middle. The teacher had written some instructions on the blackboard, and these first-grade children were silently reading them. The principal was puzzled, afterwards, at our amazement, saying, "But they have been in school for a whole year!" We saw other advisory work going on in science and in math. The advisers we met were not schoolteachers, but one step removed: an eminent physicist, a devoted mathematician, a young doctor on a full year's maternity leave. I have used the math materials of Varga Tamash (Thomas Varga), and though I can't read his Hungarian text, I can read his many drawings. That small country of Hungary is famous for its mathematicians. There is an old joke among them, that the Hungarian ancestors must have come from Mars. No, they were just good teachers.

In order to describe what we participated in or observed, I bring these developments together in the form of a single narrative, told as though they happened over a three-year period in a single school system. The three-year period is necessary in order to show how an advisory system, though very small to begin with, can expand over time.

I thus situate the story in an unnamed American city's school system, and have chosen a sizable city with a population of about half a million. The population is varied both ethnically and economically. Since in any such community roughly one in forty of its population is a child of given age, elementary-school children are about one-sixth of the population, in my case some 80,000. With an average class size of 25 children, there are about 3,500 teachers in all, at first glance a staggering number. But the size of the school system is not essential; it could be larger or much smaller.

One reason for my storytelling style is that I don't wish to enter the fray of debate over the massive failures of many of our schools or the many remedies proposed. I wish simply to describe one kind of remedy—the advisory—as though it were a single compact reality, and to do so in enough detail to invite your recognition of what is possible, your approval, your questions.

Although my story is a composite, all of it has been taken from the observations and experiences of Frances Hawkins, myself, or a few of our close associates, in the places I have described. In Boulder, Colorado, we ourselves created a center for teachers, of the kind I shall describe. In the vast world of American public education, however, I believe that such programs are still vanishingly rare. And in our country's current flurry of debate over such matters, the basic importance of advisory work seems seldom if ever discussed.

One predictable early result, in the kind of program to be described, is that requests for help came mostly from the liveliest principals and most experienced teachers, as suggested above. Others sometimes think they don't need help, or fear that to ask for help is to admit incompetence. Let me now give examples of some early requests. In one case, it was for help with a math program in which the topic of measurement seemed to be falling flat. An adviser was invited to visit and helped initiate some measurements of body proportions: height, girth, the distance between outstretched hands; then a graph of ten-year-old heights and weights was designed. Talk about the size of feet—children's and teacher's—led to footprints, to the difference between perimeter and area; and to weight per area, the pressure on the feet—remarkably the same for different children. The next topic was mapping the school and schoolyard.

In another school what developed, initially from the teacher's own concern and curiosity, was about an individual child, recently arrived, who did not "fit in" with other eleven-year-olds; she was shy and had talents hard to identify. In that south-facing classroom the adviser, fishing for clues, called attention to the sunlight on the floor and the shadow of the window's edge. She asked if anyone remembered where the shadow had been earlier that morning. The girl in question immediately pointed in the right direction. So had the shadow moved? A silly question. Yes, of course. Did anyone see it move? No. Why not? Is it moving now? This time the child in question took the lead. She brought paper and pencil to the floor, marking slowly and carefully the very edge of the shadow. But by the time she stood up and others had gathered round, all could see that the shadow had already moved a tiny bit. It had moved, and must still be moving! So Sarah, the child in question, had some special background and interest. The adviser then found a classroom mirror and placed it to reflect the shadow's edge on the far wall, twenty feet away, where all could see the motion, magnified. Sarah had brought with her, to this new class, something that might have gone unrecognized. Alertness to that sort of chance with children belongs deep within the teaching art.

This small episode, of finding something new in what was utterly banal, led to a continuing investigation, and in it Sarah was finding a place. It began with the shadow of the tip of a pole, in the schoolyard, marking the path of the sun through the school day. A dusty terrestrial globe got brushed off and found its rightful place in the sun: Its axis was lined up with north and south, tilted just right, so that our school was right on top—where it belonged. Latitude and longitude suddenly were full of meaning, sunrise and sunset were always somewhere quite visible. These hours required a bit of the teacher's courage, a hint of honorable disobedience to a curriculum guide that didn't mention any daytime astronomy! But then geography was there, and this was a fresh way into it. So was the children's math, and a teacher's repertoire had been extended.

Another teacher had found an interest among her children for studying plants and plant growth, a favorite interest of her own. This developed into a major enterprise that it is worth describing in some detail. The science curriculum included some botany, but was entirely bookish. This teacher was hoping to show that the work she planned could be lively science teaching. She had begun a small "indoor den" with a fluorescent light over a long table. Her children had already planted corn and were measuring its rate of growth. At an adviser's suggestion, the work was broadened to include a wider, more scientific study, beginning with plant reproduction.

A local horticulturist was consulted, who suggested a trip to the nearby supermarket. They bought a small harvest of things that these city students thought might grow: seeds and cuttings, roots and tubers, even leaves. Then came the contrast between the fate of corn seeds sprouted under the light, and others in the dark of the classroom closet, giving dramatic meaning to the word *photosynthesis*. Inevitably some children were more involved in the practical work than others, but the topic proved rich in activities. The encyclopedia, for example, led to some fresh questions. Two halves of a cabbage, one exposed to the air and one carefully wrapped in plastic, were balanced on a balance-board, and rebalanced day after day to measure the change. The conclusion was startling: "A cabbage must be mostly water, and in one half it has evaporated!" Both halves were then "cooked" in a school oven for several hours at high temperature, and what was left was a bit of black carbon. There was no safe way to burn the carbon, but an interested high school science teacher burned it for them in the calorimeter. What was left of the cabbage, finally, was a very small bit of white ash. Two of these fifth-graders posted a report with pictures and a conclusion: "Cabbages come mostly from the water and the air, and just a little from the soil."

A final example of first-year advisory encouragement involved the perennial debate over the best "system" for the teaching of reading. The advisers knew very well the importance of early literacy; they knew also that it meant far more than "decoding." They also knew, and enjoyed, the fact that different children can best learn differently. Almost a century and a half ago, Leo Tolstoy had a superb school for the peasant children of his family estate. They all became literate, one a writer of note. In a passage that one adviser had read, Tolstoy jokes about reading "methods":

It seems to be an accepted truth with everybody that the problem of the public school is to teach reading, that the knowledge of reading is the first step in education, and therefore that it is necessary to find the best method for its instruction. One will tell you that the "sound" method is very good; a second will tell you that Zolotov's method is best; a third knows a still better method, the Lancastrian, and so forth.[1]

Such progress we have made in a century and a half! Only the names have changed: Phonics, Whole Word, etc. Tolstoy's peasant children all learned to read; they differed in interests and talents, and ways of learning. This great teacher knew no other "method" than to help them engage their talents and interests with the written word. If we compare the history of the progress made in "reading methods" during the century and a half since Tolstoy's school with that of medicine, we must ask whether the contrast is due to the greater difficulty of the teaching arts than the medical, or to our history of complacency and neglect.

A return to my story: In a few primary classrooms there began to appear, with help from one adviser, diverse examples of "reading" that defied all simple systems. There were exhibits of children's work in art or science, well labeled and explained, in their own print. There evolved "science tables" with found objects that children brought, all well labeled. There evolved also a class wall-board newspaper, news dictated to and printed by the teacher, exhibited on the wall for "reporters" to read their own words, and for all others as well. Two friends would sometimes read together.

In one "low-ranking" class of seven-year-olds, where only a few already read fluently and some others hardly at all, there was relief from the tedium, and sometimes the terror, of "reading groups." Those were replaced by a diversity of activities that related the written word to many of the interests and ongoing activities of the class. Reading became a means of communication within a small classroom society, complete with storytelling and enjoyment. At the end of a term, reading scores were dramatically higher.

As word spread from some early few successes of this advisory work, demand for help increased, slowly at first, and advisers were kept busy. Some teachers valued the help they were getting, and spread the word. As in most school systems, the word, good or bad, traveled speedily.

In the second year, a new part of the program was developed. Space was found and put under the control of the advisers; a few teachers they had worked with joined them in after-school hours and weekends, creating a special kind of teachers' center. Its first equipment was a tea kettle and comfortable chairs. In other rooms, various sorts of inexpensive lab equipment, including pendulums, were collected for studying balance; there were a few low-power microscopes. There were also a simple loom, a clay table—more than I can describe in some detail. It had a room for seminars, and a small library began to grow.

The advisers delegated some of the center's life to teachers who used it, in after-school and weekend hours. It hosted small seminars, invited talks or simply social relaxation and shop talk. In many schools of that system, teachers had lost the vital habit of shop talk; here it could revive and be encouraged. Short courses were asked for, by advisers or those they invited, in fresh ways of pursuing elementary-school subject matter. As the number of interested teachers grew—still a small part of a large teacher corps—talks and demonstrations were sometimes given elsewhere for newly interested teachers, parents, and others from the community.

Teachers were increasingly aware that their own college backgrounds had too often given "surveys" over a field, with little time for lingering over the many potentially fascinating details: earthworms, beetles, spiders, batteries and bulbs; fossils from a nearby hill; the elementary arts of estimation, of local architecture and history, of the weaving arts and their beginnings. The list is long, and even the best amateurs can only sample from it. But when teachers of the young are amateurs of many subjects, their snares for catching diverse children are increased. Departments or colleges of education are often the focus of criticism for poor preparation of elementary-school teachers. But undergraduate programs for their general education could certainly do better than they mostly do, in relevant subject-matter education.

Yet another example is elementary mathematics. The curriculum, for its part, is traditionally limited to "practical" math. The true worlds of elementary math—of number and form—are rich with subject matter that is accessible to children's imaginations and talents. But few teachers have themselves had the chance to enjoy such matters, and have shied away from the dreariness of the standard fare—a revulsion that can too easily be passed on to children.

A mathematician friend of one of the advisers offered short courses, occasionally, simply for teachers dissatisfied with the shallowness of their own understanding. At first they stayed away in droves. But the word spread. She introduced them to playful ways of investigating some relations among numbers, interesting number sequences, numbers, and geometrical shapes. Some of these matters had been investigated by the early Greeks. She tied some of this more playful material into the standard curriculum, such as the multiplication table, and soon her courses were oversubscribed.

In this second year it became clear that an important part of advisory work, and of a teachers' center, is that of helping teachers to explore, and enjoy for themselves, more of the rich worlds of elementary subject matter that their "higher education" had neglected. Having known this enjoyment themselves, teachers are in a far stronger position to catch and support children's own dawning interests. Helping children get into subject matter should be the first order of a teacher's business.

For illustration, I mention a topic that one adviser introduced to three teachers who asked for help with maps and map making. A fifth-grade girl had asked a question, rather persistently, and her teacher sought advisory help: "But how do they make the maps?" The teacher knew of aerial photography, but she also knew that maps were older than airplanes! Two friends were also interested, and the result was a short course with plane table, triangular ruler, and carpenters' tape measure. There was a moment of excitement when lines to a tree had been drawn from two adjacent plane-table positions: "So the tree is on this line, and when we moved the table it was on that line; so it must be where the two lines meet!" Using geometry to measure the height of trees, or nearby mountains, or the distance to the moon, can give simple geometry an aura of romance that mere textbooks, useful as they then can be, can seldom manage alone.

The third year of our advisory program was primarily a continuation of the first two. The center was moved to more generally accessible quarters. A larger part of its space was devoted to the storage and exhibition of specialized classroom materials, materials not routinely provided within the system, and for which a special grant had been obtained from the city. The grant had been limited to "three-dimensional" materials, to exclude its use for books and workbooks, already adequately available. An experienced kindergarten teacher, returning to her profession after some years away, was told that her new school was "very academic," and was told she must use the "prereading" workbooks. She joked as she reported, in the center, that "we did use them; we weighed them dry, and we weighed them wet."

It was in such matters that the teachers discussed, and understood, that the word *curriculum* was intended to prescribe the accomplishments of a semester, or a year, and never the day-by-day sequence of "lessons." At times this created certain administrative tensions, but the relevant test scores were going up. As the advisory program continued, it was beginning to make gains throughout the system, not only among its chosen principals and teachers, but also in recognition by the school system's administrative staff. It sometimes threatened traditional, perhaps bureaucratic, habits, but was open to observation and criticism.

In this year the number of teachers seriously involved had increased. Two or three teachers would become a team who sought out new materials, new ways of cooperating, but the program could still only be evaluated in terms of its own rate of growth, surely not on any overall statistical basis. In a system with over two thousand teachers in twenty-five schools, no average effect was yet conspicuous. But the visible effect on some classrooms, some schools, and even on their standardized test scores, *was* conspicuous. Fifty teachers were now seriously involved, and an equal number were asking for advisory help or taking short courses at the center, gaining a new spirit of professionalism, learning from advisers and—increasingly—from each other. Small at first, the consequences of an advisory system do not simply add; they can multiply.

The evaluation of the program, as observed by the superintendent and an assistant who understood its rationale, was based on recognition that it was to be a permanent investment in teachers' professional growth. It was not an "experiment" that had to prove itself in two years or even ten. It needed no short-term statistical justification, though it had some. The superintendent was faced, however, with the criticism that it had so far had little or no effect in many schools and most teachers. The teachers' center was still outside the "system"—in its actual operation it belonged only to advisers and the teachers that had found it important.

The reactions of supervisors were mixed. Classrooms were often somewhat decentralized, with the teacher moving from table to table, sometimes quite differently occupied. Sometimes a single student was apart from the rest, working on some specialized task. The work was obviously less test-driven than it had been, but test scores were up. It was in this year that members of the school board interested themselves seriously in the advisory program, an investment that led to increasing liaisons, sometimes tension, with parent groups and others.

Some teachers had taken pains to explain their sometimes unorthodox ways to parents, and usually gained support when it became obvious that children were then enjoying the daily life of their class, enjoying even the rigor it had begun to require. But there were complaints and objections. "Soap bubbles are fun," said one parent, "but playing with them? That's not education!" A physicist friend of the teacher had introduced her to some of the geometry of film, and a few of her children had graduated from "just blowing bubbles" to serious study. In the school of the teacher with the indoor garden, for another example, some of that garden had moved out of doors in the springtime. A watchful neighbor—not a parent—had complained that children were in the schoolyard "beyond recess time." The principal explained, but to no avail. "Are we supposed to be training young farmers?"

Anything new in the public schools can invite some parental, and sometimes wider, public opposition and support. That can prove troublesome, but sometimes beneficial. The complaint I mentioned about outdoor gardening actually went to the city school board, which had originally approved the advisory plan. But now a member asked for an "explanation." At the superintendent's suggestion, two interested members of the board were invited to meet the class. They were shown graphs and other records of the children's work, their knowledge of plant anatomy, modes of reproduction, rates of growth. They had discovered that the main plant foods were not the "plant foods" that came in cartons, but were air, water, and sunlight.

When the visitors reported to the board, some members were pleased, the rest mollified; they still wondered how the three Rs were being learned that way, though the work had been full of them. One board member had remarked that "only three percent of the population, nowadays, were farmers." Clearly there were unresolved issues that called for public consideration. The activities of advisers and the teachers they had worked with, still a small minority, were beginning to gain attention; not only in the system itself and from parents, but in a wider public.

That episode was only a beginning; clearly the whole advisory system was to be open to public discussion, first, and most importantly, with parents. But I'll end my narrative there, and make only one final comment.

This sort of public controversy—agreement and disagreement—is inevitable, and vitally important. It must be informed by the evidence that these many ways of enlisting the commitment of children to their own education—children from widely different backgrounds, interests, talents, levels of parental commitment—can be successful with no loss, but with very real gain in the love, and the rigor, of learning. This ongoing public dialogue is needed because without public understanding and commitment, the permanence of improvements in the nature of early schooling can never be assured. There is nothing new in the kinds of effort I have described, but in our history they have often faded out, even after impressive beginnings. They have faded just from a lack of public interest and critical engagement, leaving undisciplined the school systems themselves. And at center-focus must always be a concern that children are thriving in their learning environment.

NOTE

1. The quotation is from Leo Tolstoy, *On Education* (Chicago: University of Chicago Press, 1960), p. xvii.

– 12 –

The Union of Number and Form:
Mathematics for Childhood and Beyond[1]

As we become committed to the improvement of early education in mathematics, and of the part it plays in general education, we are easily led in two directions. In one direction we find that the long human history of discovery illuminates the ways in which mathematical curiosity and insight have evolved. In the other direction, we investigate the origins and development of children's mathematical abstractions and interests, as these may be studied in the best pedagogical settings. I propose here to report on some pursuits of mine in both of these directions, and to discuss some implications that they jointly support. I believe they can illuminate some of the causes, in the United States and possibly in other parts of the world, of our widespread failure in the teaching of mathematics, and suggest a direction in which some cures may be found.

It has often been remarked that most of mathematics, even at its highest levels of development, can be traced back to beginnings either in geometry or in arithmetic. However, since these subjects are already parts of mathematics, I shall refer to beginnings that are even more primitive, and from which these subjects have been distilled. I refer, of course, to the practical arts such as the surveying of land, and the building of houses and silos and temples. Overlapping with these geometrical arts, and dealing with multiplicity and measure, are those of arithmetic. Some technologies join them intimately, such as the ancient high art of weaving.

These familiar comments remind us of the importance of the relation between practice and theory. The central abstractions of theory have their origins in the universals of practice, of what the apprentice has learned in the process of becoming the journeyman—about the horizontal and vertical, about areas and volumes, squares and triangles and circles.

But all these developments come before the explicit appearance of what we call theory. In its original Greek meaning the word *theory* implied schooling, viewing, or beholding, in contrast with doing or performing—it suggests a certain detachment. Throughout all the trades there is a kind of ethnomathematics evolved and passed on in practice. We of the academic world sometimes fail to appreciate its richness. Thus the roots of the mathematical theory of probability were long known in the world of gambling, many centuries before it was first investigated by mathematicians in the seventeenth century. They first studied what gamblers had long known, but in the process they discovered new facts about the worlds of chance that have subsequently found uses to which practice alone could never have led. So one may say that practice is potential theory, and theory is incipient practice.

In my own work with children of elementary-school age, and with the teachers of such children, I have found myself allied with others in exploring and advocating certain pedagogical reforms. These are reforms we have reduced to practice and found successful. Much more of this work needs to be done, but it has so far proved to be stimulating and engaging both to children, to their teachers, and to ourselves. This kind of success has led me, in particular, to borrow ideas and practices from the early history of mathematical theory, as the Greeks developed it in the century or two before Euclid, roughly 450-300 B.C. These early Greeks, such as Thales and Pythagoras, sought out and learned a great deal of practical mathematics from both Egypt and Mesopotamia. What they themselves contributed was a new style and art of inquiry, a dramatic turn toward theory and, therefore, many new discoveries. It is in what I believe to be the spirit and style of this early history that I myself have found the greatest teaching reward. Moreover, much of its subject matter has proved accessible to children. It has also attracted quite a few teachers I have worked with, including some for whom mathematics had otherwise been a closed and often rather frightening or repulsive book.

In reflecting on some possible reasons for this affinity between the mathematics of twenty-five centuries ago and some classrooms of today, I find it rather compelling, and wish to offer my work for further discussion and research.

To begin with, I must ask you to reflect upon the memory of your own early school mathematics. Both in Latin America and in Anglo America, this memory is dominated by paper and pencil, by being taught an arbitrary symbolic shorthand for the manipulation of numbers—practical arithmetic. Later, but only in secondary school, there was an introduction to geometry and the art of logical proof. But now I ask you to replace this imagery with another, from twenty-five hundred years ago. At that time there already were written number codes, taken especially from the Babylonians, but they were awkward in use and poorly developed compared to ours. You may remember being told that these codes lacked the idea of the number *zero*. The materials of writing, moreover, were expensive, and the art limited to the few. In place of the paper and pencil they had, however, a very powerful instrument that we, in our arrogance, think we have only recently invented—the computer! This machine, the counting board or abacus, existed in all the early civilizations and was widely used. With the learning and understanding of its use came all the arithmetical ideas of sums and differences, products and quotients, powers and roots, and with a zero as real as anything else. Here the central image of number is a dual one; it is that of a physical container and some specific contents. The container is a cup, or a column on a board, and the contents are pebbles. This is a natural symbolic code: a cup of pebbles can represent a number that *is* their number. The zero is an *empty* cup. The cups can represent units, or tens, or hundreds, etc. A number, however large, can be represented by a string of cups. One container represents units, the next may represent tens, the next hundreds, etc. To add two such numbers we simply combine the contents of corresponding cups and simplify, by removing any ten pebbles that may appear in one cup and giving back one to the cup of the next higher denomination. Subtraction is easily defined, and so then are multiplication and the rest.

But that is not the whole study. Three pebbles close together form a triangle, four a square or rhombus, and so on. So represented, the natural numbers are inseparably linked to geometrical form. It was this linkage that first opened the door to the development of ancient mathematical inquiry, and it can do the same in present-day classrooms of children, equipped with collections of pebbles, beans, plastic chips, marbles, wooden cubes, and plastic tiles cut in various shapes. All such materials can represent both number and form.

It is this very rich cross-connection that leads me to my central argument. Let me state it quite generally. The human mind has two basic and contrasting powers, or means of representations and understanding. One of these is strongly spatial and pictorial, geometrical. Its grasp is that of form or pattern, of many elements related synthetically. The other is strongly analytic; it goes step by step, in time and in logic. Its process is digital: it goes like the fingers in counting. I shall call it digital, or arithmetical, or algebraic. Each of these abilities, moreover, is strong where the other is weak. Perhaps this contrast is related to the recently fashionable discussion of the left brain and the right brain, but that is not my interest. I wish to focus not on the contrast, but on the interaction, the cooperation, between these different human talents. They are not opposed but complementary.

Let me mention here a single example. I ask you to think of a medieval church tower. It has a clock for all to see, a hand that turns full circle once in twenty-four hours, mimicking the sun's motion. This is the pure geometry of motion, the astronomy we have always known. Consider next that product of electronic technology, the digital clock or watch. It simply adds up the oscillations of a quartz crystal, and presents us with numerals that name the hour, minute, and second, the conventional measure of time. Both aesthetically and logically, these two timepieces are quite different and independent.[2] But if you trace the evolution of the science that underlies the art of timekeeping, you discover the constant interplay of these two complementary aspects of nature and of human understanding; they needed each other. Quite specifically I wish to suggest that mathematics itself can only begin with this cooperation, only so coming alive—either in our history, or in our childhood. Let me speak first of the history.

Having inherited much of the practical lore from earlier civilizations, some of the fifth-century Greeks began to look at what was known of arithmetic and geometry with a new interest, to look at each of these ancient subjects from the point of view of the other. I do not say that this had not been done before. It had not, I believe, been done with the same persistent curiosity, and not with the sense of creating a theoretical discipline. In fact the very word *mathematics* was coined—by Pythagoras—then for this synthesis. Among the half-legendary Pythagoras and his followers, the imagery of the pebbles and their patterns persisted, though in an idealized form of number-atoms. These were the units from which everything in nature was supposedly formed and could be understood.

If we now think of the numbers in the way these Greeks did, as defining various kinds of geometrical patterns, we can be led to an entirely different interest in them than that of the merchants or bookkeepers; yet it is this new interest that leads toward the understanding of the number domain that has nourished the sciences and teaching. Similarly, when practical geometry becomes cross-linked to these arithmetical patterns, a whole new world of geometry is opened for exploration. Some of these early mathematical inquiries are now often regarded as mere curiosities; they have been superseded by later developments, more powerful or more elegant. But they are in fact milestones along the road of discovery, and can still give powerful support to children's mathematics education.

So it was, for example, that the Pythagoreans discovered the existence of whole classes of numbers defined by their geometrical patterns. Thus for example the sequence 3, 6, 10, 15, 21, . . . all form triangular patterns, while the sum of any neighboring two of these defines a square or rhombus. A wider class of rectangular numbers includes all but the primes. In three dimensions, there are other progressions defined by geometric shapes, such as tetrahedral and cubic numbers. Many of these number classes have reappeared in later discoveries, such as the famous triangle of Pascal and Tartaglia, the so-called binomial coefficients.

So also new directions for geometrical inquiry were opened. The arranging of pebbles into various geometrical shapes can guide us toward discoveries concerning areas and volumes, and more generally toward the algebra of proportions and of scale transformations. In some cases I find historical evidence; in others I can only conjecture that many of the Euclidean theorems involving these ideas have their origins in the counting of pebbles or tiles. Thus, for example, the volume of pyramids and cones was said to have been found by Thales, one of the founders of Greek mathematics and science. I have no historical evidence that Thales used the pebble-counting method. His contemporary Pythagoras and his followers surely did. For parallel evidence, I can offer some personal experience with children and their teachers, who can easily learn to associate a visual gestalt with the corresponding number sequence.

In pursuing this revealing association between form and number, one is finally forced to realize that the symmetry of translation between these two modes of thought, though powerful, is imperfect. The Pythagoreans were committed to this symmetry and just for that reason were the first to discover its limitation. In the original Pythagorean metaphysics, the imagery of the pebble world had of course been idealized; they perceived all things as made of number-atoms of some kind; in particular, therefore, all lengths, areas, and volumes would be measured by some integer number of these minute atoms. These would, of course, be very small, and our senses would not tell us that the size of things can only change by jumps. We would be aware only of a continuous gradation. In reality, then, any two lengths (or areas or volumes) could be compared; their relation would be that of the ratio of two whole numbers. The fatal flaw in this belief was the discovery of counter-examples, of which the simplest was the relation between the side and the diagonal of the square. If one of these could be represented by an integer number of atoms, however small, the other, on pain of contradiction, could not. The relation between them was literally *irrational* (ir-ratio-nal). It could for practical purposes be approximated by such ratios, as accurately as desired, but never without some remainder. This discovery was so profound, it so negated the number-atomism of the Pythagoreans, that its unnamed discoverer was said to have been, in consequence, drowned at sea—drowned for revealing such dark secrets.

I mention this extraordinary and subtle discovery not necessarily because I wish to pursue it in classrooms for children, but because of its historical consequences. It led to a drastic separation of arithmetic and geometry. The linkages between them, basic to the very development of early mathematics, were then no longer regarded as trustworthy guides to its further development; indeed, it is only in modern times that these linkages have been reestablished. What concerns me here, however, is that this separation became firmly entrenched in the teaching of mathematics. Indeed, by the time of Euclid's great textbook the separation was already complete.

From the point of view of the pure mathematician this separation seemed necessary to the growth of understanding. From the point of view of pedagogy, it was, I believe, a profound and unnecessary mistake. The early Greeks had ascended a ladder of discovery that would not reach beyond a given height, becoming shaky and uncertain. Their followers then cast it away, forgetful that it had brought them so far and should therefore be available to all students who came after. In the centuries that followed, indeed to this very day, the pedagogical separation has remained.

In this new geometry, which we find in Euclid, the number-atoms have disappeared and the algebra of length, area, and volume is erected on new foundations. The elements now are no longer numbers, but geometrical abstractions—line segments, surfaces, and volumes. A line segment a can be extended by another line segment b, and the resulting segment is $a + b$. A segment b may be removed from a longer segment a, leaving a segment $a - b$. The a's and b's are not numbers at all. As the number-atoms had been idealizations of countable pebbles, so the line segments were idealizations for thin rods; again, "practice." The "+" and "−" were not arithmetical operations, but idealized physical operations of joining or segmenting these rods. The shift becomes very clear with the next step, which is the definition of $a \times b$. Two rods, combined by this operation, are at right angles.

They give something new; not a rod at all, but a rectangular surface bounded by the rods a and b. Similarly, the product $a \times b \times c$ defines the space filling a box whose edges are respectively the rods a, b, and c. Numbers enter this scheme *only* in a secondary way, through the introduction of arbitrary congruent units; ratios of counts based on these units (of length, or area, or volume) will in general only approximate the true relations.

It was, in fact, a theory of approximation that gave the Greeks the idea of what we would call irrational numbers; but in their new thinking the ratio was a pair of geometrical magnitudes, not a number at all. You can find all this in Euclid; but it was a part of Euclid we seldom studied in high school.

The separation of geometry from the world of numbers was, of course, only the beginning of the pedagogical separation I have complained about; it hardly explains why that separation continued for over two thousand years until the present. Part of the explanation, I suppose, lies in the enormous prestige, throughout subsequent history, of Euclid's great text and its later extensions by mathematicians such as Apollonius and Archimedes. A part of the explanation is the fact that our own mathematical tradition, deriving from the Greeks but also coming from Indian and Arabian traditions, developed first in directions away from classical geometry, and was focused instead on the numerical side. Geometry thus remained relatively unchanged until nearly the time of Fermat, Descartes, and Newton—from them began the great modern reunion, the synthesis of the worlds of number and form that we call "mathematical analysis." The spirit of this synthesis has permeated all the immense territory of modern mathematics. It is in many ways a recapitulation, though at a far more advanced level, of the ancient Pythagorean mathematics, the union of number and form. There is seemingly only one area that this synthesis has not touched: the mathematics curriculum of our elementary schools!

Children's curiosity and investigative talents can lead them into genuinely mathematical subject matter. This induction can and should take place along with, or even well ahead of, their mastery of the arbitrary, shorthand, written code and rules of operation that we now impose and wrongly call mathematics. There is by now a considerable body of research that shows that a major source of many children's difficulty in acquiring these arithmetical skills is a matter of unmotivated rote learning. This learning is often dissociated from their native understanding and so also from their talents for extending it. It is for this reason that I was first led to explore the work of the ancient Greeks, and to discover that children of today can be led into mathematics in the same way. In doing so I have inevitably overemphasized the particulars of what I have called pebble-mathematics. There are other sorts of phenomena, at once geometrical and arithmetical, accessible to control by children's hands and eyes. These equally can lead into mathematics. I mentioned one such beginning, in the art of weaving, in which again the geometry and arithmetic are inseparable. Here the root metaphor is not the pebble but the *line*, of wool or cotton or silk. The mathematical insight implicit in the art of the ancient Chinese or the great weavers of Peru was (and remains) deep and subtle. Indeed, most of the preindustrial arts and crafts, if introduced in schools, can open doorways into mathematical subject matter at an intellectual level. These can also give fresh meaning to the manipulation of those chalk marks or pencil marks our children now so often fail to enjoy or understand.

In emphasizing my own work with children and with their teachers, I have also failed to describe a substantial body of work that contributes to the kind of early mathematics teaching many of us wish to develop farther. The work I am familiar with has been done in England, France, Holland, and to a lesser degree in the United States and Canada. Typically it has provided wooden or plastic materials that children can use for playful constructions and investigations. These materials have been designed primarily to enlist children's geometrical intuition for the learning of arithmetic. Since geometry is still absent from the typical elementary-school curriculum, there has been less emphasis, unfortunately, on the uses of arithmetical understanding for the study of geometry. Commercially manufactured, such materials can be well used in classrooms, but they are also quite expensive. For myself, I prefer the kinds of materials that can be found or made locally, or bought cheaply, such as plastic tokens. In every community, in every part of the world, there are local crafts of a mathematical character, and local materials of farm or city. There are also children ready to be engaged in the kinds of mathematical investigations that such materials, attractive to their eyes and hands—and minds—can invite.

I do not underestimate the difficulties in bringing about this sort of improvement in the early teaching of mathematics. There are administrative difficulties in persuading ministries and local authorities that such changes are desirable. If that is accomplished, then there is needed a major investment of effort by mathematicians and by others to whom they give professional support. Their investment is to work collegially with the elementary schoolteachers whose interest they can attract. This work can give teachers the opportunity to know and enjoy the content and style of a way of teaching that may be quite unfamiliar to them. The purpose of such work is also equally to learn *from* teachers and to receive the criticisms and further ideas that result from this association. In my own case at least, this continuing work has led me to a new enjoyment and understanding of mathematics itself—new topics, new problems, and new estimates of the mathematical intelligence both of teachers and of children.

NOTES

1. This chapter was originally presented as a paper at the University of Costa Rica, San José, Costa Rica, in 1987.

2. I owe this description of clocks—geometrical and digital—to my friend Philip Morisson.

– 13 –

Early Roots[1]

The fact that many famous mathematicians began their careers early in life is well known. It is often dealt with by speaking of their extraordinary talent or even genius, but as though it had nothing to do with the nature of the discipline itself, in comparison, for example, with historiography or jurisprudence or statecraft. By its nature, mathematics offers some special modes of access, and sometimes of invitation, to the young. I know of no census as to the precocity of the many who could be called just good at this trade, but suspect the story would be similar. In any case, early talent cannot be estimated retrospectively, mostly lost among the competing concerns of growing up. One must observe it directly. But the record of such observations is sparse, and we have not much beyond conjecture, in which I intend happily to engage.

I believe that the study of children's mathematical insights can bring one to a view of mathematics itself that might at first seem close to Platonism, which for that reason, if no other, one should treat it with some special interest. I made that suggestion in a 1985 review article.[2] But the philosophy of Plato, read two millennia later, exists in more versions than one. I will slant a special version that, as debated by Plato scholars, allows divergence from the metaphysics of an ideal world of forms.

The competing line of interpretation leads first to Aristotle, who was for many years Plato's student, almost always neglected in modern discussions of mathematics. By a shortcut, I will bring it to some recent philosophy, that of Charles Saunders Peirce (1839–1914). Peirce was the acknowledged founder of the general philosophical outlook he called pragmaticism, or pragmatism, that claimed the allegiance (with variations) of William James (1842–1910), John Dewey (1859–1952), George Herbert Mead (1863–1931), and many others. Contemporary discussions in the philosophy of mathematics have generally overlooked the latter three, who generally followed Peirce in their discussions of the subject.

But first, Plato. In the minds of the young, inborn mathematical forms or ideas are the least obscured, Plato seems to say, but all those shadows on the cave wall at best suggest some *déjà vu*, some reminiscence of the true Ideas. For children, the access to these Ideas is least hindered. In his discussion of the *Meno*, David Wheeler gives a detailed account of Socrates's impeccable art in evoking the slave boy's latent geometrical understanding.[3] Wheeler leaves aside the context of Platonic metaphysics. In my story, the metaphysics needs to be considered but only as a way of opening doors to inquiry about the nature of mathematical ideas, whether children's or adults'.

By all reports—not just those of his best student—the historical Socrates was indeed a great teacher, as such both loved and feared. His art appeared, however—as still it seems to many—to violate all sensible beliefs about teaching. Teaching must—must it not?—be a process by which admonition and knowledge are conveyed from teacher to student. That is common sense, what everyone has experienced and takes for granted. How, then, can one be a great teacher who only asks questions? Aha! The questions are sneaky, loaded, sophistical. That was a common reaction, as Plato's dialogues frequently reveal, from those discomfited by the Socratic art. Plato puts forward the only possible defense: what such a teacher may teach indeed cannot convey knowledge; that knowledge must be already latent, somehow, in the minds of those taught. The Socratic art, he says, is a kind of midwifery; what is taught is there ready to be born, needing only that patient questioning to assist in parturition.

Plato's earlier dialogues were devoted to recording and dramatizing his master's art, even sometimes leaving an examination half-finished, where questioning reached some pause. In these dialogues Plato vividly evokes the intent and style of the master. Along the way, however, the messenger is sometimes tempted to extend the message, digging more deeply under the paradox of the teacher who did not seem to instruct. I believe it was this hermeneutic temptation that led in the end to the full-blown metaphysical doctrine we today call Platonism.

I spoke of doors that Plato opened but his metaphysics passed by. Opening them, one can begin to develop a view of the roots of mathematics in childhood, a view that suggests, I think almost compels, a more general view of the nature of mathematics itself, of its history, and of the network of converging and branching tracks evolved from such beginnings. In the observation of childhood one can recognize a kind of learning-by-abstraction that is vital, but perhaps less easily recognized, in adult experience.

In contrast with official Platonism, Aristotle's philosophy was essentially empirical. But his understanding of experience was very different from what we usually call "empiricism." The young Aristotle was for many years a student of Plato, as Plato had been of Socrates. He rejected Plato's view of a world of Ideas known independently of the world of nature. The Ideas were, rather, essential forms of things we find in nature, some of which we earliest learn. He rejected Plato's metaphysics rather casually, however, as though it had never seemed to him to be crucial to Plato's thought.

But to bring Aristotle's views of mathematics adequately into the context of the present discussion is too large a job. I quote only one remark, appropriate to the present text. Speaking of practical wisdom, which as he says depends on mature experience of complex affairs, Aristotle contrasts it with mathematical understanding; the objects of mathematics do not evolve in that way, they underlie quite ordinary experience and are special distillations from it. They "exist by abstractions." Concerning the complexities of practical life, the young, he says, lack adequate understanding: they "merely use the proper language, while the essence of mathematical objects is plain enough to them."[4]

Here is one child's version of the abstract world of number. After she had heard a name for the biggest numbers from another child—a trillion-trillion-trillion—and from a waggish physicist friend—10^{69}—she interpreted charitably: "They just meant it was the biggest numbers they had a name for." Why did she say that? "Well, you could always add one more." Many of us remember taking the comparable step to a spatial infinity, and the later trouble about a world that might be finite but unbounded. Could the numbers loop around like that? Never! One knew that.

Quite rigorously, I believe, one can show that any formal elucidation of the natural numbers must—not as a sufficient condition, but as one irreplaceably necessary—involve some literal and reproducible instantiation of them; of the first few, at least, and their sequence. In one of many stories one can invent, an early-times hunter-gatherer fisherman tied knots in a rawhide string—remote ancestor perhaps of the Inca *quipu*—for each member of his small band. He then tried to catch at least one fish for each knot. The first crucial step is that knotted string, or some equivalent standardization.

As part of his general semiotic theory, Peirce gives special attention to two such kinds of mathematical signs. One kind is primary—that he calls "iconic." A sign that first represents any basic mathematical abstraction must itself possess the very structure that it represents. Thus the icon of "3" is always some standardized triple. That of any n is an n-tuple. Such icons are part and basis of any arithmetical code. By themselves they give us a monary code. An iconic sign is typically portable or reproducible from memory. Painters' color charts are also icons. The charts that present primary-color mixtures, additive or subtractive, are icons of a mathematical kind.

But the use of iconic signs is not a sufficient condition for conceptual understanding; they are necessary, and in a way that deserves remark. The necessary possession and use of icons can be understood, of course, as a means only, a practical necessity. But what has previously been assimilated as means later becomes an object of reflective investigation. That brings about a reversal of ends and means characteristic of reflective thought.

But there are other mathematical signs that Peirce calls "indexical": they just point to what is signified. Some are like demonstrative pronouns in that they have meaning only when the thing meant is literally present in the discourse. If a sentence contains a demonstrative "this" or "that," and an apple is displayed, or a quintuple, or a mountain pointed to, then the apple or quintuple or mountain is its own icon, itself part of the sentence. Another kind of index points intelligibly to something that need not then and there be exhibited, a name or descriptive expression: thus the "3" serves to indicate some icon (*, *, *), while the indices

1, 2, 3 can in turn be elements of the icon (1, 2, 3), giving us back the cardinal icon composed of the ordinal indices. In such ways we have invented number codes other than the purely iconic. Thus the definition of a number in the decimal code is an even more complex organization of indices and icons; the sequence of digits is an icon for the powers (0, 1, 2, etc.) of ten, and the digits indices of the corresponding multiples. In any such code, happily, large numbers no longer need to be signified by icons, but by formulas that serve, inter alia, for constructing or identifying an icon (knots, pebbles) that would or does exemplify it. In that way, defined first by the monary code, large numbers need no longer be exemplified. But always, by hypothesis, they could be. They are well defined, waiting if you wish to be exemplified, but in any case already inhabiting a world of potentiality, standing arrayed there by themselves. They have mathematical existence independently of the contingencies of nature.

In discussing such matters, Peirce emphasizes what Charles Quine later recognized as "metaphysical commitment" to the reality of numbers as objects, entities in their own right, no longer mere attributes of things in nature. Peirce makes light of it. "Honey is sweet" can be transformed into "Honey possesses sweetness." What was a property (of honey) has become a kind of thing, and the statement that of a relation between two things, one "possessing" the other. Such transformations he calls "hypostatic" abstractions, turning properties into things. Detached from adjectival use, hypostatized, the sweetness is still not fictitious, it is just as real as the taste! And there are different kinds of sweetness, just as there are of honey. The numbers, similarly, now can be qualified by their own kinds or properties, and the study of them transforms arithmetic into number theory.

So my central topic must be abstraction, meant in just the way Peirce (and Aristotle) intended it. For a first look, I go back to a fortunate two-year-old who, sitting on the kitchen floor with a few pots and pans and spoons, has dropped a spoon in a pot, then removed it, repeating this pair of operations over and over again: interactively, each time pleasurably. Adults may wonder how this monotonous repetition, thirty or sixty times, can be so absorbing. Could it be, to catch gravity napping?

You would think a few times would be enough! But should you? For a second look, observe a preschool four-year-old building a long roadway across the block room, from one "city" to another. Iteration again, but now additive as well. A kind of entertainment often repeated in different contexts.

Along such developmental tracks the roots of two mathematical ideas are laid down: iteration and sequence among others, all underlined by repetition and accessible to abstraction. Those of number can come next, depending, of course, on the child and the human ambience: sequential ordering, then the one-to-one correspondence. In some such way young children may evolve the kind of meaning my fisherman knew, with portable or reproducible standards. Thus far, I think, abstraction of a distinctively mathematical kind need not have occurred, although an instrument has been found that can be taken from one kind of situation and dappled in others.

That abstractive step does take place, however, when the sequence of counters is acknowledged in detachment from practical use and considered, reflectively, as an object in its own right. Young children, morally supported in their investigations, are able to find and enjoy the essence of this abstraction. Whether or by how much they choose to explore beyond it, the door has been opened.

Peirce rejected, as emphatically as anyone else, John Stuart Mill's notion that the propositions of arithmetic are simply well-tested empirical generalizations. Indeed, they do have verisimilitude; they are reflections of generic patterns of the world around us as we experience it, yet are detached from it. When mathematical generalizations are "applied" in the sciences, they are describing the very kinds of experience that first gave birth to them. But such applications have wholly hypothetical status; the mathematics generalizes, by its art of definitions, beyond that empirical world. If certain empirical assumptions were correct, then certain empirical conclusions would follow. Thus, when considered in abstracto, every number has a successor, and the sequence is infinite. It is imaginable that of every enumerable set of things in nature, there is only a finite number. That would not affect, say, the infinity of primes. Held apart from such questions, the numerical infinity neither accords with nor contradicts empirical fact. The hypothetical "if n, then $n+1$" is an axiom. A child has laid it down: you could always add one more.

This seems a proper place to remark that the arithmetical apprehension of some small children may be "much stronger than their prompt [and] producible vocabulary."[5] Much of their thought and expression is enactive, iconic; the acquisition of speech is second language, not first. I want to say that the essential mathematical ideas of childhood belong to the first language, then only derivatively to the second.

How, next, to describe young children's available powers of geometrical iconography? Sometimes it seems more related to those of Picasso than of Euclid; they can become intelligible to adults as the latter learn (or relearn) the language of play—play with materials found eolithically or introduced by observant adults; sometimes also in painting or sculpture.

A town is sketched out on the ground in an area of a few square meters, complete with roads and road signs, an airport and a river. The river is made of thin small blocks. Waves on the water, deemed necessary, are made by the way the blocks slightly overlap. It is all an icon, or what Peirce sometimes calls a schema, a system of icons, proto-architecture, proto-geometry, with much attention to direction, to symmetry and dissymmetry. One of the planners brings for the zoo a too-large giraffe from the schoolroom. Despite its off-scale size, his partner accepts it, but with hesitant politeness.[6]

None of this iconic play needs as yet to be judged mathematical, reflectively abstracted from its early representative intent. We need suppose no sharp transitions, hard to catch even when they occur. Yet as with the early stages of arithmetical construction, geometry is on the way. Slice a raw potato once, for a plane; twice for a line; three times for a point. Shrink the potato to small size, and consider its location in relation to two walls and a ceiling.[7] Invariance to scale is one inescapable facet of the learning, scaling the big world down.

Mathematics, Peirce repeatedly asserts, is an experimental science. Since mathematical signs are iconic abstractions from empirical reality, they can be manipulated much as scientists manipulate natural processes in the laboratory. I believe what Peirce had in mind were such "experiments" as we can make, for example, in searching for prime numbers, combining algebraic equations, inventing new geometrical designs. Conjectures arrived at in this way are not in the end established by empirical tests, but they can lay out the way to formal definitions and proof, often strongly suggestive of some idea of proof.

It makes matters clearer here to invoke a distinction of Peirce's between two kinds of deductive inference, which—with Euclid in mind—he calls "corollarial" and "theorematic," and to which he attaches great importance. Corollaries are immediate inferences, special cases of more general propositions. Theorems, on the other hand, are found as consequences of some experimentally discovered combination of different and previously unrelated icons. He might have been thinking of the Pythagorean theorem.

There are a good many proofs of that theorem, some more immediate than Euclid's *pons asinorum*, but all depend on subsidiary constructions that either embed the right triangle in some larger structure already understood, or else subdivide it, as in the elegantly equivalent theorem that divides the triangle into two smaller similars in which a single added perpendicular serves the "theorematic" need most simply. By dividing the triangle into two that are similar, it reminds us that what is true of the triangles will be true of their embedding squares.

More generally, we all know the experience that by some analogy, hunch, or sheer chance we "bring to mind" together two facts previously but separately known, then discover something new, something that they only jointly entail. Granted that p and q together entail r, it does not follow from "A knows p" and "A knows q" that "A knows r." Such two facts may well have been stored on different occasions and in different parts of the mind's library; yet must be brought out together, attended to, before cross-indexing and discovery are possible. This, I believe, is the basis of Peirce's account of mathematics as an experimental science. One does not know in advance which propositions, previously isolated, will combine to form new conclusions. Deduction is the end result, but not the method.

Learning a few geometrical constructions, fourth-grade students were challenged to find ways of subdividing a given figure into congruent parts. Equilateral triangles were readily subdivided into 2, 3, 6 such parts, then finally into 4. With that construction, one student announced that she could also divide it into 9, or 16, or 25, on and on. She had previously discovered, in playing with plastic equilateral triangles, that when you put them together you can make larger triangles. With some urging from her teacher she had found, to her great surprise, that the numbers were not the triangular numbers that she and others had previously found. They were instead the numbers they had gotten when poker chips were packed in squares, now expressed in triangular shapes. She saw that you get the sequence by adding successive odd numbers (the Pythagorean *gnomons*). Instead of subdividing the big triangle into smaller ones, she reversed the process, and built it up from them. Theorem? Corollary?

In any case, there was found what Peirce calls a schema, a generative procedure that can produce square numbers of triangles to make larger triangles, or squares to make squares, just by adding each time the successive odds. The actual procedure with the tiles might eventually fail, cumulatively, from slight irregularities in the plastic shapes, if not from boredom. But that would no longer matter; the schema itself does not fail. This is mathematics! Yet it derives, palpably, from children's experience, from geometrical play.

I use that story as a reminder that at the beginning of Greek mathematics there was one rather grand "theorematic" development in which two whole clusters of prior knowledge, stored separately within the practical culture of ancient Greece, were brought together. Quite a bit of geometry had early been learned and reduced to practice by builders and surveyors, and of arithmetic, by merchants and other keepers of books. But there was no name for the union of these two arts that the Pythagoreans and others discovered; it could only be passed on and developed in teaching. Hence it was called *mathematica*, a word originally meaning, merely, that which can only be learned from teachers. I think "theory" was being invented.

A long tradition has robbed schoolchildren of the richness of this Pythagorean discipline, well within their reach. Leaving out any but the most trivial elementary-school geometry, as we generally do, we concentrate many hundreds of childhood hours on algorithms of computation, calling this mathematics. The early Greeks knew better.

We know some of those early discoveries that came from this union of number and form, each complementing the other. The fourth-grade class of my story was "right on" to one of them. The discovery that most numbers can be classified under many kinds of shapes—triangular, rectangular, square, cube, and "prime"—led not only to numerology but also to the beginnings of number theory and of measure theory, depending as it does jointly on multiplicative and additive properties. The Pythagorean theorem and the discovery of the irrational numbers may have been conjectured first from such identities as $3^2 + 4^2 = 5^2$; or the reverse. Some basic theorems about areas and volumes could be derived from number patterns—for example, the volume of the pyramid, the tetrahedron, and other solids.

It stretches Peirce's term only slightly to say that this early junction of arithmetic and geometry was "theorematic" on a grand scale. In the subsequent history, quite a few other areas of practical and scientific investigation have given rise to new orders of what Peirce called "hypostatic abstraction." In confrontation with the older mathematics these became themselves mathematized. A beautiful illustration of this extension is Archimedes's discovery that his theory of the unequal-arm balance could be used for "weighing" the volume of the sphere. The law of moments enabled him to extend the long-known properties of the circle to those of the sphere. This was no ordinary balance, but one he had mathematized: it weighed no solid weights, but abstract measures, areas and volumes. Metaphorically, also, he added a third dimension to the two that the Pythagoreans had brought together.

It does not denigrate Archimedes's genius to mention that this new abstraction can be very close to the enactive understanding, when they have been given ample opportunity to explore it, of young children. One should mention also that the theory of the balance gave Galileo a mathematical imagery for investigations in mechanics, and his geometry of motion represented the beginning of another major synthesis, later developed by Fermat, Newton, and Leibniz: analysis.

A fourth domain was brought under mathematical scrutiny by Jacques Bernoulli and others. His theorem pointed toward new syntheses far beyond the simple mathematics of gaming; that was another beginning that led to "theorematic" confrontations, those between areas of experience previously isolated, and with results as radical as those the Pythagoreans had initiated long before. When abstractions from such diverse areas of experience converge, new branches of mathematics, and new levels of abstraction, emerge.

When we begin to open the doors that Plato first dramatized but then passed by, and begin to explore the experiential sources of this rich quasi-world of abstraction, we can begin to understand, I believe, how mathematics can at once help to extend our experience and reduce it to order—stand apart from the empirical sciences and yet, at the same time, map cities in the sand.

NOTES

1. This chapter was originally published in *For the Learning of Mathematics* 13(1), 1993: 15–18.

2. David Hawkins, "The Edge of Platonism," *For the Learning of Mathematics* 5(2), 1985: pp. 2–6.

3. David Wheeler, "Teaching for Discovery," *Outlook* 14, 1974: pp. 53–54

4. Aristotle, *Nicomachean Ethics*, book VI, 1142a, in The Complete Works of Aristotle, Revised Oxford Translation (Princeton: 1894), vol. II, p. 1803.

5. This quote is from Henry James, *What Maisie Knew* (New York: Penguin Books, 1974), p. 7.

6. Frances Hawkins, "Turn Here," *Outlook* 25, 1977: pp. 23–35.

7. M. Vicentini, personal communication.

– 14 –

The View From Below[1]

There is a story about the late E. T. Bell, the mathematician. His son asked, "Daddy, why do they put that plus sign on the top of churches?" Bell also remarked, in one of his popular books, that medieval theologians could be regarded as frustrated mathematicians in an age when that discipline was not fashionable. The joke is convertible. Perhaps mathematicians are also frustrated theologians.

I start this chapter with such jokes because I believe that the sources of mathematical knowledge and invention are in fact rather mysterious. I have some ideas about how such mysteries can be resolved, but I don't think the task is easy.

Let me start with a paradigm case. The Euclidean style of geometry is restricted to pencil-compass and straightedge. Working once in a fifth grade class, we had introduced these ancient implements with an initial encouragement to produce any kinds of designs. One of the things that happens under these constraints is a multiplicity of circles of the same radius, sometimes secondary circles centered on the circumference of the first one drawn. Two girls had in fact walked the compass around its circle and come back after six steps almost exactly to their starting point. I happened to be near and caught the question that hovered between

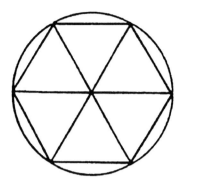 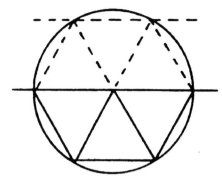

them: "How come?" My intervention was honest and it worked. We walked another circle with great care and the point of the compass landed, by luck, in the hole it had started from. After drawing the lines we ended with the hexagon dissected into equilateral triangles (see above). At one point Suzie said: "This [pointing to a radial line segment] is the same as that [a hexagonal edge], so it *has* to be just six."

I regard this as a paradigmatic case because of the implied transition from the empirical *is* to the emphatic *has to be*. I assumed at the time—and still do—that Suzie had shown some flash of understanding of a kind that marks the transition from fact as empirical to fact as mathematical. I have chosen it as a paradigm case because Suzie, like Plato's slave boy, could be presumed to lack any knowledge of formal geometry. She did give some reason for her apparent insight; she had noticed that since the pencil compass had not been readjusted, it had produced what we would call a cluster of equilateral triangles. At the time, I did no lightning-quick analysis of her apparent insight; unlike Socrates, I did not proceed to elicit from her the complete steps of a formal proof. I got her to show me that she was looking at half the circle, three triangles. I looked at them later myself, quite hard. I didn't yet wish to lead too strongly, and we went on instead to further partitions of the hexagon. When I now try to imagine what I might have elicited, I am fascinated. The first obvious proof I see depends on the formal Euclidean proposition that the sum of the interior angles of a triangle is a straight angle, or that for any polygon the sum of the supplementary exterior angles is one full rotation. Is there some similar formal proof that would plausibly interpret and support Suzie's apparent mathematical insight, without imputing to her any acquaintance with high-school geometry? Since symmetry is so powerful an idea, yet accessible to visual perception, is there a direct symmetry argument here that would establish her very emphatic conclusion? I leave this, as mathematicians often say, as an "exercise for the reader," though her drawing may be suggestive.

Maybe that particular Suzie, at that particular moment, *was* only guessing. It doesn't matter now. The story itself makes my first point. If Suzie's insight was valid, she was already in the domain of the mathematician; in a basic sense they could meet as equals. If it was not valid, that first step was yet to be taken. What then is this transition, so special to mathematics, from the merely empirical fact to the mathematical fact?

In any case, Suzie still had a long way to go, even if she was momentarily in the mathematician's domain. There are myriad other facts to be recognized, of the kind I think she saw. When enough of these facts are recognized and held together they are, as a cluster, the substance of classical geometry. For they are not independent, isolated facts, each true or false independently of the others. They are empirical facts, but not what the early Wittgenstein called "atomic" facts; they are internally related to each other. One, by itself, or two or three together, will lead to and perhaps require still another. If some can be noticed first as isolated empirical facts, they can still come together by some magnetic affinity, providing guides for further investigation; and the power of the process is multiplicative rather than additive in its potential rate of growth. As this clustering develops, some facts stand out as central; they lead to the recognition of many others.

This organization is what gets formalized as a deductive system. I see that as a later and quite distinctive development. It involves an abstracting, elucidation, and definition of what we call ideas or concepts. They are not facts but universal terms, the elements, properties and relations involved in the perception and statement of many facts, all the potential infinity of which can be stated in this common language. Suzie's construction can be described formally in this language by a few specialized terms: *points, lines, congruences, rotations*, etc. These same ideas will be implicit also in the perception of many other geometrical facts and will be expressed, at first spontaneously, in stating them. The new interest in analyzing and defining such ideas leads to another sort of clustering and ordering. Some ideas emerge as primitive, central, while others can be defined in terms of them. This development puts the affinities among geometrical facts in a new light. Though endlessly diverse as facts, they share a common domain and some can be transformed into others. Taking a few of them as primitives, the rest can all be demonstrated. The perception of mathematics as a deductive *system*, first clearly exemplified in Euclid's *Elements*, has been a paradigm and challenge for all subsequent mathematics, science, and philosophy. Can all knowledge be so organized? Can reason become a substitute for experience? A stubborn empiricist might insist on counting edges, faces, and vertices of as many kinds of convex polyhedra as she could lay hands on, and so far notice that the number of faces always happens to be two greater than the difference between the number of edges and the number of vertices. Euler's theorem says more; it implies that nature is not free to make exceptions, the difference *must* be just two. To the empiricist this is a kind of indignity.

At this point I have outlined two developments. The first, and most primitive, is that some kinds of empirical facts get recognized somehow as facts that must be so; like Suzie, we shift them from the state of *is* to *has to be*. The second stage is that clusters of such facts, which in one way or another seem to require each other, lead to the explication and ordering of a conceptual domain to which all these facts belong. When they are stated uniformly in the terms of this domain it becomes apparent that they are not independent of each other but are linked by bonds of implication in some orderly system. Facts now become theorems. Some theorems are chosen—as primitives sufficient to generate all the others— to be axioms.

If we wish to speak more formally about the relationship between ideas and theorems, we can describe these as a linkage between two domains. Ideas are related in their own domain by relations of meaning and definition. Some of these can be taken as primitive, and others defined in terms of them. Theorems are related in their own domain by relations of entailment, in which again some are primitive and others derived. But the two domains are also essentially cross-linked in one-many relations. A given idea is involved in stating several theorems, and the statement of a given theorem involves several ideas. Each domain has its own internal connective tissue, of definition in the one case and implication in the other. But the connective tissue in each domain is enriched and elucidated by cross-reference to the other.

Suzie's apparent insight started from a particular drawing that could be described as an affair of circles, lines, and points. This drawing was

not in her mind an *example* of anything geometrical. It was not a consequence but a starting point. But after we have developed some theorems
the drawings become examples, in retrospect. Philosophical and pedagogical accounts of mathematics often treat examples as inessential. They
are mere starting points, aids to the imagination, etc.; but they have
nothing to do with the essence of mathematics, which is entirely an
affair of abstractions detached from their humbler origins, like the modern trigonometry text that has no pictures of right triangles in the unit
circle. Lewis Carroll complained about this sort of thing in *Alice in Wonder-
land*, and he was quite right. In the View from Above, examples may seem to
have no essential place. In the View from Below, on the other hand,
they are of the essence. They are not only vital sources of knowledge but
they have a continuing and quite indispensable place all along the way.

Corresponding to any mathematical system of ideas and theorems
there is, therefore, always also a third domain, one-many related to the
other two. It may be called the domain of examples. In the View from
Below, it would be better called the domain of proto-examples, of originals. Any concrete example of a theorem is very likely to turn out to be
an example of several more theorems. These may be closely connected in
the domain of theorems, but also they may not have been seen to be,
and their coincidence may suggest new theorems, or new connections
between old theorems. I don't know who first looked at the drawing I
reproduce here and noticed in it the possibility of a new and immediate
proof of the old *pons asinorum*, the Pythagorean theorem:

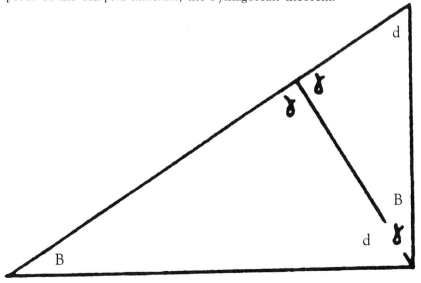

Instead of constructing *squares* on the sides of the right triangle, it makes use of the three similar *triangles,* two of which together "have to be" equal in area to the third. The famous theorem is seen as a direct consequence of the more general fact that the areas of arbitrary similar figures are proportional to the squares of any corresponding linear dimensions—a consequence of the flatness of the plane.

In their domain, examples or originals are directly related to each other by similarities and differences, or by part-whole relations. They come also to be indirectly related to each other through the domains of ideas or of theorems. Thus the cube and octahedron are indirectly related by the fact that the description of the one is transformed into the description of the other by simply interchanging the words *faces* and *vertices,* and this duality immediately suggests a way of constructing the one from the other or vice versa.

I would like at this point to acknowledge a substantial debt to the work of Edwina Michener,[2] from which I have taken the above three-fold partitioning of elements in the structure of mathematics. Her clear definition and discussion of these three domains provides a most useful frame for my discussions. She demonstrates this usefulness in several ways, illustrated from several fields of mathematics, elementary and more advanced. A key aspect of her work is to elucidate the nature of mathematical understanding. Rather than trying to summarize her discussion, I will continue on my own track but with that same concern for the meaning and importance of the verb to *understand.*

I grew up with a somewhat rebellious acceptance of the notion that mathematics was by its nature a highly sequential affair. I gained this impression first from the format of courses and textbooks, and later from some study of formal logic and the foundations. The pecking order of pure and applied math was then the order of the day, and the dominant positivist trend in philosophy, following some traditions of research in mathematics itself, was to declare that what was real was empirical and what was rational was—however elegantly—empty. This emptiness was to be demonstrated by the exhibition of completely formalized mathematical systems bled of all conceptual or factual content, yet with no loss of formal coherence. In such a demonstration the theorem domain could be disconnected from those of ideas and examples by depriving its formulae of any taint of vulgar meaning.

This movement can be considered from two points of view. As a special movement *within* logic and mathematics, it has been part of a whole new investigation of a metaformal character concerning the logical nature of mathematical systems, dealing with problems of consistency, completeness, the relation of axiom systems to models, etc. As a *special* mathematical discipline it clearly fits the general framework of Michener's analysis; it has its own genres of theorems, concepts, its originals being the mathematical systems. But the general philosophy I have alluded to, which for its own ends identified the theorem-structure of formulae with the whole of mathematics and left other aspects uncultivated, no longer seems very fresh or intriguing. Yet its legacy is still with us, the image of an essential part of mathematics mistaken for the whole.

Having been strongly influenced by that philosophical movement, though never embracing it, I tend to be inhibited in any outright opposition to it. Such opposition seems to embrace some allegedly outmoded philosophy of Platonic, Aristotelian, or Spinozistic rationalism. Yet the desire to oppose has grown steadily. Apart from my own roots in those older philosophical traditions, I have been strengthened in this desire by endless professional curiosity about the thought habits and commitments of physicists, biologists, economists, children, and mathematicians. Having been a student of the last two, I have found I frequently come back to mathematics from a new point of view, usually misnamed *applied*. Whenever this happens I find that though the formal academic background has helped, I frequently arrive, after some struggle, at a sense that I have not merely applied some mathematics but in the process and with help have invented or reinvented or extended it along shortened pathways quite different from those I was taught. Indeed, I have often reinvented the wheel, but have come in the process to realize that in such matters—the wheel is a good example—no one has yet quite said the last word on the subject or its implications. These pathways typically start from "applications," but also typically bring close together ideas and theorems that have been treated in quite different parts of the book or in different books. I have begun to get a clear sense that the mathematical territory is not so much like the directed graphs or trees of the theorem-space, but much more like a network in which one could go from A to B by a variety of routes and back again along still others.

Treelike structures there are, but they are so interestingly cross-indexed by analogy and reference that no simple metric of distance or closeness, such as that represented by the numbering of theorems in a book, seems appropriate. One is involved in a network somewhat like a map of airline routes, and like the airlines it brings many things close together. The map is, of course, a high-order abstract. To know the landscape and the culture one must get there in person. I have also realized, however, that the image of the network needs major constraints. If every node is connected directly to every other node one is informationally swamped in finding the relevant connections. Nodes must be graded by importance, by generality of relevance. Nodes are not all of the same kind, moreover, nor are their connections. What is first seen as a connection—for instance, the idea of a shared property relating different examples—can thereby itself become a node connecting to other ideas, sometimes by shared examples. This sort of duality transformation seems to blur the image of the network. Michener's representation helps; it allows three planes or spaces in each of which the items and relations are of the same kind, but with cross-referencing by specific dual relations to items in the other two. I think that then the image becomes sharp again.

Michener is concerned primarily to use the network as a framework for improving our understanding of mathematical *understanding,* and thus for a description of the personal qualities that we call fluency, resourcefulness, and competence. Understanding, of course, implies knowledge, and knowledge implies subject matter, some independent domain of fact that is just there. Though understanding implies knowledge, I think it need not imply formal proof. Indeed, understanding is often the guide to the invention of a proof, or a better one.

If the goal of mathematics education were really to work for active understanding on the part of students, what would the consequences be? Michener has experimented successfully with the deliberate and conscious use of her scheme among university math students. No doubt many good teachers do something like that implicitly. With the emphasis on understanding, on fluency, what does the picture look like for the early years? I cannot give a research report, but can only suggest the outcome of a good many years of elementary-school work, some with children, some with their teachers. One result is to see a need to modify or amplify the foregoing account. It is one thing to try to extend mathematical understanding among those who already have some formal education, but perhaps quite another to give access to it in the first place. I believe there are two complementary answers. One is from Plato's myth of reminiscence, that children *already* have some mathematical knowledge and understanding, and that we can learn to recognize this and as teachers resonate with it. The other is that this understanding is typically implicit. Henry James says it with characteristic rigor in the preface to *What Maisie Knew:* "Small children have many more perceptions than they have terms to translate them; their vision is at any moment much richer, their apprehension even constantly stronger, than their prompt, their at all producible, vocabulary."[3] In building bridges for communicating with children, one needs, therefore, to learn (in part by reminiscence?) their characteristic ways of thinking and this, I claim, involves a genuine extension of our own mathematical thinking.

This bridge building also requires, as a result, some qualifications to Michener's scheme.[4] For children, theorems are not yet theorems, concepts are not yet concepts, examples, above all, are not yet examples. To say this in a less Zen-ish language, they can and will often employ patterns of recognition and thought, yet be unable to scrutinize them, or communicate about them in anything resembling adult language. What one discovers, through trial and error in teaching, is that their powers of communication are immensely greater when they and the teacher are in the immediate company of the concrete situations, the originals, out of which their understanding has manifested itself. Jean Piaget talks about this phenomenon as reflecting a concrete operational stage of thought, which in one sense it does. But this is often taken to mean that children are incapable of having and using high-order abstraction. This is another claim altogether, and I think a false one. Suzie's symmetry argument, as I call it, is rather deep, though she could not at all spell it out. She can only communicate it to me by pointing to elements of the diagram we have produced, using gestures and demonstrative pronouns, appealing to my visual perceptions. I can't quite partition her insight into theorem, concept, and example, though I can—after some effort—validate it that way.

So for present purposes, as I noted earlier, the term *example* is ill-chosen. An example becomes an example only after it is an example of something previously named and recognized in the domains of theorem and concept. What is seen is a concrete particular is seen as something understandable. The understanding is still implicit. For me the particular is an example; for her it is still a concrete—though somehow pleasing—particular, an intriguing fact. I led her along the pathway of my kind of analysis as far as I dared, hoping to help her build bridges into an adult world.

A mathematician's own understanding is extended only by active search, by being personally in charge. The mathematician can accept help from talk and print and can follow an argument if some of its turf is already shared. But the individual alone develops understanding. How does this translate into the childhood context? The major change, I believe, is that we must learn to share the childhood turf. A part of this can be at times almost adult, a thing of paper and pencil, of books, even at times, I suppose, of workbooks. For most children most of the time, the turf is different. It is the world of concrete experience, presentational rather than linguistically representational. In this world, the activity that leads to understanding is not yet separated from overt activity. It is directly perceptual and—a term of Jerome Bruner's—enactive.

In our own work, for such reasons, we have made ample use of the now-commercial concrete math materials and added others as we were bright enough to think of them: pegboard and golf tees for lattices and graphs and for Mary Boole's curve stitchery; many each of several shapes of geometrical tiles for tessellations and growth patterns; various looms for weaving (originally, *com-plications*); marbles for 3-D patterns; cards for making polyhedra; poker chips for graphs and patterns, etc.

An interesting fact about the commercial materials is that often their most appealing uses are those not intended by the designers. The Cuisenaire rods were intended primarily for arithmetic, but I have never seen children first use them for that purpose. The intended use is representational; they were, I think, conceived as examples of the little number facts of early arithmetic and the 2-D and 3-D extensions of these. They were conceived, in short, as new tools for the didactic teaching of arithmetic. What they get spontaneously used for, however, is presentational rather than representational; they are fine for building complicated and elegant patterns, some of which may happen, along the way, to raise some very nice questions of arithmetic or geometry. We assign a sort of figure of merit to these commercial materials, the ratio of their unintended usefulness to that intended. In these unintended uses, children show you some of the rich turf you have to learn. Natural materials—such as mud cracks and growth patterns—are often better.

It has been a great help and moral support to me in this work to realize that much of early Greek geometry and arithmetic can be developed by the use of Cuisenaire rods. John Trivett and his students found they could represent the sum of successive squares by a rectangle built of rods, but only if they combined three such sequences together. He told me that he then really *understood* why that algebraic formula has a six in the denominator! They had, in fact, rediscovered a theorem of the Pythagoreans, who also extended the method to find the sum of cubes. I gave these problems once to a class of students in an analysis course; only four solved them, using analytic methods. I regard such students as underprivileged. When you are first inventing geometry (or is this number theory?), you don't use standard methods. You have to develop your understanding.

One of the results of working in this style is that you get into mathematics, not just computational routine. The computation comes along, and quite a bit of it could be called practice. In finding tetrahedral numbers, the sum of successive triangular numbers, you can do a lot of sums before you see the pattern. And when you encounter those sums again in random-walk investigations, also after much numerical calculation, you are on the edge of a deeper understanding. I emphasize the computational aspect because it is, among other things, of some importance; but also because if you thought someone on the school board would regard your work as time-wasting play you could point with pride, inter alia, to the number skills.

My purpose has been to try to map a useful and plausible account of the structure of adult mathematics into the childhood milieu. If that doesn't work, something is wrong with the account itself. If it does work, it still may qualify the description of the structure of mathematics and mathematical understanding. If my interpretation of the story of Suzie— and we all know other such stories—is correct, we should look more carefully at the ways in which the domain of mathematics—which in some essential sense is discursive, symbolic, digital in its mode of expression—nevertheless is linked to that which is perceptual, presentational, implicit. Such a linkage is required, I suggest, by any account of the historical origins of mathematics or of its successful pedagogy. I think it is also needed in any account of later major developments within mathematics itself. If one traces the origins—the originals—of such development, one finds that they very often turn upon some fresh success in discursive explication of the perceptual and intuitive. Greek geometry surely depended on such an explication. Its axioms, once explicated, were "evident." The parallel postulate in particular is an explication of the perceptual symmetries of certain lines and angles, themselves defined by symmetries. Archimedes introduced novelty by his derivation of the hidden symmetry of the law of moments from the intuitive symmetry of the equal-arm balance, and used this as a new tool of investigation in geometry. Bernoulli appealed to the intuitive symmetries of gambling devices, and from this derived his famous theorem, probably the first major mathematical step beyond the practical lore of gamblers. Connected to the idea of groups and invariance, the symmetry principle became the basis for whole new developments in geometry and also in theoretical physics. Still more recently, it has legitimated the use of probability theory within number theory and in geometry itself.

If one takes such a series of examples of the way in which our understanding can sometimes be mathematized, one is—or can be—tempted to return to those older rationalistic philosophies that I have mentioned earlier. They reserved a place, at least, for the notion that at any given stage in its career the mind possesses some furniture that is in no obvious way simply the outcome of empirical induction, but which it can bring to any new experience as a means for reducing that experience to order, of reducing the apparent redundancy of experience. If one does not like the classical rationalism with its appeal to innate ideas, one can try the move initiated by Immanuel Kant and treated developmentally by Piaget.

If one is temperamentally suspicious of all such grand philosophical moves, however, there is another track to try to follow, more modest and in its own way empirical. The one example I have suggested is a kind of examination, from historical and contemporary sources, of the ways in which arguments from symmetry have contributed to the mathematizing of otherwise only empirical subject matter. I have mentioned examples from Suzie (and Euclid), from Archimedes, from Bernoulli and those who followed. I could also mention the many fascinating examples of symmetry and invariance that have been first postulated, in an apparently high-handed a priori fashion, by theoretical physicists and often enough (though not in every case) empirically confirmed. Rather recently, it seems, good formal arguments have been developed that derive the classical conservation laws from the symmetries of space. I don't understand these arguments yet, but they seem at first sight to be legerdemain, at variance with good old-fashioned empiricism. At any rate and in the meantime, this whole history seems to suggest something important about the process of mathematizing, at least one long and tough thread of continuity between what Suzie knew and the most recent higher development of some parts of mathematics and physics. I don't know how to assess this, although it would have delighted the hearts of the old rationalists. If they are wrong, we need to find some adequate account of such matters, one that among other things might be pedagogically important.

I think that in fact the old rationalists *were* wrong, though the standard empiricism is wrong, too. Even along the one line of continuity I have suggested there are incursions of novelty into the development of geometry—modifications of, extensions of, and attacks upon preconception. The most cherished intuitions, once axiomatized, are open to revision. This is very far from saying they are arbitrary; the intuitive symmetries can be played with, and new pathways explored, or the old symmetries subtly modified, as in non-Euclidean geometry. Some "firsts" are so important we should learn to be playful about them—but not before we understand their power.

NOTES

1. This chapter was originally published in *For the Learning of Mathematics* 1(2), 1980: pp. 15-19.

2. Edwina Rissland Michener, *The Structure of Mathematics*, MIT Artificial Intelligence Laboratory, A.I. Technical Report No. 472, 1978.

3. Henry James, *What Maisie Knew* (New York: Penguin Books, 1974), p. 32.

4. Qualifications to which I hope she would agree. Cf. Edwina Michener, "Understanding Understanding Mathematics," *Cognitive Science* 2, 1978: pp. 361-383. Compare David Hawkins, "Understanding the Understanding of Children," *American Journal of Diseases of Children* 119, 1967; reprinted in *The Informed Vision: Essays on Learning and Human Nature* (New York: Agathon Press, Inc., 1974), pp. 195-206.

– 15 –

Critical Barriers to Science Learning[1]

To investigate the ideas people have about mirror vision, I have sometimes asked subjects to imagine that one wall of the room we are
sitting in is a large mirror and then to draw, on a map of the room, the
direction in which they would look to see a given object "in the mirror."
If the object requires an oblique viewing angle I have found that subjects
draw a wide range of directions that cluster bimodally near two extreme
positions. There is a small peak clustered near the direction that geometrical optics requires (A in page 180 figure) and a larger peak near the
place defined by a line drawn perpendicularly from the object to the
mirror (B in page 180 figure). For this larger group of subjects, the mirror image of the object is apparently thought of as analogous to the
picture of the object pasted onto the surface of the mirror "where it
would see itself," or else the depth-dimension in the "Looking Glass
Room" is radically foreshortened in subjects' conception of it.

I have found approximately the same statistics with upper-elementary-
school children, elementary-school teachers, and two graduate classes in
the philosophy of science. About 15 percent cluster at the small, correct
peak, 50 percent at the other extreme, and the rest scatter in between. In
the two graduate classes, the 15 percent were mostly students in physics

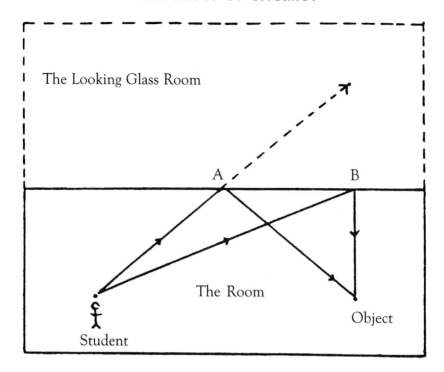

or mathematics, while the rest were from sociology, philosophy, psychology, or other disciplines. The prevailing adult conceptualization of mirror vision, and vision in general, is a gold mine of the kind of phenomena I want to discuss here.

This difficulty in understanding mirror vision illustrates a class of what I call critical-barrier phenomena, or simply critical barriers, in present-day science teaching. These phenomena are easily observed in many contexts and represent barriers to learning for at least a clear majority of precollege, college, and adult students. Though diverse in content, the phenomena share certain characteristics that I believe are uniform enough to sustain some reliable generalizations.

They appear early in any standard science curriculum, and are associated with extremely "elementary" science topics. I put the word in quotes because *elementary* is often taken to mean "easy" or "obvious," and thus appropriate to begin with. In fact, as I will try to show, some "elementary" ideas are exceedingly unobvious to those who have not yet assimilated them and are themselves only lately won in the history of science.

Elementary ideas are often deep. Students who fail to assimilate them must often come to regard them as barriers to entry into any further science learning. Often they give up, becoming frustrated and typically either dropping out or dropping up—that is, continuing the course and managing to pass it without any valued or valuable precipitate of understanding.

Some students manage to avoid this impasse. They may have had early, self-directed interests and talents; they may have had early successful teaching. They have already assimilated and can readily use elementary ideas that, for others, are formidably opaque. In the few cases where I have some recorded statistics, this group is small and typically consists of those who already have a conscious bent toward science as a career or an avocation.

My concern is with the general level of science education, not with the advanced education of scientific specialists—it is with the size of the base of a social pyramid, not the height of its peak, though I am mindful of the relation between the two measures. I believe that by carefully examining the class of critical-barrier phenomena it is possible to arrive at some conclusions about present levels of scientific culture and modes of science teaching at all levels except the highest. These conclusions do not automatically define remedies, though they suggest some. My concern is, rather, to use them to define goals for science education policies, goals that I believe are crisp and definite enough to suggest useful criteria for decisions about ways of working toward them.

In the following section I will further illustrate, define, and interpret the class of critical-barrier phenomena. In the final section, I will attempt to define policy goals I have in mind. Chief among these is the need for much more basic research, analysis, and experimentation. The experiments with mirrors, and others I will cite, were casually done and should be repeated with a more carefully stratified sampling of subjects. I believe I am describing only the tip of an iceberg.

FURTHER EXAMPLES OF CRITICAL-BARRIER PHENOMENA

My other examples of critical barriers come from contexts as rich and illuminating as the mirror difficulties. They involve size and scale, air and water, heat, and elementary mechanics.

181

SIZE AND SCALE

In some fifteen years of teaching a general physical science course for nonscience college majors, and in an equal period of time devoted to in-service teaching of general science to elementary-school teachers, I have found in both groups a marked conceptual difficulty in grasping, or gaining fluency with, the elementary relations between length, area, and volume. The frequency with which this difficulty appears (if one looks for it) is high; it affects something in the neighborhood of 80 or 90 percent of both groups. Reasonably patient explanation is no cure. For this reason, a teacher concerned to "cover the subject"—meaning, of course, to get through a textbook or promised outline—will become exasperated with students' disabilities or with the teacher's own inability to make such elementary things clear. The fact that patient explanation is no immediate cure is a hallmark of the class of critical-barrier phenomena. One *can* break through, but not easily or uniformly, and failure may lead a teacher to say that some people are just dumb. Another hallmark of the class, however, is that when the breakthrough does come with students they often have a high emotional release, a true joy in discovery: "Is that what it means?" There is often a marked change in later performance, as though a hitherto hidden secret had been revealed.

Returning to length, area, and volume (L, L^2, and L^3) and their relations to each other, both the resistance to explanation and the subsequent joy of discovery suggest that the student is not lacking in knowledge so much as he or she is habituated or addicted to some congenial alternative way of thinking. My work with children of middle- and upper-elementary ages reveals that with materials, time, and supportive interest they can arrive at these relations through honest empiricism—not yet firmly built-in, perhaps, but without confusion or conflict. Generalization may be difficult; it is one thing to see the scale-relations with larger cubes built out of smaller cubes and quite another to recognize them in the scaling up or down of spheres of different sizes, of irregular shapes of dough or plasticine, of models, or of dollhouses. That takes time.

Let me inspect this example in terms of what we call common sense or common knowledge. Length, considered in isolation, is no problem. But, though farming, carpet laying, and painting involve area, area is indeed problematic, especially in relation to length or as a characteristic of irregular shapes. "You can't find the area of a footprint; it's not a rectangle" is the supposition. An eight-by-ten rug is an eight-by-ten rug, but "is it really *eighty* square feet?" Volume (*pace* Piaget) is well understood in typical adult volumetric contexts, but *not* as L^3.

With such shaky foundations, the next steps—the principle of similarity and the elementary scaling relations—are quite inaccessible, and here I think I have support from history. The ancient Greeks had formulated these ideas. Euclid establishes them formally, though we would say awkwardly. Galileo was the first to elucidate their relevance to the properties of material things in his discussion of the strength of beams. Extended to include time and mass, they are implicit in Newton and were more or less formulated in nineteenth-century physics. D'Arcy Thompson in the early twentieth century was, so far as I know, the first to see living things as phenomena of scale. At about the same time, Lord Rayleigh elaborated dimensional analysis as a style of simplified physical analysis.

I mention this history because it shows how long a time was required for a simple and widely illuminating idea to show its full implications, even among the learned. At a relatively elementary level, the now-old P.S.S.C. (Physical Science Study Committee) physics text for high schools was written in the spirit of the scaling laws. Philip Morrison, one of its coauthors, gave the Christmas lectures at the Royal Institution of London on this subject for British schoolchildren some years ago. Ironically, the P.S.S.C.'s opening chapter on the scale of nature has been eliminated from commercial editions, apparently because these ultimately simple considerations that give rough intelligibility to the whole face of nature are still not considered to be physics.

I have used this example of a critical-barrier phenomenon of science as part of my introduction to the discussion of our failure to achieve a wide dissemination of scientific ideas and attitudes; it suggests that we are up against something rather deep in the relation between science and common sense—we are up against a barrier to teaching in the didactic mode that has hardly been recognized, or if recognized has been seen mainly as a challenge to ingenuity in teaching rather than as a challenge to a deeper understanding of human learning. It is the sort of phenomenon we tend to acknowledge only in a spirit of despairing humor or complaint; we tend not to focus on such matters as worthy of intellectual curiosity and excitement. Why *are* these difficulties at once so elementary and so abundant? That question is too seldom asked.

As a first step of analysis, I suggest that the verb *to learn* implies a time scale; some things can be learned in five minutes, while some come only on a long developmental time scale. It is the great merit of Jean Piaget to have emphasized the importance of the latter kind of learning, and his great demerit to have popularized the belief that what takes place is not really learning at all but an age-specific biological development independent of a society's educative potential; if an intellectual skill or scheme cannot be taught, just wait a while and it will appear anyway. This does not reflect Piaget's best thinking, but he has never repudiated it. The whole class of barrier phenomena I am concerned with here represents the apparent inability of most adults in our society to get beyond what would have to be classified as limitations that belong to early stages in the Piagetian taxonomy.

With respect to length, area, and volume, most adults have something in mind that is quite different from, and potentially conflicting with, the geometrical sense for invariance and variation in scale. They have a perceptual common-sense way of taking things as "big" and "little" without reliance on the analytically defined concepts of length, area, and volume. From the common-sense perceptual point of view, this is entirely reasonable. Immediate common-sense judgment is geared to a great variety of perceptual cues, and its practical reliability is typically very high. Since over the range of normal experience length, area, and volume are highly correlated, it is plausible that in the common-sense scale of big and little there is for most practical judgments of size no focal consciousness of any one of them. When challenged to measure the area of a footprint, most students, most adults, will suggest measuring *around* it, measuring its perimeter. The notions of perimeter and area are not clearly distinguished from one another.

In order to compel attention to such distinctions, there are many ways of using the principle of the extreme case, such as artificial or naturally occuring shapes with large perimeters and small areas, large areas and small volumes, etc. This is not only an exercise; it leads naturally to the many biological examples of adaptation to scale—the roots and leaf area of green plants, the elaborately branching lung tissues and guts of large animals, etc. In extending curiosity and experience to these ranges of phenomena—many of them everyday phenomena accepted incuriously by common sense—ordinary incurious perceptual habits of thought can be gradually cross-linked to those that are more analytic and more consonant with the newly extended range of experience for which the history of science is responsible.

A deepening grasp of the significance for scale of invariance and variation is one of the major gateways to the modern world of science. It represents the acceptance of an intellectual discipline upon the extraordinary subtlety and pattern-recognizing capacities of ordinary perceptual learning, capacities that are geared to the great variety and complexity of the human world and are basic to many forms of understanding and of art. In such perceptual matters, the axiomatic simplicity of geometrical scale is by itself almost useless; yet in extending our knowledge and intuition of the ampler world of science—with which our life as a society must be increasingly concerned—the failure to develop these axiomatic thought-habits and to link them fluently to perceptual modes will inevitably rob the mind of a power it increasingly needs. The failure to grasp the planetary impact of present-day activities and practices—the failure to understand what it means to scale an explosion by a thousand or a million—can be fatal to a society. Beyond that, however, it is a failure that robs most of us of the possibility of any aesthetic and moral framework within which we can understand and enjoy, and thus be full participants in, the great and problematic era our history has created. Without it, most of us will remain or increasingly become what Arnold Toynbee called a "cultural proletariat," in but not of the society we unwittingly constitute.

AIR AND WATER AND BEYOND

My third critical-barrier phenomenon of present-day science education has an equally interesting and varied history. It is the scientific conceptualization of the states of matter. Aristotle sorts them out as a matter of course, with fire suggestive of our "energy." Nothing is more obvious, and common sense has no immediate trouble with the traditional introduction to the elementary text that began with the sorting into solids, liquids, and gasses. Yet here again a large majority of "nonscientific" college students and adults develop deep difficulties. Let me begin with the atmosphere. We live in it like the fishes in water, and its very constancy as the medium of our life renders it mainly unnoticeable except for special circumstances that common sense recognizes in its usual piecemeal perceptual fashion. From history, again, we know that scientifically "obvious" things about the air are recent in any human consciousness. The Greek astronomers appear to have deduced the "ocean of air," a terrestrial mantle of limited thickness. This, I believe, was to explain the remarkable fact that an object so distant as the moon (whose diameter and distance they had fixed from the geometry of the eclipse data) was still clearly visible, while distant mountains, so close by comparison, were almost lost in the atmospheric haze. At any rate, Plato weaves a myth around the ocean of air. Yet the impact of the idea—otherwise long forgotten—came back to scholars full force only after Torricelli's and Pascal's investigations and the visible fact of the Torricelli vacuum.

The elementary-school science text or demonstration can prove that air has weight, and usually does so badly, with balloons, avoiding the consideration of the ocean in which the weighing is done, of buoyancy and density. High schools can evacuate a flask weighed before and after, and that is a neater demonstration; but neither demonstration can produce any resonance in a mind that is unprepared, as most are. The siphon is a familiar phenomenon on the edge of everyday experience, but for most of the group I speak of it is another of those mysteries that is only deepened by patient scientific explanation. Elevate the top of a water siphon to thirty-odd feet, a silly trick just beyond the edge of common experience; now the sense of mystery at the result will become palpable.

We often discuss, pro and con, the educational impact of television. News programs are characteristically climaxed by a discussion of the national and local weather, complete with those marvelous satellite pictures, accounts of new "systems" moving in or out, of the jet stream, of highs and lows. Some, at least, of those weather experts are indeed good meteorologists, but like many scientific experts they have long since forgotten what most of their audience does not know it needs to learn, the early slow steps by which they themselves assimilated a conceptual structure that meteorology already presupposes. I discussed this once with a TV weatherman, a good meteorologist indeed, and suggested some televised byplay with water barometers, rotating dishpan models of the atmosphere, and the like. He thought it would be fun but explained that time constraints required rapid speech and bare daily essentials. Yet today good climatologists are raising questions about man's own impact on the climate. What sense will these concerns make to intelligent citizens for whom the global circulation of air and water is unreal—for whom water evaporates and condenses only up and down, locally, and for whom, half the time, air is literally nothing, half the time reaches on to the moon, and all the time is mysteriously able to support the flight of airplanes?

Another aspect of this topic concerns the elements of biochemistry and their relation to the green cover of the globe. For thousands of years farmers have farmed well in the belief that their crops are earthy, pushing up from the maternal soil and somehow composed of it. Water and the heat of the sun were necessary, but the stuff of life came from below. That view, like some Jungian ancestral memory, still dominates the thought processes of most of us. It is only a few generations since there was a scientific realization that trees are essentially shaped from air and water, that sunlight drives their circulatory systems, that they grow from the outside in. A large majority of our adult students will tend to believe the opposite: that plants—grasses or trees—push up out of the ground, their blades or branches slowly rising, their newest growth in the center, and all this despite a forgotten course in biology.

At a slightly more sophisticated level are the ways of conceptualizing the interphase characteristics of things, the simplest and most accessible being the water-air or water-oil boundaries. The idea of a "skin on water," being of negligible significance on the human scale, is hardly credible to common sense, though intelligent discussion of it often raises up the phrase "surface tension" from some otherwise forgotten science lesson. This leads nowhere. Soap films are not credited with thickness, and their colors are rarely provocative. Here again scale is of the essence, and a sense for it is lacking. Evaporation and condensation—up and down—are believed in separately but are not understood as shifts of equilibrium in an always two-way exchange.

The missing ingredient here is any insistent realization of atomicity. Atoms are known about in the verbal store as something to be believed in but not as things to be imagined in conceptualizing everyday physical, biological, or chemical processes. The simplest reasoning of John Dalton, or even of Lucretius, is again a critical impasse for most; explanation only heightens the impasse, though such now-accepted terms as "carbon monoxide" and "carbon dioxide" are familiar.

Here again there is ample historical evidence of the recentness of such ideas and of the discrepancy or unresolved conflict between the scientific and the common-sense perceptual modes of thought and imagery. The everyday physics of qualitative change is still predominantly in the mode of the early Aristotelians and alchemists, a metaphysics of dispositions and qualities—thus drying, cooking, dyeing, melting, dissolving.

HEAT

Heat is another critical area, with temperature as associate. Thermometers are historically recent but are widely assimilated into the common-sense world. For most, what they measure is perceived as a refinement upon Aristotle and the medical investigators of Galileo's time. Temperature is a measure of "temperament" in human bodies and outside, of the balance between two principles called the hot and the cold. This ancient conceptual predilection is indeed a nice match to the animal temperature sense, which measures something that *is not* physical temperature, although correlated with it. What it measures is approximated by the scientific notion of heat flow, in or out, but at this level common sense conflicts with any notion of heat as substance, whether in the early form of "caloric" or the modern one of thermal energy.

This congenial notion of the hot and the cold conflicts with physics so long as we fail to recognize that here again the common-sense perceptual categories are inherently a different sectioning of experience than that of modern science, more discriminating for many of the purposes of common life but less significant as abstractly universal. This common-sense notion of the hot and the cold can be mapped into the scientific framework only after we know a great deal not only about physical heat and thermodynamics but also about the temperature sense, its linking role in the homeostatic regulating mechanisms of the animal body, and its purely psychological aspects. If the physical concept of heat appears to common sense as inaccessibly recondite, the common-sense notion of heat can be represented scientifically only by a complex and perhaps still incomplete model. The transformation from one conceptual domain to the other is not one-to-one, is not simple; it is one-to-many and many-to-one. Here as elsewhere, of course, the scientific concept has its roots in common experience and thought, but the steps by which it has evolved took two centuries or more of analysis and research, reaching into the last decades of the nineteenth century.

ELEMENTARY MECHANICS

Historically the earliest modern science, mechanics is beset by many similar pedagogical troubles. Even the idea of balance of forces, which goes back to the Greeks and is treated as a dull little subject introductory to the older texts, is in fact a fascinating thicket of these troubles. Archimedes derived the law of the balance from pure considerations of symmetry, by a style of argument that is powerful and deep, anticipating that of Leibniz and of modern theoretical physics; it is close to common sense, but not as a formal intuition, not for predicting the stability or instability of structures made of wooden blocks or Tinkertoys. Almost none of our subjects knew ways of thinking about the stability or instability of balance. In this context, the image of the center of mass lying at the bottom of a potential well or on top of a potential hill is radically difficult to reach. This does not imply the technical vocabulary I use; the image can be that of a marble in a bowl, but the linkage of analogy is unavailable. Similarly, the transition from Aristotle to Galileo in the discussion of motion is equally unavailable. For perceptual common sense, motion is always and inevitably in a medium; air may not be thought of as real, but space is definitely full, not empty. Mechanics derives Stokes's law for falling bodies by adding a resisting medium to Galileo's law. Common sense, like Aristotle, has to go the opposite route, but it abhors the distinction between air and the vacuum.

Mechanics is full of examples of things that for most of my subjects are unteachable by standard means and, if so taught, hardly go below the level of verbal discourse and artificial problem solving. They certainly do not become what Piaget called "schemes," penetrating to what Dewey calls "the subsoil of the mind." Common sense says that the wall does not push back on me when I lean on it; the flight of the airplane moves nothing downward to keep the plane up. Perhaps the textbook science is stored for a while in some basket of recall, but much of this learning can be unlearned; it is not irreversible.

An alert and apparently very lively college sophomore had what appeared to be incurable difficulties with the idea of the relativity of motion. The context was that of an introduction to astronomy, but homely examples were to no avail, nor was patient explanation after class. An imaginative tutor finally got the student to pirouette counterclockwise while observing the walls and ceiling, inviting her to imagine that she was stationary and the room rotating clockwise. After two or three trials, it suddenly worked, with the characteristic high emotional release. In this case the change was major and unusually dramatic; she moved from failing grades to a very adequate final paper on the kinematic equivalence relation between the Ptolemaic and the Copernican models of the solar system. It is not always so simple; students more often must relive such transitions repeatedly. A teacher for whom kinematic relativity is second nature may fail entirely to grasp the intellectual nature of this difficulty or to understand that explanation with diagrams, no matter how patient, inevitably presupposes the very conceptual transition it seeks to explain. Historically, we are reminded that even Galileo did not describe inertial motion with full generality of context, but only on a horizontal plane. The thought experiment that requires a body moving arbitrarily in empty space was apparently not available to him.

INTERPRETATION

It seems evident that in considering these critical barriers we must avoid a confusion of *levels* in learning. In many cases less obvious than those discussed above, verbal structures are often received and in some ways assimilated by students. These structures may be returned on examinations or even applied to the solution of simple problems, but what has been so learned does not prove retrievable or applicable in new situations, especially those arising outside of class or in later years. The loss rate of isolated knowledge transmitted in science classes is often about equal to the rate at which the knowledge is gained. The partial recognition of these problems is very old, probably as old as formal instruction, but somehow they have not been brought into sharp focus.

It is not appropriate to discuss here the psychology of educationally significant learning, for which in fact we have no widely received and powerful theory. It is, however, appropriate to distinguish between learning conceived of as the reception, retention, and recall of verbally coded and transmitted information, and learning understood as the development of intellectual habits for *transforming* sensory or verbal information to bring it into congruence or conflict with prior general knowledge or belief. The critical-barrier phenomena suggest that it is this latter kind of learning that has failed to take place. If such matters have been taught in a superficial way—verbally transmitted, momentarily understood, and retrievable as fact but not transformed into tools or disciplines for further learning—then loss or burial is unavoidable. A teacher who had been taught about the conservation of mass, in high school or college, could maintain without conflict that a terrarium sealed for seven years now weighed more than when she had planted and sealed it "because the plants are bigger." She could be reminded of her earlier learning, but only very slowly did she acknowledge, with final delight, the logical quandary involved.

I have deliberately emphasized the prevalence of learning failures of the most elementary kind, but such failures also occur at higher levels, even among the scientifically learned. The very high energies of cosmic rays were for a long time regarded as a prime mystery. Only two or three decades ago, Enrico Fermi pointed out that dynamic equilibrium between stars and free atoms in space would imply even larger cosmic-ray energies than those observed—the principle of equipartition. Suddenly, as a result of Fermi's observation, the question was reversed: Why aren't the cosmic-ray energies larger? In a popular television program on man-powered flight, many fine technical details were mentioned, but no one thought to dramatize the simple fact that even a bird geometrically scaled up to the mass of a human being couldn't fly. The difference between a bird and the man-powered Gossamer Condor is of a piece with the anatomical contrast between mice and elephants. These two examples are at very different levels of scientific knowledge and sophistication, but the latter was as unavailable to the learned of three centuries ago as was the former to those of three decades past.

I have emphasized elementary examples for several reasons. First, they are commonly overlooked prerequisites for even the kind of basic scientific culture we deem necessary to life in our present world. Second, what is elementary from a scientific point of view was often unavailable even to the learned of a relatively recent past. "Elementary" should not be thought of as meaning easy or innately understandable. A sense for powerful elementary ideas is not the beginning of scientific knowledge but is typically a late product of its evolution. Individual learning does not have to recapitulate history, but history can tell us a lot, commonly overlooked, about the dimensions of the learning and teaching tasks we face.

A third reason for my emphasis is to combat the commonly received notion that widespread scientific education and culture are increasingly problematic because of the vast increase in scientific knowledge, which allegedly requires specialization beyond any layman's possible understanding. But the power of even simple scientific ideas, fully mastered and enjoyed, can make the scientific world-picture intelligible overall and in first approximation, and that is the level at which I believe we have mostly failed. How else can we understand the prevailing level of PR about something called the neutron bomb?

Since the immediate purpose of this chapter is to propose a definition of goals sharp enough to suggest directions of search and research into means of achieving these goals, I think it is proper to emphasize still further the distinction between the two levels of learning mentioned above—the "verbal structure" level and the level of true conceptual understanding, of easy insight. It has been the historical aim of science both to extend our experience and to reduce it to order, these two aspects being always interconnected. The ancient astronomers—early Greek or pre-Greek—extended their experience by carefully mapping the sky and its motions over centuries. At some point this suggested, or allowed, the strange notion that Earth was not an indefinitely extended cosmological boundary but a thing, a body, perhaps a sphere, poised in space. This was proposed as a fact that fit all the data, but it was much more; it was a reduction to order of many otherwise unrelated astronomical phenomena. But this new order conflicted with commonsense intuition, which required a universal cosmological up and down. The conflation of these two ways of thinking created the uneasy question about why *the* Earth, now a body among bodies rather than a cosmographic division, didn't fall, and a question about upside-down inhabitants of the antipodes. Even Dante put the entrance to Hell *down* there. A century or two after the early Greek discoveries, Aristotle announced, with a lingering note of triumphant understanding, that "down is toward the center." The round Earth-body was not simply a new fact to be stored along with other facts; it was a fact that required a radical reorganization of the whole category structure of geographical and cosmological thinking. If it were taught merely as a fact, without appreciation of the need to help it penetrate into the subsoil of understanding and to rebuild the mind's category structures in the process, it would remain something merely bookish and abstract, to be entertained nervously and then forgotten. Perhaps children of today can grow up without this particular conflict of understanding, one that many of us can remember from our own childhoods. The educational time scale here, that of the transition from opaque fact to intuitive widespread grasp, has been at least a couple of millenia. We ought to do better.

This familiar example illustrates the nature of the distinction of levels of learning that needs to be developed. The relation between the two levels can be compared to that between a filing system and the contents filed in it. The invention of a filing system will in general involve arbitrary or conventional decisions, but to be efficient the system must in certain basic respects be adapted to the nature of the contents to be filed and to the range of uses the contents will be put to. As either content or use change, the system itself must be modified. Things previously filed together may increasingly need to be divided. Things previously filed in different categories may later be recognized as belonging together. Categories that once contained vital information fall into disuse and are cast out or put in some remote dead file. Input once discarded as inessential acquires new value and requires new categories. Librarians, bureaucrats, and scholars know all these problems and can at times show great ingenuity in reorganizing, cross-indexing, or even evolving dual or multiple systems—alphabetical, chronological, topical, cross-linked. In some fields, it proves possible to discard large amounts of useful information by the discovery of algorithms or other procedures for regenerating information on demand rather than storing it; in the simplest case this is called mathematics.

If one follows the filing system analogy one can understand at least some aspects of the class of critical-barrier phenomena I have been concerned to define. A great deal of formal instruction can be described as transmission of new information into a filing system—the mind of the student, whether child or adult—without adequate recognition that this information can be filed or retrieved well only if (1) there is some sufficient match between its implicit structure or order and the category structure of the receiving mind, and (2) there is some consonance between the uses for which the transmitted knowledge structure was evolved and those to which the student will be moved to employ it.

But the task is not easy. The prime agent of this needed reorganization is the learner, not the teacher. The description of a new way of filing information can itself be codified and transmitted to the learner. But the learner will receive this instruction as new information and initially be able to receive and store it only within his existing category structure. This is communication—teaching—at a level essentially different from what is needed, namely, assistance in adapting or reorganizing the existing structure. I believe that the critical barriers I have cited all illustrate the disparity between these two levels of teaching and learning, and the inadequacy of the first, by itself, to affect the second. The elementary mathematics of size and scale can be taught by instruction to almost all children and adults, as facts to be filed and retrieved, but its potential for helping to provide a new way of receiving and organizing information about the natural world is not thereby realized. Clearly we do not have to relive history in order to achieve such a reconstruction; there are short-cuts, even radical ones; in that sense, the reorganization of categories *can* be taught. In his famous dialogues, Plato blocks this problem by arguing that "ideas"—read here as "ways of organizing experience coherently"—are innate and cannot be taught but can only be brought forth by a kind of midwifery. In the end he admits, however, that such midwifery *can* be called teaching, though it is not of the didactic kind.

So it is with the other examples I have given. Rather than go over them in detail I will only observe that the characteristic resistance to patient explanation has a ready source in the radical difference between the two meanings of "learn" that I have emphasized. At some crucial junctures, language adapted to one category structure cannot be received within another without conspicuous incoherency and conflict. Trees made of air and water or heat as a substantial fluid are examples of this difficulty, as is the flow of momentum to the planet from an accelerating automobile.

It is not my purpose here to discuss the teaching art but only to emphasize the nature of one major problem to which such a discussion must respond, and from this to arrive at a statement of goals. There are, I believe, two closely related conclusions that bear directly on science teaching and the kinds of direction and support it should be given. Both are implicit in the foregoing.

The first conclusion is that much greater and more systematic attention should be given to description and analysis of the whole class of barrier phenomena I have illustrated and partially defined. If I am correct, this investigation is concerned with the ways in which relatively long-term, developmental learning is inhibited or advanced.

The second conclusion is that in giving full and unembarrassed recognition to these barriers and in probing for ways of overcoming them, we stand to make substantial gains in the art and theory of science teaching. To succeed well in helping more students overcome these barriers is to open doors for them into further learning, to help them find paths in which the growth of their scientific understanding is nearly multiplicative and irreversible rather than additive and reversible. However great the practical difficulties in pursuing greater understanding in this area or in effectively communicating it, the potential gain is large.

Both of these conclusions imply a somewhat different conception of science education than those that have traditionally prevailed, one that gives ample time and attention to the reconstruction of intellectual habits. If it is the aim of science itself to extend our experience and reduce it to order, it should not be the aim of science teaching to push rapidly beyond or to deprecate those pre- or nonscientific modes of organization that I have earlier referred to as common-sense perceptual, inherited through the common culture and reinforced by daily experience. The aim should be not to deprecate but to enrich and extend the common-sense perceptual. It is these modes that give us the middle-sized world, our daily world, from which science itself starts and to which it must return. The problem of goal in science education is not one that can be formulated in terms of some art of filling scientifically empty heads with new knowledge or new processes and attitudes; it is, rather, the problem of thinking about the kinds of bridges that can and should be built *between* the common culture and the much newer scientific subculture. This is a different and more basic problem than the derivative problem that C. P. Snow made famous, the gap between the scientific and the literary-artistic subcultures, between high art and high science.

POLICY

If the kinds of critical barriers I have spoken of are accepted at face value as reflecting an intelligent disposition characteristic of a large part of our adolescent and adult population, what is to be made of this? A traditional interpretation would be to suppose that the grasp of scientific principles inherently requires a level of intelligence well above average. Such a conclusion would foreclose without evidence a whole array of alternative explanations that need investigation—including the alternative that describes intelligence itself as a function of developmentally significant learning.

Another interpretation, opposed to the traditional one, is that the prevalence of such critical phenomena is a reflection of a deplorable average level of science teaching in our society. This was the predominant view of the curriculum reform movements of the 1960s in which I myself was a participant. One essential weakness of this view was not that it was wrong but that it incorporated too uncritically a belief that the reformers themselves knew, or could soon evolve, a cure. A great deal of imaginative work went into the reorganization of texts, the redesign of laboratory materials, the preparation of teachers' guides, and the planning of in-service courses for teachers. Many of the people brought into the reform movement shared the spirit of research and were determined to transmit the investigative spirit of science as a human activity and not merely its precipitate of organized factual knowledge.

The principal failure of the reformers, I believe, was their failure to extend that very spirit of investigation far enough to become radically troubled about the dimensions of the task at hand. I believe a good many of us were intuitively rather good teachers at our own academic levels, but we did not look hard to find the rare masters of the more "elementary" art we set out to improve. Some, indeed, spoke of preparing materials so good they would be "teacher-proof," thus at one step breaking the historical continuity of teachers and taught. Others were less arrogant and, recognizing the important role of the teacher, spoke about "retraining" or "retreading" teachers through summer workshops. This was less arrogant, perhaps, but not much less. Obliging teachers were indeed consulted, teachers who tried out the newly developed materials, usually at a stage when only minor revisions were possible. But the science teaching art itself as reduced to practice by the best teachers went largely unexamined. That was the essential arrogance.

Despite these severe limitations, gains were made in the intrinsic quality of subject matter and the emphasis on investigative style and methodology. Perhaps the greatest gain, and no mean thing at that, was a reeducation of some of those who took part in the venture and learned the hard way of some unanticipated dimensions of the problem. The most important neglected dimension was, I believe, that of the causes and cures of the kinds of failure I have tried to underline and emphasize.

John Dewey, in an old essay widely listed and widely ignored, shrewdly analyzes the conflict we are addressing. In "The Child and the Curriculum," and elsewhere in his voluminous writings, Dewey speaks of a needed reconstruction within science itself, aimed at increasing its permeability by the common understanding. The logical organization of subjects isolates them from wider use and relevance in daily life; it is useful for professionals who have already mastered the thought-habits it presupposes but not for entry from the outside. The needed reorganization involves the design of a working ambience for students that invites them to begin to practice the ways of thought that science has evolved. Such an ambience does not directly instruct students except in special phases; rather, it "directs by indirection." Dewey remains vague about the character of this needed reorganization or "psychologizing" of science. The style of teaching implied is not simply didactic, nor on the other hand is it passive, laissez-faire. But what it *is* he does not say.

In reacting against the didactic teaching of science as an organized collection of facts or a body of knowledge, Dewey led the ranks of those asking that science teaching be transformed into an emphasis on investigation by learners, designed to allow and motivate them to move toward a full use of the intellectual resources they have already developed, ready along the way to assimilate what others have already learned. But this last requirement was in the end neglected by the progressive movement that Dewey led and tried to redirect. The necessity of a *transmission* of substantive knowledge was overlooked in favor of the practice of scientific *method*, the process of inquiry. But the scientific method is the use of knowledge to gain more knowledge; if not much knowledge is organized and available for use, not much will be learned.

Reacting against this limited methodologizing view, others in turn have proposed a "concepts approach," a curriculum organized in successive phases, each explaining and illustrating some basic scientific concept. When the course is finished students will have risen to a higher level of scientific literacy and will possess a foundation for understanding scientific statements and explanations. This view, like the method view, represents conditions necessary but not sufficient. It suffers from the ambiguity or confusion, already discussed, of two very different levels of "learn" and "understand." Verbal transmission and reception focused on the use and illustration of scientific concepts are not the same as teaching and learning that succeed in reconstructing older thought-habits.

I believe that a careful analysis of the critical-barrier phenomena discussed above shows clearly that scientific thinking gains in power primarily through the recognition and assimilation of *generally* relevant facts about the natural world, but that this happens only when these facts have been assimilated in such a way as to ready the mind for new habits of thinking; when they have stimulated a reorganization of ways of thinking required by such general facts, they have penetrated into the subsoil. The examples of geometrical optics, of atomicity, of the transformations and interactions of the states of matter, all imply the substantive dependence of even quite elementary scientific thought-habits upon accrued scientific knowledge. What has been wrong with traditional didactic instruction has not been its emphasis upon the transmission of factual knowledge but its neglect of the developmental preconditions for genuine and productive assimilation of this knowledge. There is a time for didactic teaching, but it is a time that presupposes that thought-habits which can accept, store, and retrieve for new uses are already developed or developing. Optimal teaching must, therefore, be both diagnostic and nurturing.

I have sought to sharpen this emphasis on diagnosis and nurture by insisting on a wide class of critical-barrier phenomena associated with students' entry into the world of science. These are epistemological phenomena widely prevalent but typically glossed over or too superficially recognized by teachers and *their* teachers, even by those whose scientific knowledge and comprehension is by ordinary standards quite adequate. I have tried to underline the often surprisingly elementary levels of scientific knowledge at which these phenomena appear, and to suggest that the very concept or stereotype of what is elementary needs serious reexamination in the light of closer historical and epistemological investigation.

I repeat that these phenomena are closely associated with an essential characteristic of science—with both its history and its continuing commitment, the commitment to extend experience *beyond* the range of common experience and to find *new* ways of ordering this extended experience that will in turn be tested by, modify, and enrich the common understanding. The old-fashioned term was enlightenment. Our society is committed technologically, aesthetically, and politically to exploit and further explore many of the new dimensions of experience that science has made accessible, and yet our common culture is not adequately tuned to this commitment.

I suggest that this whole class of barrier phenomena needs wide and cooperative study and research and that such a focus should represent a major policy direction. As a philosopher of science and an amateur in science with a considerable range of elementary teaching experience, I have had the good fortune to stumble onto many of these phenomena. I have become sensitized to their prevalence in the student and adult populations, and have confirmed my otherwise perhaps idiosyncratic emphasis on them by frequent informal shoptalk with other science teachers. I do not believe the ideas I have tried to organize in this chapter would have come to definition without occasional success in the science-teaching art itself; an art in which I have learned much from others more deeply involved in that art than myself. The art is essential to the research. Yet this sort of consensual evidence needs much additional support or modification from more highly disciplined research. I believe that the history and epistemology of science has much to offer such research by way of suggestive conceptual framework and analogy.

Once a barrier phenomenon has been observed in the course of teaching, it is often possible to investigate it further by means external to the classroom. Such investigation can in turn contribute to the refinement of teachers' own diagnostic skills. But an investigator who is also a teacher has access to other sorts of information hard to come by outside a tutorial or classroom environment. This is the evidence of success, the evidence that a diagnosis has been correctly matched by the nurturant provisions a teacher has made on the basis of diagnosis. Failure is evidence also, and in teaching it counts equally as it leads to revised diagnosis and fresh provision.

For the above reason, it seems urgent that the research I recommend should not be too often or too long detached from the teaching ambience. If my analysis of barrier phenomena is at all correct, significant teaching success in helping students overcome such barriers has a time-scale intrinsic to it that is not that of the ordinary laboratory or the journal article, though it can fruitfully involve them. This means that skilled and insightful teaching is indispensible to the research, that the normal academic boundaries between teaching and research must be broken down.

Clearly such research must be highly interdisciplinary, combining resources from philosophy, from developmental and cognitive psychology, from those deeply versed in subject matter and in its history, and from practitioners who teach—the last-named being especially crucial to the investigation needed. I would suggest, finally, that in the course of such research the history of science education itself, in philosophy and sometimes in substantive detail, could fruitfully come under review. I would anticipate that studying earlier curriculum development efforts could contribute to this research, but the research should not be aimed prematurely at providing better teaching strategies, better curricula, or better supporting materials. It should be research aimed at producing greater understanding, stimulating wide discussion and a wide multiplicity of practical trials and developments. Like many other teachers, I have views about what some of these trials and developments would be and have been a propagandist for them. Here I have put such views aside in order to emphasize that we need a rather radical reconstruction of our own ideas about the nature of science and of effective science teaching. The common sense of teaching experience is where we must start; we simply have not extended it far enough, nor do we yet know how to reduce it to order. I offer the critical-barrier phenomena as a major clue and a promising start.

NOTE

1. This chapter is an edited version of a paper written for the Directorate for Science Education, Division of Science Education Development and Research, National Science Foundation, 1980. It was commissioned during the course of a study attempting to define needed research into the area of scientific literacy.

– 16 –

Science for All Our Children: A Perspective[1]

In celebrating the life of Robert Oppenheimer, a man who was a powerful teacher, I wish in this chapter to examine some needs of our institutions of education, in particular those wherein we can examine the roots of human development in our society, and the nourishment we provide, or fail to provide, for its improvement.

Robert Oppenheimer's whole life, in the several parts he played, brought him to a vivid awareness of the intensity of change in our present-day world: as a student in the United States and Europe between the wars, during the revolutionary development of quantum mechanics; as a California professor during the European turmoil of Mussolini, Hitler, and the Spanish Civil War; then as first director of the Los Alamos Scientific Laboratory, with its portentous history. Then he was director of the Institute for Advanced Study, aware of and helping sponsor extraordinary growth in several different fields.

But the military world still dominated his attention. As some of you know, Oppenheimer had believed that the nuclear explosives being developed at Los Alamos should be used as a weapon in World War II— so that their nature and portent would be indelibly written, and lastingly understood, worldwide. This terrible but one-time use should not be a nationalistic assertion of American invincibility but a kind of mathematical proof of impossibility: that its very destructiveness made it unusable as a weapon among great warring countries, a weapon in some disastrous World War III. To Oppenheimer, the human control of nuclear energies altered the very nature of the world. It would—if we could learn—teach us that such great wars as our century had known were no longer within the range of intelligible military planning.

So Oppenheimer carried on that commitment from Los Alamos, becoming a persuasive advocate of international openness in all matters of nuclear technology and policy. Making many forays into the political turmoil of postwar Washington, he paid the cost, tragically, of having created too great a disturbance within the circles of then prevailing military policies and ambitions. The world was not yet ready to understand that its nature had already changed.

During the following years Oppenheimer wrote an essay—probably first a talk—in which he spoke of the high rate of change in our society, sketching the many novelties we are simultaneously confronted with. I think that essay was a mirror of his life. The central novelty among all the others, he said, is the sheer acceleration of novelty itself. Our cultural traditions do not adequately prepare us to face this new world, he said; or define the need for more steadfast ways of thought and action than they can easily provide. This great fact of novelty should be at the center of all our concerns, our education. That need is what I wish to focus on.

If the roots of education are like those of a tree, Oppenheimer was a person who moved easily among the upper branches, whether of physics or philosophy or politics or poetry. When we go down to the roots of this same tree, to education, we must have in mind some very different and always diverse talents, those of childhood. These talents are innate in our kind, and our new world needs especially to value them, but also to inquire, more deeply than in the past, into their power and their fragility. This is a kind of inquiry, so far, that we support very superficially, either for children or for those who teach them. In learning how better to support and protect children's talents, I believe we can find the beginnings of that more stable human character and culture that Oppenheimer was thinking about.

Because I pay homage to Oppenheimer, I am bound to talk mainly about science, and science education, linked, as they always should be, to children's talents for the arts and humanities. Here many scientists can make serious contributions—perhaps are already doing so. It is an avocation in which they, together with science amateurs and our children's teachers, can join. It is the job of finding ways and topics that can attract and engage many children and youth, rather than—as often at present— repel them.

REPERTOIRES FOR TEACHING

Here is one place we can help. Teachers need to have decent-sized repertoires of good matters to investigate, with good and often impro- vised lab equipment. Computers should be in evidence, but never as convenient substitutes for live subject matter. All of us need to learn, through work with children and teachers, the siren songs, the entryways into good subject matter, avoiding at all costs the hard outer shell pre- sented by most textbooks and their traditions of teaching. There are many topics that we scientists and teachers and children can find, ex- plore, and enjoy, inviting the investigative curiosity and talent of chil- dren, and helping reawaken that of teachers who ask for help. To find good topics, you have to try them out, and more than once.

Most scientists, I believe, are persons who have enjoyed that kind of work, or play, in their own childhoods and youth, and who were there- fore prepared for the routines and rigors of the kinds of didactic coursework that, for most other students, has simply turned off the light. But as successful students in formal coursework, most scientists think that the way they learned is the right way, forgetting the earlier, more self- directed work, or play, that first got them into good subject matter on their own. The amount of formal instruction we can fruitfully assimilate depends on our age and our own previous learning. But even at the most advanced levels the best teacher is the student, helped in one way or another to take over the direction of his or her own learning.

I hope my many earlier examples will have suggested something of a style of early science teaching that Victor Weisskopf once formulated for teaching at the most advanced levels. The aim, he said, is not to cover the subject, but to help students uncover some part of it. I repeat here a story told by an eminent theoretical physicist of the following genera- tion. He studied, he said, under three masters of the trade: Eugene Wigner, Enrico Fermi, and Weisskopf. Wigner wrote everything out, in correct detail. Fermi gave marvelous simplified analogies that got to the heart of things. But he always had written everything out first, for himself, to be sure his analogies and imagery were correct. Weisskopf also gave appealing intuitive explanations, but sometimes got the formalism wrong. Then the students had to work it all out for themselves and correct his errors. "That way," my informant said, "you really learned physics!"

And now, in that same spirit, I come back to children's science. From a good deal of practical experience—my own, and others'—I have evolved a kind of framework for all of this that is quite different from teaching specialized advanced subjects, where some measure of logical order and sequence is essential. For children's first entries, formal order is not crucial: no "prerequisites" are assumed or required. This framework is emphatically not what gets called a "science curriculum." The word *curriculum* is from the Latin, meaning "a little racecourse." In fact, what I have worked at, and propose, is the exact opposite of a curriculum: it is a scheme for *choosing* science content that invites children not to race but to stop, to browse and ruminate wherever they, and we who help them, find the grass is greenest. I shall give examples of some topics I have found that attract both children and teachers. Others will find others, and we ought to pool our findings into a kind of super-repertoire.

THE SCHEME

The many things of nature that can prove to be open to children, for observation and experimenting, can be mapped on a grid of three dimensions, all potentially important. Where a topic lies on this grid can tell you, the adult, pretty much how it can be made open to children's investigation and what it can contribute to the understanding of nature, to scientific literacy for a new generation.

SCALE

The first dimension of this grid, or map, is a scale of the size of things. Many properties of things, their dominant characteristics, depend on size, from atoms to galaxies. The importance of this scale for education has been dramatized by a Dutch teacher, Kees Boeke, in a little book on the size of things. The subject was enriched more recently in a video and book by Charles Eames and Philip and Phylis Morrison, *The Powers of Ten*.[2] For early science, one needs to know only that this quite elementary domain can be a very live beginning of deeper understanding.

Before I discuss the general scheme, let me tell a story about a group of elementary schoolteachers in a summer course. They could just as well have been a group of fifth-graders, and Galileo and Borelli would have loved it. Like many elementary teachers, their education had been—except for some forgotten "survey" course—remote from science, but they were eager to learn. We began with talk about some obvious changes, with age, of human body proportions. Painters and sculptors of the early Italian Renaissance often represented the body proportions of infants and small children quite wrongly, resembling those of adults. In East Africa, we once learned, children are old enough to go to school when they can reach over their heads and touch the opposite ear. My teachers and I got on to these and other ratios, like those of arm-spread to girth, to height, etc. Finally, we got to the pressure on our feet, the ratio of our weight to our foot area.

You can't predict, but sometimes a topic like this takes off and makes you put aside your so-called lesson plans. The idea of area was first a trouble. Some had to discover—to my naive amazement—that area is not the same as perimeter. Some finally outlined a foot on graph paper and counted the squares, a rather tedious method for finding area. The best was to outline the foot on cardboard, cut it out, and weigh it against a standard square of the same cardboard.

One teacher raised an innocent-looking question: What about pressure on the feet of a cat? A dog? A cow? I said, "Wow!" She and a friend got us the data, since she lived on a farm. Then in a next-door class they had some gerbils. What about them? Technical problems, but they were overcome. Then what about elephants? We had none handy, but a children's encyclopedia gave us weights and photographs from which foot area could be estimated. And finally, what about a brontosaurus? That took us to toy plastic models, and some expert's estimation of body weight.

It had been fun, but what to do with all these dozens of data? We could make graphs, of course, but the teachers soon recognized that the changes in scale ruled out ordinary graphing. They had never heard of logarithmic graphs, much less the log-log kind. So one teacher, then others, introduced the idea: plot both axes, of weight and area, with the indices 2, 4, 8, 16, . . . etc. Such a graph accommodated both the gerbil and the dinosaur! We should have sent the resulting paper to *Nature* for publication! Two parallel straight lines, one for soft-footed animals, one for hoofed. In both cases, a scaling law: pressure on feet increases as the square root of weight! Ideas these teachers, all college graduates, had never encountered—length, area, and volume in relation to each other; then pressure and above all, the exponential arithmetic—all came into play from a simple experiment in finding the area of a human foot.

I now come back to space scale with a discussion of some needed geometry. Some twenty-six centuries ago, a Greek story tells us, Thales learned how to measure the height of a pyramid in Egypt. He compared the length of its afternoon shadow with that of his own. Shadow triangles later gave Greeks the size of the Earth, the size and distance of its moon, and a very difficult estimate of the distance to the sun. That last estimate was very inaccurate, but you can also say it was only off by an order of magnitude; enough to give them the idea of the heliocentric solar system, a millennium and a half before Copernicus. Some older elementary-school children have happily learned to use the method of Thales for finding the heights of trees, tall buildings, even nearby hills. It was Edward Teller who suggested to me that my students could find the size of the Earth by timing the sunrise on our nearby mountain. We did it, and with the moonrise as well—to within 10 percent accuracy! For older children, there are various ways of tracking the sun—graphing its path in the schoolyard, for example, by tracing the shadow, on a flat surface, of the tip of a pole. Why is it blurrier at the tip, not near the base? When you have traced the shadow's tip through the day, and then week by week, these graphs provide good mysteries to solve. The school's terrestrial globe belongs outside, set to the school's latitude and longitude. It becomes a scaled-down mimic of the Earth for solar time, latitude and longitude, time zones, and the paradox of the dateline.

Two or more schools at different latitudes can compare shadows at high noons and find the size of the Earth in the way the old Greeks did. We might follow their lead also by finding the size of the moon and getting its distance, when the Earth's shadow crosses over it in an eclipse. If you cheat a bit and use the almanac to find the precise time when we see the moon half in shade, then use a good sextant, could you improve on the Greeks' estimate of the distance and size of the sun? We didn't try.

How far any child or group can get into solar-system astronomy, or beyond, one shouldn't decide ahead of time. A telescope will help, even spy glasses. Astronomy can help children make a first empirical step to get the sizes of things, and at least the lower edge of the astronomical time scale, from months to years. The rest is inevitably, properly, rather bookish, and I leave it there. With shadow geometry we can get at least to the moon and sun, and begin to bring much more into focus.

For scale changes of animals and for the shift from our daily world to the solar system, we need something that does not change with scale. Euclid did not prove that earthly and celestial shadow triangles had the same geometry; it was only assumed, as an axiom. We all assume it, intuitively, whether you go down or up in the scale of sizes.

This idea of geometrical invariance can grow with children's interests. One of the grandest examples, of course, is the making and using of maps. For some older ones the plane table can produce first-rate geometry: with one or a few distances measured, and many sightings, you can draw many more angles and distances. They come free; you don't have to measure them.

A profile map of New Mexico is a monstrous scale-transformation of the state itself—abstract to be sure, with some conventions. Science itself is rather like that. But the textbook, like the finished map, tells very little about the labors that produced it, or the limits of its reliability. I offer two examples of a different kind for the geometry of scale: a skillful older brother was building a model sailing ship, and asked his younger sister, now Frances Hawkins, to go find some thread or string that would scale correctly for the ship's rigging. She was at first deeply puzzled and uncertain. What did "scale" mean? When she finally understood, the memory lasted as a reminder of scale relations that children's lives are full of; for her own early life as a mistress of dolls and their possessions, and her later life as a teacher of young children. Their intuitions of scale are still coming to order, and it is a phase of development she sees celebrated in the draftsmanship of a great artist such as Picasso.

The invariance to scale we name after Euclid lies well within the range of children's learning, as do amusing violations of it in their play, as with a doll twice too big for its chair. As they grow older we can help them go up or down in the scale of sizes.

On the microscopic scale there is much, to begin with, at low powers: fluff from the floor, sand grains, then pond plants and animals, the anatomy of flowers, whatever young children bring. At higher powers, crystals of salt or of metallic silver, and growth rates, of course, are magnified as well as size. For the macroscopic scale of things, I would of course suggest some astronomy. But first, the second dimension of the map.

The second dimension of my map is that of time, of duration. I remember still vividly when my own childhood friend, Berlyn Brixner, now of the Los Alamos laboratory, stopped the wings of a hummingbird with his new Leica camera. Since then, I know, he has invented cameras that were considerably faster.

For long times as well, such as those of human history, or the still longer history of nature, human imagination and invention also needs stretching. I tell the story of one fine teacher's patient encouragement. Her fourth-graders literally invented their way back to the origin of a nearby limestone stratum in which they had found some fossils. A visiting geologist had said it was about 30 million years old. Their invention used a roll of paper tape. After several false starts, they found a way. On successive ten-foot lengths of the tape, they represented the successive powers of ten: first ten years, then ten decades, ten centuries, then millennia, and so on.

The tape went more than halfway around the classroom wall. The children had in fact invented our standard powers-of-ten notation, and by the time they got into it the limestone was almost forgotten. They worked hard, by questioning and reading, to fill in the tape as they unrolled it; first year by year, with personal histories; then decade by decade, for family and community happenings; then some American and earlier history, then past the beginnings of agriculture, and into an ice age. In these ever-grander steps, they soon got up to the limestone's age, 3×10^7 years. Two more decades of tape could have gotten them to the Earth's very origin. This can be heady stuff, and our schools dismally fail to provide even the beginnings of it.

For both the time scale and that of size, we need an arithmetic that children can easily be taught and almost never are. My two examples, so far, must be generalized. Most children, even when they grow up to be teachers, are robbed of the joys of large-number arithmetic. It is tens in the first grade, hundreds in the second; add them, subtract them, multiply, divide, in endless monotony.

There is a splendid children's fantasy by the Bohemian author Wanda Gaag about an old couple who loved cats and accumulated them, logarithmically, to cover hillsides: "Cats and kittens everywhere; hundreds of cats, thousands of cats, millions and billions and trillions of cats."[3] A four-year-old in my wife Frances Hawkins's nursery school was standing one day on a hillside, and pinched a cattail he was carrying, watched the tight package of its micro-seeds explode into the wind, and exclaimed, "Now we can say, 'Hundreds of cattails, thousands of cattails, millions and billions and trillions of cattails!'"

With the right enticement, children will join you in estimating the number of beans in a jar, leaves on a tree, even the number of sand grains in the sandbox, which is about the number of stars in our galaxy. The great Archimedes took time to explain to the young Pharaoh a way of estimating the number of sand grains that would fill the whole universe known to astronomers of his day. Many quite young children, unstressed by poverty, neglect, or violence, may show their enjoyment of the natural numbers by looking for the "biggest number," and find infinity instead.

For both size and duration, then, large numbers require the arts of approximation. Educational investments in large numbers can provide one broad avenue to these great arts. We can first ask children, and their teachers, for guesses as to the number of leaves on a large tree. More than a hundred? Less than a million? Are you sure? Can you narrow the bounds? Count branch by branch, then count the branches. Wait until fall, and count them on the ground? Don't wait, but measure the shadows instead! Other methods can now evolve.

Is this a trivial subject? It can be just useful arithmetical fun. But wait. The leaf area of a tropical forest can be estimated from samples of the noonday darkness on its floor. Water transpires through all those leaves at rates we can approximate. For the ecologist, these playful exercises can get us into deep understanding about the vitality of rainforests. Children's simple investigations can come near to scientifically sacred ground, and teachers' own education should prepare them to recognize it.

FUNICITY

The conception and the definition of this third dimension of the grand map of natural phenomena owes its origin to two friends from wartime Los Alamos. It came in a discussion I had with Victor Weisskopf, theoretical physicist, and Cyril Smith, metallurgist. Richard Feynman had said somewhere that all the sciences were becoming historical—even, he feared, physics itself. Weisskopf was probably thinking of DNA, Cyril Smith of his beloved Chinese bronzes. For the degree to which anything embodies a record of its history, we looked for words. We tried *historicity* and *historicality*, both words awkward and misleading. We tried *hysteresis*, a relevant word, but from a different root and too narrow in meaning. Then simultaneously the two remembered a story by Jorge Luis Borges, the Argentinian writer of fantasy.[4] "Funes the memorious" was a man who could forget nothing that happened to him, and had to sit quietly, for long periods, in a dark room, to avoid some terrible overloading of his memory. So, half seriously, a new technical term was born, *funicity*. I propose it, seriously, to honor the two of them.

I offer the following examples for the application of funicity. Two sodium atoms may have been born in different stars at different times, wandered on different courses ever since, and happen to end up in my left thumb. But they are identical, marked by none of their postpartem history. Atoms are low on the funicity scale. If there are immortal quarks, they have funicity of zero. At the opposite extreme may be such things as animal brains, their whole character a record of biological history and individual experience. We all remember William Blake's poem "The Tyger," "burning bright, in the forests of the night." Then the poet asks, "In what furnace was thy brain?"[5] The answer, we well believe, can be traced through some billion years of history. The physics and chemistry do not explain it; they only make it possible.

Within biology, at least, there is a well-defined physical measure of funicity. The great twentieth-century discovery, going back to the biologist Aristotle, is the concept of information, the transmission of form. The twentieth-century idea was first developed by Leo Szilard, later by Claude Shannon, then applied in biology by George Gamov, Frank Watson, Francis Crick, and others ever since. When a nucleic acid gets copied in a cell, or a specific protein constructed, there is always a cost of the information, a selection of one next unit to be put in place, from among several that would otherwise be equally likely to go there. This selection has a free-energy cost in coin of the physical real, kT, a constant time temperature, per unit of choice. For a whole organism, that is a substantial part of its food supply. Thus in the biological world funicity can have a well-defined measure. Another example: that a vast number of molecules on this planet are all left-handed, rather than a 50-50 mix, may only be possible because they had a single ancestor. So the principle holds for evolution as well as reproduction.

The chain of chemical reactions that produces carbohydrates in green plants, put with other evidence, writes whole chapters of biological history from the time of the simplest cells to those of later times. In the macroscopic world beyond biology, the same principle holds, though qualitative comparisons are all we can afford. Parallel scratches in some high-mountain rock virtually demand the age of glaciers. The craters on the moon would be absurdly improbable without the hypothesis of a multitude of impacts from beyond.

In using this dimension for my map of good science for children, one can think of an array of topics that span the scale of funicity but are accessible to the classroom scales of space and time. At the high end of the scale they range from classroom and schoolyard biology, down through some local geology, and near the low end to purely physical phenomena of air, earth, water, and fire. The abstract idea of funicity, of course, isn't for children; it simply helps us define a place for the worlds of biology and geology. We need that idea, or something like it, as a reminder that there can be a strong link between the worlds of high biological science and those of children's enjoyment and understanding, their potential literacy. Our rapidly changing world needs both.

For the high end of the funicity scale there are, again, a few classroom stories. These center around the work of a biologist and teacher, Ronald Colton. Through his influence, teachers working in our center in Boulder, Colorado, equipped their classrooms for the nurture and growth of green plants—little more, at first, than a table under a low-hanging fluorescent fixture, supplied with potting soil and water. Their classroom work could start, for example, with what he called "supermarket botany." A trip to the market invites children to pick anything they think might grow: seeds, roots and tubers, even leaves and stems. The very thought is surprising to some, that given soil and water and light, so many things we buy as food will respond by growing. Such work can open doors into the world of the green planet—that our urban world, to its peril, can too easily ignore.

Some teachers already have a love of gardening, and only need recognition that this art belongs in schools. Others need help, and there are usually helpers available, green-thumbed friends and neighbors. One immediate contrast with other sciences is that of tempo, which is set by the plants themselves, not the experimenter. Corn grows rapidly enough from seed, and its growth is easily graphed. The very young need have no numerical measures. But Miguel Savage, later from Africa, suggested they match the successive heights of their corn with strips of paper, which they simply kept in bundles. Some time later he asked these six-year-olds to compare the growth of their respective plants, and they had trouble with the matching. He then gave each child some cards and paste and suggested they mount their strips. The result was the invention of several kinds of graphs. One bar graph reached the edge of the card too soon, so the rest of the bars were mounted horizontally. Another child mounted her strips in clockwise fashion—simulating polar coordinates, perhaps.

The textbook told a group of junior-high students something about photosynthesis and something called a "starch test four" to demonstrate the plant's ability to manufacture the carbohydrates necessary to growth. They wanted better evidence, and designed an experiment that would show, if successful, that you can grow up a corn plant, in the dark, by feeding its leaves with sugar! Some botanists I've told don't want to believe it.

Common-sense ideas about plant growth can die hard; one of the great facts of plant life, of course, is that they don't grow out of the ground, but into it, feeding on water, air, and sunlight. Humans have farmed for many millennia, but the recognition that air is a plant food still defies most people's common sense. The first surprising demonstration was as recent as two centuries ago, with Stephen Hales.[6] We can start by balancing half of a fresh cabbage against the other half, the one wrapped in plastic, the other open to the air. The loss of weight in the unwrapped half is dramatic; you have to keep moving the other closer to the fulcrum of the balance. For young children, evaporation itself can be an important discovery. A large part of the plant, at least, was water. I don't know how to take it from there, to repeat Hales's experiment or improve on it. I think I might cook the dried cabbage to death in the oven and examine the black stuff that is left. Could that have come from the ground? If I burn it, a small bit of ash will be left, from the Earth? What happened to the rest?

For the long-time scale of funicity there are great geological chapters in the book of nature, some accessible to children. Every locality, even in cities, has some text that children can begin to decipher. Here at the end, now, we are near the great Jemez caldera; three hundred miles south the Trinity test site sits in a great rift valley where crustal plates once spread apart, leaving behind many other relics of fire and brimstone. Erosion is everywhere, and there are plenty of rocks for study. The great problem here is not the geology; it is how to get children comfortably and safely out of the classroom. Indoor geology, for example with stream tables, can be a lively subject for many ages, and I leave it there.

NOTES

1. This chapter was originally presented as the Oppenheimer Lecture at the Los Alamos Scientific Laboratory in 1995. The Oppenheimer Lecture is an invited annual lecture given each year on the anniversary of the Hiroshima-Nagasaki bombings. This year was the fiftieth anniversary.

2. Philip and Phylis Morrison and the Office of Charles and Ray Eames, *Powers of Ten* (New York: Scientific American Library, 1982).

3. Wanda Gaag, *Millions of Cats* (New York: Coward-McCann, 1928).

4. Jorge Luis Borges, "Funes the Memorious," in *Labyrinths: Selected Stories and Other Writings,* James E. Irby and Donald A. Yates, eds. (New York: Random House, 1984).

5. William Blake, "Auguries of Innocence," in *Great English Poets: William Blake* (New York, Clarkson H. Potter, 1986).

6. Stephen Hales, *Vegetable Staticks* (London and New York: Macdonald & Co./American Elsevier, 1969).

– 17 –

Human Equality: Matters of Philosophy, Questions of Fact, Practices of Education

TRADITIONS[1]

As is true of other deep issues, that of human equality waxes and wanes, appears and disappears like a comet, to return again in some later epoch. Like a comet, it has been altered by every perihelion passage.

Egalitarian ideas are very old. From the first written history they appear, and reappear throughout the evolution of urban society, though usually in a form conditioned by the universality of gross and obvious inequalities. Marcus Aurelius the emperor and Epictitus the slave saw themselves, saw all human beings, as equally sparks of the divine Zeus, and as equally condemned to the inequality of their stations and duties. In Hindu traditions, human beings have an equal, ultimate destiny through the cycles of reincarnation, their differences corresponding to unequal progression along that very long road.

Jesus of Nazareth had taught that the meek would inherit the Earth. Saint Paul announced the equality of all, though he could imagine it flourishing only in the country of Heaven. Three centuries later, in Saint Augustine's lottery of divine grace, all persons—not just those of self-proclaimed virtue—have, so to speak, equal a priori probability of being chosen to fill the heavenly thrones left empty by the expulsion of Satan and his followers. The Lord's ways are mysterious; mere humans cannot predict them. Since Augustine, many revivals have reaffirmed that belief: the meek and lowly have opportunity for salvation as great (if not perhaps greater) as do the aggressive and powerful. Condemned as we all are by Augustinian original sin, we have no basis in wealth or station, or even in manifest moral virtue, to regard ourselves as favored recipients of that grace or election that might tip the divine scales in our favor.

In both Buddhism and Christianity, this acknowledgment of an ultimate equality is coupled to another basic idea, without which it is empty: that of fraternity. Salvation is not only (as in most forms of mysticism) an individual matter. Rather, those who might be saved or redeemed would choose to stay behind to help the less favored.

In these religious contexts (as in Plato's allegory of the cave) there is an acknowledgment that the equivalence or equality of human beings is to be conceived not as we stand in isolation from one another (where their de facto inequalities may be manifest enough), but rather as an equivalence that has vitality and meaning within the domain of their interchange and mutual influence. The idea of fraternity, therefore, carries with it the acknowledgment of human diversity. In the domain of our interchange, because of our very differences, we can always learn. The great seventeenth-century philosopher Baruch Spinoza puts it simply: "Nothing is more useful to a human being than another human being guided by reason."[2]

If we wish to look deeply into the processes of education, these ideas—equality, diversity, fraternity—can discipline our thinking, and to this discipline I will return.

Though it was grandly proclaimed in the French and American Revolutions, the recognition of this linkage is much older. An ancient Hindu formulation states it simply as the law of sympathy: *Tat tvam asi*, "That art thou." Other ways of saying it have come around. John Donne referred to the individuals of our human kind as "books open to one another." He added then his more famous injunction, "Ask not for whom the bell tolls, it tolls for thee."[3]

The linkage of equality and fraternity is a clue to any adequate discussion of human equality. Thus in the rise of modern secular thought, the axiom of equality continued to serve as a standpoint from which the wide spread of social inequality was to be faced as a problem, explained;

not as a fact of nature, but as consequence of our history to be condemned or somehow justified. Thomas Hobbes and René Descartes had announced equality as an axiom, Hobbes in political theory and Descartes in the theory of knowledge.

But the great figure, coming not long before the French and American Revolutions, was that of Jean-Jacques Rousseau. His *The Social Contract*, appearing in 1762, was the first substantial development of the principal of government by consent, and fueled the ideas of both revolutions.

In American history the Founding Fathers laid down the principle of equality as an axiom in a sense they had learned from Euclidian geometry, a common first principle: "We hold these truths to be self-evident . . ." They took it as a precondition of rational political existence and of constitutional law. Yet even as a principle, our constitutional equality was never unqualified. It clearly did not exclude economic or other forms of inequality lying outside the sphere of governmental power, as that power was implicitly defined by the Declaration of Independence and the Constitution. To the profound and silent embarrassment of our founders, it did seem to exclude the institution of African slavery, which flourished indeed for three-quarters of a century thereafter.

Amid all these qualifications and compromises, Rousseau himself was set aside—with some embarrassment. In his earlier *Discourse on the Origins of Inequality*, he had announced that all human inequalities had originated only when savage societies (we say "neolithic") turned to agriculture and the private ownership of land. This argument, that human inequalities were historical inventions, rather than inherent in human nature, came, I believe, from Europe's still-new acquaintance with America's neolithic societies, long gone, in fact and in imagination, from Europe. In this *Second Discourse*, politically ignored at the time, Rousseau anticipated careful accounts that came nearly a century later, to which I will return. Still, as our government and our economic system has evolved, limitations on political equality have been repeatedly up for debate and revision. Extensions of egalitarian logic and sentiment, going beyond eighteenth-century laissez-faire, are still central in our debates, embraced or denounced.

In the face of gross economic differences, equality can clearly become an empty principle, as in Anatole France's famous jibe about the magnificent equality of the law that forbids the rich no less than the poor to sleep under bridges or steal a loaf of bread. In all historical versions of the axiom of equality, indeed, its assertion (even when linked to that of fraternity) has a polemical appearance.

So the axiom of equality has survived not as a truism, but as a claim, a challenge to be set somehow underneath what is obvious, the generally established inequality—in status or achievement—of persons; their moral or intellectual capabilities, their powers over others, their station in society. So if the axiom is accepted, then it must follow that differences in human powers and capacities—excepting gross birth defects—arise from the ways in which those powers and capacities are, from birth, educationally developed and economically supported or neglected.

According to modern classical thought, then, the origins of inequality are historical and institutional, and lie in the specific kinds of nurture or deprivation, and of status, that a society affords. Born diverse, but equal in fraternal potentiality, we can become radically unequal through differences of station, early nurture, or education. Institutional inequality perpetuates itself as new generations appear. Accepted, the axiom of equality must require an increasingly egalitarian commitment to break the chain that ties each generation to the inequalities of its past.

It is a very strong statement to call the principle of equality an axiom, "self-evident," as our political ancestors did. What is the real power of this axiom? It supports, we must remember, the whole system of legal rights and obligations in democratic society. But beyond that it keeps open a system of possibilities that otherwise—by all kinds of arguments— might be put down. And why is this so important to ethics and politics? It is like the scientific axiom that every phenomenon can be understood; i.e., to deny it shuts off vital possibilities for social invention and reform. The axiom is grounded, I believe, in the fact that we are deeply social creatures—as deeply social, it may seem strange to say, as the ants or bees or termites.

The social insects are small automata that can signal, and respond to signals, with no powers of choice. We, on the contrary, are endowed with a new kind of bonding to each other, at a vastly higher level. We are individually helpless, on the one hand, without the means and products of livelihood widely shared; including shared intelligence, invention, and enjoyment. Voice to ear, and hand to eye, can transfer the mind-code of thinking from one to another, as though by neural tissues connecting our very brains—including even those of anarchists and libertarians.

But how well can these ideas—of equality and fraternity—be sustained, now at the beginning of the twenty-first century? For this I need to discuss one more period of our historical background, the most recent and the most important. A century and a half ago there began to appear a new perspective on the discussion of human character, and so a further return of the comet—of debate about equality. It brought interests of a new kind into examination of the classical axiom; there began then a discussion of human equality and human differences from a more historical, evolutionary, and now for the first time, purportedly scientific context. It began, of course, with that great adventure led off by Charles Darwin and Alfred Wallace.

Twelve years after *The Origin of Species*, Darwin published *The Descent of Man* (1871). To place our human origins in the same great stream of biological history—as we now can estimate, at least three thousand million years of it—was for many Christian theologians, and congregations, to commit a profound heresy. It seemed to describe us as just one more mammalian species, though to be sure a quite novel one: a species that had the power, among many others, to investigate its own history. Here was a biography that seemed at first reckoning to leave no place for the human soul, for the spiritual riches and agonies of human life, for questions of freedom and destination.

After Darwin, however, there began to be pieced together the story of a uniquely human evolution, an odyssey far more ancient than Homer's. It was based on new sources of historical evidence, and has led to new disciplines: anthropology, ethnography, archaeology, etc. Lewis Henry Morgan, an American contemporary of Darwin, described an advanced neolithic society (*The League of the Iroquois*, 1851). This new-world society was of a kind, as I have said, long since vanished from the memories of Europe. Rousseau had, indeed, invented the story of such a society, out of little more than his own fertile brain; here, in America, was the reality. I should mention also the last vestige of one much later neolithic world, destroyed by our own westward expansion. So early communication could have facilitated the evolution of the language-capable brain, while development of that brain could have stimulated the (cultural) evolution of language.

Almost a century later, informed for the first time by the accumulation of reliable archaeological evidence, Gordon Childe's *Man Makes Himself* (1947) recognized and gave careful definition to an essential characteristic of our species that distinguishes us as a uniquely social creature with biological capacities for a new kind of evolution, essentially different from, and eventually far more rapid than, that of genetic variation and natural selection.

The capacities for invention and transmission within a human society, with its language-borne world, altering institutions and technologies, have thus led us to a kind of evolution that cumulatively alters our ways of livelihood and of association; but with essentially no late changes in our genetic makeup. Societies have sometimes remained essentially unchanged for millennia; but they can be altered radically in far shorter periods, as in Rome from republic to empire, and in modern Europe and America. Tools have long been "extra-corporeal and detachable," transferable from one to another, master to master, master to apprentice. Human language, essentially unlike other modes of mammalian communication,[4] is equally transferable, and children master it early. What is said by one can be repeated by another: extended, qualified, rejected, evolved in discussion; and "put into practice." Language, Hegel said, is the public consciousness. And only through language does consciousness itself become a shared and public fact, as does, then, the domain of reflection, when habit is perturbed by uncertainty, and uncertainty is resolved, sometimes, by observation, reflection, and debate. So also there appears a world of questions that can reach beyond resolution. Geological history leaves us little to tell of the subjectivity of early humans, but from a few remnants we can tell much, as from early painting and sculpture; and from the sheer fact that they undertook the burial of their dead.

Through storytelling, through the discussion of ends, as of means, there can evolve both new ways of working and of living, new divisions of labor, of human intimacy, of association or alienation. So it is that our hands-on, minds-on human talents, socially shared, have made possible a kind of evolution wholly new to the planet.

The continuity of history has required, of course, an early period in which cultural change, though potentially far more rapid than the genetic, was paced and at first limited by the slower biological changes that it must in turn have continued, selectively, to stimulate. The evolution of our unique language capacity is a major case in point. The linguistic brain could only have evolved, on Darwinian principles, under "selective pressure" from the biological utility of increased powers of communal action; but languages themselves, culturally evolved, must at first have been limited by the more slowly developing linguistic brain.

We know, of course, very little about that early period of our history during which the two modes of evolution—communication and technology—must have proceeded slowly together, before culture change could accelerate; before it could begin to distinguish us so sharply from the rest of the primate world. From archaeological evidence, to date, this period of rapidly accelerating culture change seems to have begun only a few tens of millennia before the present, whereas the period that goes back to our earliest (*Homo sapiens sapiens*) ancestry, as identified so far, is at least fifty or a hundred millennia.

In the fullness of time, there have thus come about new means of livelihood, new social groupings, new variations of human character and, on the dark side, new modes and means of intergroup conflict. And our uniquely human mode of social life has required, and enabled, the evolution of morality, the discipline that surrounds and makes possible our capacities for deliberative choice; choice not of means only, but of ends; and so of morality and its ongoing debates. It is just here, in this account, that the evolutionary story can join that of the Judeo-Christian and other religious traditions, when Eve and Adam discovered they were on their own; and when, in consequence, God expelled them from the paternal estate of His garden.

What we can say, in retrospect, is that while the biological capacity for human education—for culture transmission—is genetic, a result surely of Darwinian evolution, education itself has been the vehicle, as it were the cultural genetics, of our history, our character. Corresponding to genetic mutations that make biological evolution possible, cultural evolution depends upon the inquiries and inventions of individuals. Like biological mutations, most individual or small-group deviation from prevailing norms of culture are lost in the hubbub of social existence. Here or there some invention, some burst of wisdom or folly, gains a following, but is soon to disappear. More rarely, with favoring circumstances, it catches on, and enters the mainstream of social existence. Of these social changes, most perhaps are anonymous, the record lost; only a few give personal names to the pages of history. But some innovations happened repeatedly, in different parts of the world—for instance, the beginning of agriculture.

Over fifty or seventy or a hundred millennia, at least twenty times those of any written history, these at-first slow but accelerating processes of cultural evolution have made possible the transformation from many small bands of hunter-gatherers to our own now-massive world society. In Darwin's time, even the most learned Europeans or Americans knew only what had come their way from three or four centuries of exploration, trade, and conquest. They duly observed the cultural diversity scattered around the planet, from hunter-gatherers to farmers to those of an urban life far older, though technologically less sophisticated, than their own. These observations gave Europeans support, quite typically, for claims of self-superiority. After the conquest of Mexico, the Spanish Church had to be cajoled by devoted missionaries to decide that the people of Mexico were human and deserving, therefore, of Christian charity.

Also in Darwin's later time, cultural differences were assumed, often enough, to reflect different degrees of "progress" along a single track of purely Darwinian biological evolution. The genetic differences among present-day "races," where these differences can be at all reliably defined (skin color, hair, minor body proportions, etc.) are one measure of the amount and kind of Darwinian, genetic changes the human species has undergone in those millennia back to their common ancestors. After the domestication of cattle, for example, some Darwinian variation and selection of the digestive system made it possible for the tribes involved to consume cows' milk and cheese. They could then migrate and take live cattle with them, while others found such migration impossible. The most extreme case of human isolation is that of the native Australians, unknown, apparently, to the rest of humanity for many millennia. Their talents—linguistic, artistic, even mathematical—are only recently gaining adequate recognition, beginning to overcome immigrant Eurocentric prejudices. Yet even their great cultural divergence can be grasped and—when we are open to it—enjoyed, by the rest of us.

But the traditions of hereditary superiority die hard. In Darwin's times—those of the American Civil War—T. H. Huxley, one of Darwin's great supporters, viewed Lincoln's Emancipation Proclamation with alarm. It was morally correct, he had to concede. But he viewed with alarm the suggestion, what he called an absurdity, of any implication of mental equality between Africans and Anglo-Saxons. In that same lecture, Huxley found it equally distressing that some persons should equate the intelligence of women with that of men.[5] Even gentle Darwin could reflect some of Huxley's then-fashionable racism, though it was not to his taste.

One should not speak too gently about the attitudes and beliefs that clothed the European domination of the rest of the planet, from the sixteenth century; imposing on much of it the institutions of colonial misrule. But neither should one underestimate the depth of such attitudes and beliefs, as they pervade the language, the unwitting presuppositions of our own culture. Huxley's pompous declarations, about Africans in particular and women in general, shocked many of his time. But the same attitudes lie buried, like a permafrost under the good soil, in the minds of those of us far more enlightened. Among the European-American missionaries who had lived close to peoples of other cultures, some few came back as converts themselves; not to another religion, but to the depth and humanity of other cultures.

It is a kind of historical joke to say that these returning missionaries became the first anthropologists, messengers that would expand our sense of humanity. Yet even when enlightenment has come, more of it may yet be needed. At the turn of the century Ishi, the lone survivor of a band of neolithic tribesmen in northern California, threw himself, near starvation, on the mercy of a local community whose sheriff communicated with A. L. Kroeber, anthropologist at the University of California. Ishi then came to live out his life in the university's anthropology museum, becoming a friend and teacher of the Kroebers and their associates, giving public demonstrations of Yahi life and culture. In her marvelous account of Ishi's life and accommodation to his new life,[6] Theoddora Kroeber remarks that her husband was so shaken by the plain story of Ishi's life, by the high levels of human cultivation and talent it revealed, that for a time he contemplated resigning from his own profession in protest against its ignorance and deprecation of "savage" humanity.

Our very vocabulary is loaded against the recognition of Ishi, "the last savage in North America," a chance friend of these Euro-Americans. Was Ishi "civilized"? Yes! But no, the Romans gave us that word from *civis*, "city," along with the implied superiority of city-dwellers over "barbarians," the neolithic people of Europe. Was Ishi a "cultivated"person? Indeed he was; but no, the word derives from the arts of farming. Ishi's people had not learned to farm, but they had long harvested acorns, for bread, from the oak forest.

THE AGE OF MEASUREMENT

In any present-day discussion of human equality and fraternity we must, then, acknowledge the traditional European (and Euro-American) traditions of self-superiority. In the not-remote past they have justified conquest and colonization, and they still linger on the dusty bookshelves of that "civilized" mind. These traditions led to an intellectualized interest that grew stronger in the late nineteenth and twentieth centuries. This interest was in the background of attempts at a scientific study of human differences, individual or racial, and some of these studies brought a new challenge to the axiom of equality.

Thus Francis Galton, a cousin of Charles Darwin, was among the first to examine his own society with statistical measures.[7] His statistical studies led him to—or supported him in—the belief that differences in human talents are largely hereditary. Not surprisingly, such a belief has seldom been questioned by the elite in any society. But in Galton's case it came from careful study, disclosing the high frequency with which Englishmen of recognized talent were the children of men also talented. Not distinguishing between biological and purely esucational inheritance, Galton came to the conclusion that such talents were hereditary.

So far as I know, Galton did not concern himself with racial differences, but his notions provided obvious support for beliefs that were already abundant in the Western world. Once in my own youth (in 1928) I was taken to meet a well-known American anthropologist; his popular book on evolution had been on a shelf in our house. Among other pictures it contained a prominent one of busts then in the Museum of Natural History, purporting to represent three stages of human evolution: the ape, the African Negro, and the European! Even a half-century after Lincoln's proclamation, it was, evidently, a "scientific" belief still prevalent in some learned circles.

Perhaps unwittingly on his part, Galton's conclusions helped strengthen a claim, in the name of science, that later became the basis of the eugenics movement.[8] This movement has been embraced by many, more or less innocently. Far less innocently, it provided what was alleged to be scientific support for the general notion that creative human beings appear mainly because they share the genetics of creative ancestry. It was used, with fully evil intent, as justification for the anti-Semitic and anti-Gypsy horrors of Germany's National Socialism.[9]

Quite independently of such corruptions, there has been a long history of Galtonian studies and controversies. These studies have attempted to sort out, as neither Galton nor the eugenicists did, the relative contributions of "heredity" and "environment" to the talents of maturing youth. The intelligence quotient (IQ) and related measures have given answers of a kind to the questions Galton failed to ask. The statistical distribution of such measures of human intelligence—as defined by the usual IQ test scores—has seemed to confirm Galton's general belief, while correcting his omissions.

Thus "intelligence"—roughly speaking, is the age-rate at which a large multiplicity of different matters, available in the culture, have been learned. Differences of IQ score, on average, are least for identical twins; greater for same-sex fraternal twins; greatest for pairs of persons not closely related. A statistical model of such results is based on the "best fit" discovery that about two-thirds of these scores—high or low—can be attributed, on average, to the degree of shared immediate ancestry, while the remaining one-third is imputed to whatever is not congenital, hence called "environment."[10] Such findings have been statistically refined over three-quarters of a century. They are, of course, welcomed by those of surviving eugenic persuasion.

But this relation is not a fact of nature; it is an artifact of IQ-test statistical methods. In point of fact, the relation of an infant's heredity—temperament, ways of responding, etc.—and her or his maternal and material environment, is not "additive" except in extreme cases of deprivation. It is, instead, one of interaction, not addition or subtraction. Nor does this interaction cease with advancing age. At each new stage of development the same environment can affect different children differently; different environments, likewise, can bring similar development. Within obvious limits, this *complementary* relation can continue through any life of learning.

Here is an example of the "additive" fallacy: African Americans do poorly, on gross average, compared to European Americans. An argument, from the above interpretation of IQ scores, depends for the appearance of validity on this notion that heredity and environment are additive in their contribution to intelligence. Thus one treats African-Americans as though their "heredity" was that of some shared parenthood—rather than their obvious social heredity of a shared history, from slavery and continuing ostracism, segregation and hardship. Such a view is put forward, however, in apparent ignorance of studies that give important evidence about children in our society who are from *reluctant minorities*. These children, with of course notable but too-rare exceptions, have been correspondingly reluctant attendees in our schools. With high absenteeism and dropout-rates, low academic commitment and IQ-test scores do indeed follow.[11] One should mention another minority that tests well *above* the U.S. average: the Oriental Americans. They are, I believe, youth who want to be here: an eager minority. To this whole discussion of Galton and the tradition that has evolved after him, I wish now to say farewell. But one last comment is in order.

The tradition of the IQ and related psychometric techniques has continued, and blossomed, in three-quarters of a century, despite the fact they offer very little in fundamental scientific contributions about human development, and very much as part of the normal educational administration of our schools and colleges. What began as a psychometric investigation of "intelligence" very soon grew into an administrative tool of our educational establishments, all the way from tests of "kindergarten readiness" to the SAT tests that can so powerfully govern college admissions. Rather than adapting our education to the given diversity of our young, we tend to filter out those who do not fit the patterns of a preconceived meritocracy.

DIVERSITY AS CHALLENGE

The understanding of equality that I wish now to explore may seem more complex, and more interesting, than that of the classics; or that of my first conclusions (in agreement with the classics): that our gross inequalities of status and abilities stem, for the most part, from the poverty or wealth of our nurture and are rarely congenital; that they have originated in the radically uneven dynamics of our social and political history; that they represent a grossly unequal investment in children's human potential.

What is still missing from that account, however, is an explicit consideration of the kinds of equivalence or equality we can and ought unqualifiedly to approve of, and so seek to realize. First, equality need not be sameness of talents or character; in fact it must depend on our individuality, and so as much on the diversity of character and talent as on their similarities. Try to imagine a society of persons literally indistinguishable from each other (identical in the manner, say, of sodium atoms). I think it is clear that such members would have no need either to belittle or to applaud each other. Perhaps the grimmest version of this thought experiment is to imagine a society consisting entirely of duplicates of oneself—undeniably equal.

A second image, equally attractive, is that of a society in which just one person is in all ways superior to the others, superior in the rather strong sense that for this supreme individual there is literally nothing to be learned from others, nothing not already experienced or understood or mastered, through association with any of the lesser multitude. In his zeal to describe an ideal embodiment of all the human virtues, Aristotle in his *Ethics* came perilously close to this in his image of the ideal "great-minded" man. By very definition, this paragon has nothing to learn from the lives of others, nothing to emulate, to be intrigued or challenged by. A canny philosophical critic could thus immediately create a logical paradox, pointing out that in claiming all excellence for the "great-minded" one, Aristotle was inevitably extending the definition of virtues to include one that his hero lacked: the great art of learning from others.

One aspect of this art—of learning from others—is implied in Immanuel Kant's principle of obligation: that we should respect others as ends in themselves, never as means only to our own ends. As we violate Kant's principle, we cut ourselves off, and those we only exploit, from the human sources out of which all social well-being arises. The subject is vital, so let me quote from the other philosophers. I mentioned Spinoza earlier, on the idea of equality. Here is the full passage:

> There is nothing more profitable to man for the preservation of his being and the enjoyment of a rational life than a man who is guided by reason. Again, since there is no single thing we know which is more excellent than a man who is guided by reason, it follows that there is nothing by which a person can better show much skill and talent he possesses than by so educating others that at last they will live under the direct authority of reason.[12]

But neither Spinoza nor Kant puts emphasis upon the importance of diversity in human talents and achievements. This diversity, as I remarked before, is what links together the ideas of equality and fraternity, lying somewhere between the Kantian respect for others and of the Spinozistic enjoyment of its fruits.

Here, therefore, I defer to John Stuart Mill, whose defense of political liberty was to argue for the tolerance and even the support of divergent perspectives, persuasions, and commitments. Such diversity can give robustness and stability to a society when it faces unexpected challenges. The same is true of biological species that possess a great amount of internal genetic diversity. They can adapt, or rather they are "preadapted," to environmental changes in which others cannot survive. Whatever may be the genetic diversity that arose from early human separations and migrations around the planet to different environments, the cultural diversity we now inherit is still greater. Our cultural profiles of talent and learning are likewise jagged and uneven. In this fact lies some of the robustness, in a changing world, that our welfare requires. What counts is a richness of preadaptation, a diversity that can help prepare us for an uncertain future. But of course, mere diversity is not enough. What counts for cultural robustness, as for biological, is a pool of cultural choices, not random variety. Thus have arisen new modes of knowledge, of artistic expression, of organization, of technology.

The deepest meaning of equality, as I have argued, lies across a domain of human transactions at many levels; we do not by nature outrank one another uniformly, around the profiles of our talents and achievements. Rankings will and should appear in this or that special context; some can be leaders and some followers, but by turns. Where universal rankings seem unavoidable, these may be regarded as symptoms of personal or social ill-health. Institutions that foster such social illnesses are therefore to be challenged. I have mentioned one example: our test-driven establishments of education, which can range all the way from "kindergarten-readiness" to SAT scores for university admission. If one wants to measure human abilities, it is necessary that the logical structure of the measure should match that of the things measured. One of the less interesting examples, as I have already suggested, is the IQ-test score. To an observant teacher of young children it tells nothing new, and offers no guidance for work among the rich diversity each group of children can reveal and profit by. Discovery of special interests or talents can always be part of the teacher's duty and delight. But that art also includes, at best, a far richer discernment, both of possibilities and limitations.

To suggest how much more complex a child's profile of abilities may be, I print here a quite imaginary profile (in polar coordinates) of any one child's talents and limitations (see figure). Each radial line represents some interest or talent, weak or strong. Among fifteen or fifty, no psychologist, or no teacher, could actually plot such a curve. The idea of it

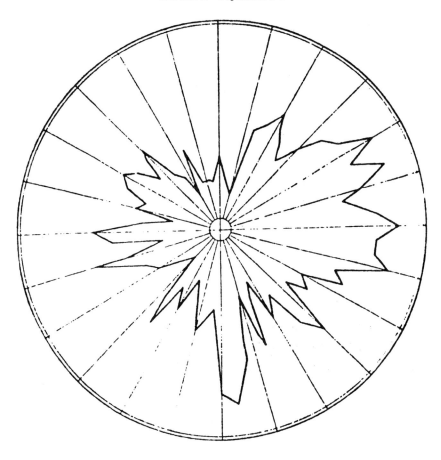

is simply a reminder that—when the right kind of social ambience is present—each child may have a special place, to be recognized by the others, and can contribute in some special way to their learning.[13]

This array of many conceivable measures cannot be reduced to any single aggregate measure without a loss of its essence. Any good measure of human abilities is thus a vector, a cluster, of different and interacting components, not a single all-important measure of worth that would provide a single important ranking. We all know, in simple terms, what this means, but I can illustrate it by a memorable story from decades past. We four parents, on holiday with our children, heard them, of ages six to eight, relaxing from their play and discussing their respective virtues.

They took turns in summarizing: Julie is best at telling stories; Tom (the oldest) is best at numbers; and Karen (the youngest) is best at catching frogs.

In human affairs generally, both large and local, equality surely means that everyone must have some place, some voice. This is a pronouncement that should, of course, accompany our classic demand for "life, liberty, and the pursuit of happiness." Of the essence of democracy, it is, oddly, missing from our American litany. Its absence allows a bit of political nonsense, which is that we should all just be let alone to engage in "the pursuit of happiness." Yet one has no voice if one is silenced or excluded. That was Mill's concern. One also has no voice if one has nothing to say, or if the voice only plays back what the ear has recorded. And this is where education comes back into the argument, especially when it is about children far less fortunate than the three I spoke of.

The discernment of special talents, and of individual needs, can begin in many ways: from a child's stories or drawings, from participation or withdrawal, even from the fact of exclusion by others. Whatever the special talent or need, that child can potentially become a participant in classroom society, adding something to its resources. Gaining some special status in the eyes of others, children become genuinely members of the class. Good teachers can have many stories to tell about the ways in which individual children have contributed to the ambience of a classroom. Today, with the increasing knowledge of human genetics, of infant development and behavior, of the human brain, it becomes possible to hear the voices of science confirm what has long been grasped by devoted and observant mothers, nurses, and teachers of the young. There are stories that tell of redemption, even of apparently "feeble-minded" children, in a classroom ambience that gives values to their lives. For one remarkable example, I followed the two-year transformation of a "closet child" (IQ 40, expressionless, and with no speech) in the kindergarten of a young teacher, Frances Pockman.[14]

Such persons embody the prescience, literally the "pre-science," of what comes now from the disciplines that are exploring pre- and postnatal development. I would like to compare this "pre-science" with other examples we can find in history. From ancient times, soldiers knew and passed on much of the gambling art, calculating chances in games of cards, bones, and dice. It was from that background that the mathematics of probability evolved, from pre-science to science. There were metallurgists in the Middle Ages who knew much practical chemistry, while the learned were still tinkering with alchemy. Successful practice can thus precede and lead to science, and science can then extend the practice from which it grew, while remaining still open to further learning.

The wisdom of infants lies in their extraordinary developmental plasticity—child development is never simply growth along a predetermined pathway.[15] We are then in a position to reach beyond the traditional and still-persistent view of "heredity" as something merely helped or hindered somewhat by the overall quality of "environment," but largely predetermining the quality of individual accomplishment. But this is not at all to say that our differences, at birth, are less important than the old hereditarian beliefs have allowed. The newborn infant is already uniquely individual, already accepting or rejecting what is offered; not a tabula rasa, a blank slate on which a given "environment" will somehow, for good or ill, write down that infant's character. The entire course of individual development, instead, is essentially one of interaction with specific adults and other children in specific material and social environments. The outcome of each such phase of experience can then determine the direction and potential further development. And this development, again, may depend on restrictions and opportunities that surround it for direction and promise.

This relationship is as remote as possible from the notion that accompanied the old IQ paradigm, i.e., that human achievement is somehow the sum of hereditary and environmental "variables." It can be, instead, quite radically interactive. Such interaction can grow into a unique fabric of character, woven by experience on the warp of native character. Here I go back once more to Aristotle. Discussing humankind as a biologist—Darwin called him the greatest of all time—he commented on the greatly prolonged infancy of our species, as compared to that of others. It is, he observed, a condition necessary for the continuation, generation after generation, of our very existence as a biological species. He wanted to put the sheer fact of education into its biological perspective. Without education we humans cannot survive. He might have added that with bad education we survive badly.

The human being is the product, first, of biological evolution, from a distinct primate line that reaches back several million years to any ancestry shared with other present-day primates. Increasingly, along that long way we are also the product of cultural evolution, emerging at first slowly, from biological change. We are apt for learning, for shaping ourselves by it. And so the stories of our lifetime careers, measured only in years and decades, are tales as fully evolutionary as the others.

When they are free of hunger and pain, safe within their adult surroundings, infants show us that from birth they are already programmed for learning.[16] Aristotle knew that too, as had Plato, who represented it by a kind of myth. Plato was so amazed by infants' aptness for learning that he could only attribute it to knowledge they seemed already to possess, from some prenatal heaven. This idea has rattled around among philosophers ever since, that of "innate ideas." Infants' *aptness* for learning is the important fact.

The prolongation that Aristotle observed of infancy and childhood has been a kind of evolutionary change associated with cultural evolution going far back in human history. Biologists use the term *neoteny* for any developmental sidetrack that can branch from an ancestor species; characteristics of some early stage of maturation remain dominant, prolonged into adulthood. Thus our domestic dogs, of wolf ancestry, maintain many of the characteristics that wolf-puppies have, but later lose. So also we humans can maintain, through life, the early learning-abilities that our primate cousins more early lose.

But Aristotle had no conception of evolutionary change, except for a crude version he could easily refute. We can understand, as he did not, that the human neoteny, emerging from our long-ago primate ancestry, not only allows the ongoing reproduction of our present societies and cultures, but also for their changes—their responses, wise or foolish, to external or internal stresses and opportunities.

When we consider the sheer present-day fact that a new kind of world society is emerging from our still postcolonial habits, we must look not only beyond Aristotle, but beyond, as well, our present educational commitments, resources, and mistakes regarding the equality of human aptitude for being educated.

NOTES

1. Originally published as Chapter 1 of David Hawkins, *The Science and Ethics of Equality* (New York: Basic Books Inc., 1974).

2. Baruch Spinoza, *Ethics*, W. Hale, tr., revised by Amelia Hutchison Sterling, James Gutman, ed. (New York: Hafner Publishing Co), p. 244.

3. John Donne, *The Complete Poetry and Selected Prose of John Donne* (New York: Modern Library, Random House, 1941), Sermon LXXX, p. 241.

4. Several recent works reveal fresh perspectives and information on the nature and origins of human language. I list here three works: Steven Pinker, *The Language Instinct* (New York: W. Morrow and Company, 1994); Terrence William Deacon, *The Syboptic Species: The Coevolution of Language and the Brain* (New York: W. W. Norton); Steven Pinker, *Words and Rules: The Ingredients of Language* (New York: Basic Books, 1999).

5. T. H. Huxley, *Science and Education* (D. Appleton and Co., 1897), from the essay "Black and White," p. 66.

6. Theoroda Kroeber, *Ishi in Two Worlds: Biography of the Last Wild Indian in North America* (Berkeley: University of California Press, 1961; reprint 1976).

7. Galton's cast of thought and manner of inquiry can be caught in his *Heredity: An Inquiry Onto its Laws and Consequences* (London: Macmillan, 1885, and Gloucester, Mass.: Peter Smith, 1972), and his later reflections in *Inquiry into Human Faculties, and Its [sic] Development* (London: Macmillan, 1883, and New York: AMS Press, 1973).

8. "Eugenics" derives from the Greek *eu* ("good"), *genos* ("race," "descent").

9. Within only two weeks after Hitler seized power, the rector of the University of Berlin was replaced by another professor whose specialty was "eugenics." For firsthand background by a man who was living in the Kaiserhof Hotel, as was Hitler himself, see George Norlin, *Fascism and Citizenship* (Chapel Hill: North Carolina Press, 1934). Norlin, then president of the University of Colorado, was giving a series of lectures on American political life. This specific report is among his literary remains at Norlin Library, University of Colorado, Boulder.

10. Average IQ scores differ somewhat for American groups of different socioeconomic status. A classic study, affecting the belief that such differences are "largely hereditary," is that of Skodak, with follow-up studies. This first study was of radical intervention in the lives of "feeble-minded" orphans, normally doomed to institutional care.

The original and classic study was by H. M. Skeels and Skodak, "A Study of the Effects of Differentiated Stimulation on Mentally Retarded Children," *Proceedings and Addresses of the American Association of Mental Deficiency*, 1939, vol. 44, pp. 114–136.

A twenty-year follow-up study was "Adult Status of Children in Contrasting Early-life Experiences," *Society for Research in Child Development Monographs*, 1966, vol. 31, no. 31.

11. See John U. Ogbu, and H. D. Simons, "Voluntary and Involuntary Minorities: A Cultural-Ecological Theory of School Performance With Some Implications for Education," *Anthropology and Education Quarterly* 29(2): 155–188.

12. Spinoza, *Ethics*, W. Hale, tr., revised by Amelia Hutchison Sterling, Book IV, Appendix IX (New York: Hafner Publishing Co., 1949), p. 244.

13. I owe the recognition of this special understanding of classroom life to Frances Pockman Hawkins. She has recognized it during her many years of work with young children, and has formulated it in her writings.

14. In Frances (Pockman) Lothrop Hawkins, *Journey With Children: The Autobiography of a Teacher* (Niwot: University Press of Colorado, 1997).

15. Eugene S. Gollin, "Development and Plasticity," in *Behavioral and Biological Aspects of Variation in Development*, Eugene S. Gollin, ed. (New York: Academic Press, 1981), pp. 231–251.

16. Stanley I. Greenspan, with Beryl Lieff Benderly, *The Growth of the Mind, and the Endangered Origins of Intelligence* (Reading, Mass.: Addison Wesley Press, Inc., 1996). This book provides a fully developmental perspective on matters of human development generally, and on education in the context of present-day society.